Multimodal Literacy

new literacies
AND DIGITAL EPISTEMOLOGIES

Colin Lankshear, Michele Knobel,
Chris Bigum, and Michael Peters
General Editors

Vol. 4

PETER LANG
New York • Washington, D.C./Baltimore • Bern
Frankfurt am Main • Berlin • Brussels • Vienna • Oxford

Multimodal Literacy

EDITED BY
Carey Jewitt & Gunther Kress

PETER LANG
New York • Washington, D.C./Baltimore • Bern
Frankfurt am Main • Berlin • Brussels • Vienna • Oxford

Library of Congress Cataloging-in-Publication Data

Multimodal literacy / [edited by] Carey Jewitt, Gunther Kress.
p. cm. — (New literacies and digital epistemologies; v. 4)
Includes bibliographical references and index.
1. Critical pedagogy. 2. Knowledge, Theory of. 3. Literacy.
I. Jewitt, Carey. II. Kress, Gunther R. III. Series.
LC196.M86   370.11'5—dc21   2002156036
ISBN 0-8204-5224-6
ISSN 1523-9543

Bibliographic information published by **Die Deutsche Bibliothek**.
Die Deutsche Bibliothek lists this publication in the "Deutsche Nationalbibliografie"; detailed bibliographic data is available on the Internet at http://dnb.ddb.de/.

Cover design by Lisa Barfield

The paper in this book meets the guidelines for permanence and durability of the Committee on Production Guidelines for Book Longevity of the Council of Library Resources.

© 2003 Peter Lang Publishing, Inc., New York
275 Seventh Avenue, 28th Floor, New York, NY 10001
www.peterlangusa.com

All rights reserved.
Reprint or reproduction, even partially, in all forms such as microfilm, xerography, microfiche, microcard, and offset strictly prohibited.

Printed in the United States of America

CONTENTS

Chapter 1: Introduction   1
GUNTHER KRESS AND CAREY JEWITT

Chapter 2: Communicating Meanings through Image Composition, Spatial Arrangement and Links in Primary School Student Mind Maps   19
DIANE MAVERS

Chapter 3: Computer-Mediated Learning: The Multimodal Construction of Mathematical Entities on Screen   34
CAREY JEWITT

Chapter 4: Tiger's Big Plan: Multimodality and the Moving Image   56
ANDREW BURN AND DAVID PARKER

Chapter 5: Putting the Text Back into Practice: Junior-age Non-fiction as Objects of Design   73
GEMMA MOSS

Chapter 6: Embodied Knowledges: Young Children's Engagement with the Act of Writing   88
CHARMIAN KENNER

Chapter 7: Beginning at the Beginning: How a Young Child Constructs Time Multimodally   107
LESLEY LANCASTER

Chapter 8: The Olifantsvlei Fresh Stories Project: Multimodality, Creativity and Fixing in the Semiotic Chain 123
PIPPA STEIN

Chapter 9: Children's Text-Making at Home: Transforming Meaning across Modes 139
KATE PAHL

Chapter 10: Palmers' Kiss: Shakespeare, School Drama and Semiotics 155
ANTON FRANKS

Chapter 11: Genres and the Multimodal Production of 'Scientificness' 173
GUNTHER KRESS

List of Contributors 187
Index 189

Gunther Kress and Carey Jewitt

INTRODUCTION

The chapters in this book look at multimodality and learning in a variety of settings (primary and secondary school classrooms and the home), and across a range of curriculum subjects (school English, information and communication technologies, math, media studies, and science). The basic assumption that runs through the chapters is that meanings are made, distributed, received, interpreted and remade in interpretation through many representational and communicative modes—not just through language—whether as speech or as writing. The chapters show that the world as it is represented in different modes has a different appearance, and that such different appearances have differential effects for learning. The approach that underpins the chapters is a semiotic one. The primary focus of the chapters in this collection is therefore on signs, meaning-making, representation and communication, and interpretation. The authors who have contributed to the volume have come to multimodality and semiotics in different ways, some combining a multimodal semiotic approach with other theoretical interests and perspectives. A multimodal semiotic approach gives the chapters a continuity; however, it also highlights some interesting tensions between the chapters in what is currently an emergent area of research.

Multimodality: New Questions for Learning

A multimodal approach to learning requires us to take seriously and attend to the whole range of modes involved in representation and communication. Throughout the chapters in this book, *mode* is used to refer to a regularised organised set of resources for meaning-making, including, image, gaze, gesture, movement, music, speech and sound-effect. Modes are broadly understood to be the effect of the work of culture in shaping material into resources for representation. These resources display regularities due to that cultural work, and due to their more or less frequent use in social (inter)action. These regularities are what have been called 'grammars' traditionally. The more work a culture has put into such a resource, for whatever reasons, and the more it has been used in the social life of a particular community, the more fully and finely articulated it will have become. Speech is such a resource, as is writing, and so are the sign-languages of communities of the hearing-impaired. Likewise, images have been developed into a mode in various places in the world and at various times, whether as the character-based writing system of Chinese (and Japanese); the hieroglyphic system of ancient Egypt, itself a precursor to the alphabetic writing systems of the world; and other visual systems.

As well as asking how each mode features in specific instances of learning, each of the chapters shows that in communication, modes rarely, if ever, occur alone. Indeed, the act of writing is itself a multimodal practice that draws on visual and actional modes, in particular resources of spatiality and directionality, as Charmian Kenner demonstrates in her analysis of children's engagement with writing (Chapter 6). The complex relationship between image and writing is a focus of several chapters in the book. Diane Mavers (Chapter 2) analyses the mind maps of young students in Chapter 2 to explore the particular possibilities in communication potential of the spatiality of image on the page as against the linearity that writing affords. This theme is also addressed by Gunther Kress (Chapter 11) to examine the emergence of visual and written school science texts in relation to genre. Collectively the chapters suggest that there is no monomodal communication, and set out to challenge the implicit assumption that speech or writing are always central and sufficient for learning. We want to suggest that the commonly held view of communication and learning as being fundamentally about speech and writing is somewhat confused and contradictory. On the one hand it acknowledges that there are 'extra-linguistic' phenomena together with speech such as gesture, facial expression, tone of voice; or image and layout with writing, and that these modes are meaningful. Yet at the same time modes other than speech and writing are often regarded by educational research as ancillary, and marginal with little or no contribution to learning: 'language' is often considered to be the core of communication where rationality resides, and which defines humans as humans. As a consequence of this focus on speech and writing in the majority of research on informal and formal learning, much of what is analysed in these chapters as 'data'—the collages, drawings, music, and the three-dimensional models made by children—seldom feature in the analysis and discussion of learning.

Rather than taking talk and writing as the starting point, a multimodal approach to learning starts from a theoretical position that treats all modes as equally significant for meaning and communication, potentially so at least. Societies and specific communities may, and indeed do, value certain modes more than others. And beyond that, in any one communicational event one mode may be foregrounded and others not, so for example Anton Franks (Chapter 10) explores an instance of English teaching in which the role of gesture, movement, and voice are foregrounded. Within a multimodal approach to communication an assumption is that any mode may become fore-grounded; that different modes have potentials that make them better for certain tasks than others; and that not every mode will be equally 'useable' for a particular task. Several authors (in particular, Stein in Chapter 8 and Pahl in Chapter 9) explore children's shifts across modes and their affordances to develop narratives. The affordance of one mode over another, and how these affordances are orchestrated in instances of learning is explored in many of the chapters in this book. For instance, Andrew Burn and David Parker (Chapter 4) analyse the interplay of sound, image, movement, and so on, in a short animated film made by children about Anansi the spider, from one of the cycle of African folktales about the spider-man trickster.

An implicit assumption in much multimodal work is that *language is partial*. If, as these chapters show, there are always many modes involved in an event of communication (say, speech, gesture, posture, maybe images) then all of these modes together will be representing significant meanings of the overall message. The meaning of the message is distributed across all of these, not necessarily evenly. In short, different aspects of meaning are carried in different ways by each mode. Any one mode in that ensemble is carrying a part of the message only: each mode is *partial* in relation to the whole of the meaning—and speech or writing are, we suggest, no exception. This partiality of all modes is a significant aspect of multimodal approaches. This forces us to ask in what ways is a specific mode partial both in a specific event of communication; and maybe quite generally, it forces us to ask what a mode does and doesn't do. The question of what images do and don't do, and how young readers engage with image and writing in their literacy practices is addressed by Gemma Moss (Chapter 5). This question of how modes work together to contribute to learning is also a feature of Carey Jewitt's discussion of young children's computer programming practices (Chapter 3). In summary, the chapters in this book provide a challenge to the assumption of much research on learning that language is a full means of representation, and a challenge to all the assumptions that flowed from that in overt and in hidden ways.

So the focus of this book is to discuss the related issues of *learning* and the *semiotic forms* in which meaning is represented and through which learning happens. Two central questions are posed by the chapters in quite different ways. Firstly, how do modes shape what is represented, and how do the differences in modal representation reshape what is represented? And secondly, how are learners, and how is learning, affected, changed, shaped, by the differences in mode, the material differences entailed, and the different senses called on, engaged, in the use of a mode?

In those chapters that explore learning in formal institutional sites of learning, and the curricula that they propose, the question becomes a matter of how (curricular) knowledge is (differently) shaped in different modal realisations and what are the effects of this difference on learners and on learning. A further question, ever more urgently posed, is 'How does difference in mode interact with difference in media to affect ways and possibilities of learning?' (this question is discussed in Chapters 3 and 4). Alongside the analysis of *modes* of representation (that is, the resources that a culture makes available as *the means for making representations and meaning*—speech, writing, image, gesture, music, and others) the chapters explore the *media* of production and dissemination—that is, *the technologies for making and distributing meanings as messages* (such as, book, magazine, computer-screen, video, film, radio, billboard). What do we need to understand about the facilities offered by new communication technologies, in their configuration of modes and the users of the media? What do we need to understand about new forms of message arrangements on the 'page' or on the 'screen' and their role in learning? Gemma Moss explores the arrangement of image and writing on the page in her chapter (Chapter 5) in relation to junior non-fiction books and the implications for reading paths and young children's literacy practices more generally.

The multimodal ways of looking at learning and at the world of communication presented in this book also raise new questions for learning as much as they do for communication more generally. For instance, does 'knowledge' remain the same when it is represented in speech, in image, in gesture, in a 3D model, or in other modes? This question raises a further question: What *is* 'knowledge' prior to, or other than, in its specific appearance in a mode, or in a number of modes? How can we know that which is not (yet) made real in some outward material form, that which is not yet *realised*? Does 'learning' happen differently or in the same way when we engage with 'knowledge'—or the world much more generally—through image rather than through speech, or through writing? Can image do what writing does, or writing what image does? These questions are explored in different ways through the detailed multimodal analysis of instances of learning presented in each of the chapters. If, for example, there are two modes of communicating, what do we need to understand about what each can and cannot do, or cannot do easily?

We suggest that in order to understand the new forms of multimodal representation in a world of multimediated communication and their implications and effects on learning, new ways of thinking, new theories of meaning and communication are needed. The contributors to this book raise many of the issues that are central in beginning such a re-theorising, and do so in various ways. And yet, as we put forward our thoughts in this field, we want to be clear that these are early days as far as this enterprise is concerned. Although the theoretical domain of multimodality is developing (Kress et al., 2001; Kress and van Leeuwen, 2001), multimodality is an emergent field; there is no orthodoxy. This lack of certainty adds equally to both the excitement and usefulness of multimodality and we view the tensions and questions that its emergent status gives rise to as analytically productive. Opening up questions is, we think, more useful at this point than suggesting unsustainable certainties.

Multimodal Explorations of Learning

As we have already stated, the aim of this volume is neither to settle nor to conventionalise multimodal analysis. Rather, in this book we have brought together examples of ways in which multimodality is currently being applied in the context of educational research. In doing so, we hope to show how the approach can extend understandings of learning across a range of quite distinct areas of representation and communication and of the modes involved.

The chapters reflect the different journeys that the authors have travelled in their involvement with questions of learning. This is apparent both in the content of each chapter and in the analytical processes employed by each author. The chapters focus on learning in different ways, and in different sites, and draw on a range of texts that mediate learning. All of the chapters share a focus on text, although the kinds of texts dealt with vary widely: from the mind maps of young children (Chapter 2); to the learning of mathematical concepts via computer programming (Chapter 3); to the drawings of a young child (Chapter 7); to the bodily performance of a Shakespeare play (Chapter 10). Multimodality focuses on the modal resources that are brought into meaning-making, and the chapters in this volume focus on the range of modes that are made differently available by the various learning sites and instances described. Some of the chapters foreground specific modes for analysis: image and writing are the focus of several chapters, including those by Mavers, Moss, Kenner, and Kress; gaze is foregrounded by Lancaster; actional modes are a focus for Franks; while the multimodal 'orchestration' of a range of modes in quite different instances of learning are the focus of a number of chapters, including those by Jewitt, Burn and Parker, Stein, and Pahl.

The authors' different backgrounds and interests have led to their different uses of the concept of multimodality. Some authors see it as a methodological approach useable and distinctive in its own right—a part of a semiotic approach (e.g. Kress). Other authors combine multimodality with a theoretical perspective drawn from ethnography (e.g. Moss, Kenner, and Pahl), aspects of quantitative methodology (Mavers), an interest in sociocultural theory (e.g. Lancaster), and screen studies (Burns and Parker). Within this diversity the authors all share an interest in how the modes present in a communicational event contribute to learning in its broadest sense, and it is this that gives coherence to the volume.

The communication of meanings through image, composition, spatial arrangement and 'links' in children's drawings is the focus of the chapter by Diane Mavers 'Communicating Meanings through Image Composition, Spatial Arrangement and Links in Student Mind Maps' (Chapter 2). Mavers explores how nine- and ten-year-olds in a primary school communicated with researchers on the topic of 'Computers in My World' through making 'mind maps'. In their images, which predominantly represent objects, they have analytically condensed key defining features or 'criterial attributes' into theses maps, in a way that communicates their meanings effectively and economically. The author uses the mind maps as well as interview data to suggest that perceptual, experiential and conceptual matters are interwoven in the semiosis of drawing. The resources of size and positioning of images on the page demonstrate how children have used spatial arrangement to organise and classify their ideas via nodes into 'families'. She also examines the children's use of links between images to guide and assert directional control over the reader—that is, by constructing reading paths, or alternatively, to invite exploration of non-hierarchical groupings. The chapter concludes that the spatiality of image as against the linearity of writing affords particular possibilities in communication potential of which the children have made full use.

The question of how a range of representational modes contribute to the construction of mathematical entities and rules is explored in Carey Jewitt's chapter, entitled 'Computer-Mediated Learning: The Multimodal Construction of Mathematical Entities on Screen' (Chapter 3). She presents a detailed multimodal analysis of how the entity 'bounce' is constructed by two young students in an after-school computer club using the computer programming system Playground. The analysis centres on the impact of a range of modes—still image, gesture, posture, speech, animated movement and writing—on the emergence of the mathematical concept of bounce. Jewitt suggests that the choice of representational modes in the design of a program is central to the manner of the engagement of the user with the program. Modes provide the maker of an application and the user of it with different features for making meaning and for engaging with aspects of programming. Through a detailed multimodal analysis of the students' design process Jewitt shows that the modal resources each makes available to the user realise the entity 'bounce' in quite different ways. She concludes that a multimodal approach can offer essential insights into understanding the learning potentials of computer programming applications such as Playground.

In their chapter 'Tiger's Big Plan: Multimodality and the Moving Image' (Chapter 4), Andrew Burn and David Parker describe the ways in which modes work on screen through their analysis of a short animated film produced by young secondary school students in a specialist media school. The chapter explores how the discourses of mischief, Africanness, and pedagogy are realised through the multimodal production of the animation. They address the integrative, combinatorial assemblage of modes of the animation that has always posed theoretical problems for understanding film through the concept of design and what they have termed the 'kineikonic mode'. Burn and Parker focus on how the students designed and produced 'time' through their animated production. Using the concepts of 'boundary', 'grouping' and 'conjunction', and drawing on social semiotic theory, they analyse a short sequence of the film to see how sections of the image and soundtracks are grouped, how these groups are articulated, and how this 'tells the story'.

The multimodal construction of reading paths is the focus of Gemma Moss' chapter 'Putting the Text Back into Practice' (Chapter 5). Her emphasis is on the question of 'boys' reading', here junior-age non-fiction, as objects of design. Moss explores the complex relationship of texts of writing and image and the practices of reading. She focuses on the potentially complementary relationship between ethnography and multimodality to help her in understanding reading as a situated social practice. She argues for the aptness of the ethnographically located concept of the 'literacy event' as the means of bringing these two perspectives into play. The chapter puts ethnographic observation of literacy events in school settings side by side with analysis of the texts involved in these events in multimodal terms, and sets that in the broader environment of the shifts in the contemporary design of junior age non-fiction. In doing this she wants to 'put the text back into practice'. Moss argues that there is a strong tradition in conventional work on literacy that successful reading, in one way or another, reproduces a given text, that it is a kind of getting to grips with what is already there—without attempting to see how the 'there' is constituted internally. She argues that what is there in the text—seen multimodally—can become the central reference point against which to assess what readers do. From an ethnographic perspective, it is the interactions between participants in the literacy event which will both establish and steer what the text will mean; while from a multimodal perspective it is the reader's quite specific engagement with the modal particularities of the text which are the issue. The ethnographic approach has the effect of back-grounding the text itself. Moss goes on to argue that understanding the nature of the text that children are perusing, and its affordances and resistances as a multimodal object, gives new insights into what is happening in this event and its place in a larger textual economy. The chapter shows ways of 'building the text back into the analysis', but newly so.

Charmian Kenner combines an ethnographic perspective and a multimodal perspective in her chapter 'Embodied Knowledges: Young Children's Engagement with the Act of Writing' (Chapter 6). She approaches the physical process of young children learning how to write as a multimodal process, involving particularly the visual and actional modes. The chapter draws on examples from research with bilingual six-year-olds learning to write in Chinese, Arabic or Spanish (three writing systems with very different visual realisations), as well as English. Kenner argues that the teaching of writing promotes certain cultural patterns with regard to the writing process, spatiality and directionality, and that biliterate children therefore gain access to a variety of 'embodied knowledges' through their learning of different scripts. The chapter also considers how individual children interpret and transform these available cultural meanings.

Lesley Lancaster examines the key role that the co-ordinated use of physical and bodily resources plays in the structuring of semiotic events by very young children in her chapter "Beginning at the Beginning: How a Young Child Constructs Time Multimodally" (Chapter 7). The chapter focuses on how a concept of 'beginning and ending' is constructed by a two-year-old during sequences of activity involved in making a greetings' card. The analysis employs a micro-level multimodal description of the physical and bodily resources used by the child in the mediation of these activities. She shows that language, gaze, and action are used in systematic configurations to construct this concept. The chapter demonstrates how during this process, gaze is used to link images of past experience with anticipation of future activity, and at the same time interpersonally maintains the involvement and help of an interested adult. The significance of multimodal analysis in understanding the conceptual construction of very young children is thus one of the aims of the chapter. Lancaster considers the degree to which this systematic co-ordination of physical, bodily modes in the mediation of meaning might be a conscious, knowing process.

Pippa Stein's chapter 'The Olifantsvlei Fresh Stories Project: Multimodality, Creativity and Fixing in the Semiotic Chain' (Chapter 8) focuses on early literacy, in a project conducted in Johannesburg, South Africa, which aimed to develop a body of stories based on and arising from young children's lives and local experiences. Through her analysis of these stories she shows that multimodal pedagogies can work consciously and systematically across semiotic modes in order to unleash creativity, reshape knowledge and develop forms of learning beyond the linguistic. She shows how in this project the use of multimodal pedagogies led to the production of varying semiotic objects in sequenced stages and in different modes: 2D drawings, writing, 3D figures, spoken dialogues and multimodal play performances. The production of these textual objects was in response to a central theme that ran through the project, namely, the creation of a group of characters who would form the basis of storytelling, of play making and of writing. In the chapter she focuses on the 3D doll/child figures produced by the children in this semiotic chain. She describes how they illuminate a number of important issues in multimodality, particularly materiality and creativity in different social contexts of meaning-making. Through the ways in which the making of the doll/child figures happened—that is, the specific process of making—she raises issues around the topics of agency, cultural memory and home and school learning within the South African context.

In Kate Pahl's chapter 'Children's Text Making at Home: Transforming Meaning across Modes' (Chapter 9), we are introduced to a child who is playing on the carpet of his bedroom floor with small figures, some models of Pokémon, and assorted trucks and miniature animals, which he photographs and provides a running commentary about. These photographs are remounted with a new commentary, to create a newsletter about his favourite Pokémon creatures and a collage. The child also makes miniature Pokémon creatures out of modelling material. In this chapter, Pahl maps these descriptions onto an account of multimodality. In all the examples, the child has crossed from one mode to another, and in each mode different affordances are present and can be manipulated and used. By attending to the interplay between modes, the importance for the child of the transitions across mode can be appreciated and recognised. Moving across modes is identified by Pahl as a crucial way in which children express and uphold meaning. When the affordances of one mode begin to lose their communicative possibility, another mode can be taken up. Through Chapter 9 Pahl addresses three key questions in multimodal meaning-making: How did this child transform meaning as he took one particular theme or idea and followed it across modes? How did the choice of mode affect meaning? And, how did mode affect identity construction?

The study of Shakespearean text in schools is the focus of Anton Franks' chapter, 'Palmer's Kiss: Shakespeare, School Drama and Semiotics' (Chapter 10). He argues that learners have differential access to wider resources of cultural and specifically textual knowledge, a knowledge that can enable them to make sense of the text. At the same time, teachers often want to mobilise their students' experience and knowledge of the world, of home and school, of other texts—books, films and television—and bring them to bear on their reading of the printed page. Sometimes, teachers decide that students will better understand the meaning of the text if they move beyond 'sedentary reading' of the verbal text and move toward acting out some part of Shakespeare. The assumption is that through the processes of dramatisation—the bodily enactment of the text in voice, action and interaction—value might be added to the reading of Shakespeare. Franks argues that traditional modes of describing and analysing classroom action and interaction tend to present verbal transcripts and descriptive narrative as data. When he looks at the subtle shifts of meaning-making involved in moving between a group's reading of a 'literary' dramatic text, to social action and dramatised activity, however, something else might be needed. One way is to focus on the role and function of the body—the socially organised body—situated in particular places and social settings, as a locus of multimodal meaning-making activity. The chapter examines transitions between social action and dramatic action, focusing particularly on bodily action and interaction in its social and cultural setting, using methods of multimodal semiotic analysis.

In the final chapter in this volume, 'Genres and the Multimodal Production of "Scientificness"' (Chapter 11), Gunther Kress explores two questions in a semiotic theory of multimodality: How is knowledge reconfigured when 'it' is moved from one mode to another (the matter of transduction); and, What can we learn about learning in the process of sign-making, and the reading of signs. Kress asks whether the term genre—from linguistic descriptions and theories of language—still works when we want to apply it to other modes. Through his discussion of two secondary school student texts produced in a science classroom, as examples of ensembles of modes brought together to realise particular meanings, Kress explores genre as a matter of multimodal design.

The purpose of this introductory chapter is not, as we stated earlier, to offer a definitive or stable glossary for a multimodal perspective. Nonetheless, we think it useful to outline some of the key theoretical concepts that inform a multimodal approach to learning. These concepts are 'worked' and taken up quite differently in each of the chapters.

Multimodality: Some Key Concepts

Multimodality and Semiotics

Even though we may at times speak of multimodal theory, the theory behind multimodality and with which we (C.J., G.K.) work is *semiotic theory,* and for us the form of semiotics that we have adopted is *social semiotics* (Halliday 1978; Hodge and Kress 1988). Multimodality is the field in which we apply semiotic theory—its field of application. The adjective *social* draws attention to a criterial aspect of this version of semiotic theory—namely to the role of people in meaning-making, to their *social agency*. In the dominant forms of semiotics people are regarded as confronted with ready-made *systems* for making meaning—the linguistic system might be the example par excellence. They are seen as learning to use the resources offered by these systems in ways that are deemed 'appropriate' in terms of social convention. People are not regarded as having a role in the making or in the reshaping of these resources. In these theories, the system is 'there'; it is stable, and its stability is both produced and sustained by social power, which presents itself as convention. 'Convention' rules. People *use* the resources, but they do not *change* them.

The concept of sign (realised through a range of modal resources) and the processes of engaging in situated sign-making (again, through a range of modes) are central to the chapters brought together in this volume. The basic elements of these modal resources in traditional and social semiotics are signs—the fusions of meaning and form. In traditional semiotic theory signs are thought to be *arbitrary* conjunctions of form and meaning, arbitrary fusions of signifiers and signifieds. Within traditional semiotic theory arbitrariness is viewed as sustained by convention (that is, social power in another guise). In contrast, social semiotics views the agency of socially situated humans as central to sign-making. From a social semiotic perspective, people use the resources that are available to them in the specific socio-cultural environments in which they act to create signs, and in using them, they change these resources. In other words, signs are not viewed as arbitrary. Rather, signs are viewed as constantly newly made, in a process in which the signified (what is to be meant) is realised through the most apt signifier (that which is available to give realisation to that which is to be meant) in a specific social context.

A simple example of this aptness of sign in the field of image might be using the image of a man with a shovel (the signifier) for the meaning (the signified) 'men at work' on a roadside sign. In each case, the maker of the sign has something she or he wishes to 'express', and finds the most apt form to give realisation to that meaning. That is, we view meaning and form as always linked in a relation of *being apt for*, one for the other. The chapters in this volume provide a variety of examples of sign-making as a process in which a learner (sign-maker) uses the most apt signifier available to her or him in a specific social context and time in order to signify what is to be meant, from the dolls made of bubble wrap and other found materials discussed by Stein (Chapter 8), to Burn and Parker's analysis of the use of voice and music to indicate mischief in students' animated film (Chapter 4).

Nonetheless, the arbitrariness of signs continues to have a strong theoretical hold. The support for the arbitrariness of signs seems easily found: Why should it be that the same 'thing' has such different realisation in different languages, for instance, if it was not due to the arbitrary decision of a social and linguistic group? Social semiotics offers an alternative explanation for this different realisation: each culture looked for what seemed the apt, the most plausible existent signifier. The light-bulb, for instance, when it was introduced over a century ago, was named *light-bulb* in English, while it was called a *Gluehbirne* in German; and an *ampule* in French. So why should the English have decided to call 'it' a 'light-onion' (bulb meaning onion), the Germans to have called it a 'glowing pear' (Birne meaning pear)? and the French, a 'blister'? In these cases the *vehicle* that was available happened to be an already existing word with its meanings. These words were taken as the signifier for the new signifieds. What differs in each case is the difference in what was seen as most salient; and that salience determines the grounds for the analogy, shapes the metaphor, and the new sign. From this perspective, neither the process nor the principles are arbitrary—rather, they reflect somewhat varying *interests*. In taking the signifiers into these new signs, the potential of the signifier stuff is changed, it is *transformed*. But that which is signified is also transformed.

In many other theories of sign a *light-bulb, gluehbirne* and *ampule* are called metaphors—which they are, given that all signs are always metaphors. All meaning is made as sign, all meaning is always metaphoric. Representation is always partial, and what is represented is that which is central to the sign-maker at that particular moment. The metaphors are revealing in that context in that they tell us what the maker of the sign/metaphor saw as criterial about that which was to be represented, because it is that which is aptly represented in the vehicle/signifier. The shape of the signifier, its form, its materiality, gives the reader/viewer a clue about what the shape of the signified might be. From this perspective, reading becomes the construction of hypotheses about the shape of *the-to-be-meant* from the shape of *that which means it,* the vehicle/signifier.

Anything may come to serve as signifier, just so long as it is judged apt for the meaning-makers' purposes, in the way we have described it here. This applies to materials drawn directly from nature (such as stone, feathers, metal, wood, fruit, flowers) as much as it applies to materials drawn right from the histories of cultures (such as words, images, colours, sounds, syntactic forms, 3D objects). Culture always intervenes, and shapes both what we may wish to mean and the things that might be used to mean them.

To summarise, the principle underlying the relation of 'thing meant' and 'thing meaning it' within a social semiotic multimodal perspective is *aptness*. The shape of the signifier already suggests to the maker of the sign that it is ready to signify the to-be-signified. This is the relation of analogy, which underlies every metaphor. Signs are metaphors, and as all signs are newly made, all signs are new metaphors. What establishes the relation of analogy between signifier and signified (in other words, 'what means' and 'what is meant') is the *interest* of the maker of the sign. This relationship is realised in three ways: first, her or his interest decides what is to be signified; second, he or she decides what is the apt signifier; and third, she or he decides how the sign is made most suitable for the occasion of its communication. In all three cases metaphors provide insights into the meaning principles of a culture as much as of an individual.

Multimodality and Learning

As the concept of the motivated or 'interested' sign described above suggests, a sign functions both in representation and in communication. The sign functions as a representation of the sign makers' meanings. At the same time a sign functions in the communication of these meanings adapted to the intended reader—that is, the sign represents the sign-maker's assessment of the communicational environment, and her or his perceived relation to others. In other words, 'what is to be signified' is not the same as 'what is to be communicated'. The first is concerned with the sign maker, and with what he or she wants; the second is concerned with the sign-maker's perception of the audience and what he or she imagines they want.

It is here that we begin to come closer to the issues of learning. When a person makes a sign, in making that sign (in any mode), for example a sign of a car, they can only ever represent some aspects of what it is they want to represent. They can never fully represent all that, for instance, a car might mean to them. They have to make a selection, based on their interest, from all the features that could signal *car*: aspects of its look more than aspects of its performance—its sleekness, shine, colour, rather than its speed, its power, its petrol consumption. What a person selects as being criterial for them at that moment in signifying *car* depends on their 'interest' at that moment. What they select as being apt signifiers also depends on their interest: how they wish to represent speed and power, for instance; or the intensity, the depth, the sheen of the colour on the bodywork. And third, how they choose to signify power or speed will depend on their relations to and perceptions of their audience.

Given this sense of the sign and its making, we can turn the process around and treat it as a means of 'reading': if the sign in all its (formal and material) aspects represents the interests of its maker, we can make inferences, hypothetically, from the shape of the sign to the interests of its maker. The sign is evidence of the interests of its maker in the moment of representation, the sign-maker's engagement with the world to be represented. The sign is also evidence of its maker's interests in communication, their engagement with the social world in which the sign is a (part of a) message. From the representation of the *car*, for example, we can infer ('trace') the interests of the sign-maker in what matters to her or him about 'car'.

This view of representation and communication, a *semiotic process,* can be turned into a sense of what learners are and what learning is as an *affective/cognitive process*. There are two ways of seeing this initially. Firstly, we could, *as readers,* learn what the interests of the maker of the sign were, in the way we have suggested above. This is reading for assessment. If we are teacher-readers, for instance, this is not an inconsiderable matter as it gives access to a mode of assessment that is different to those usually at issue. The question is no longer 'How does what is here match what a teacher *expected and wanted* to be there?' but rather, 'How does what is here give a teacher insight into the *interests of the maker* of what is here?' Secondly, we could see the sign as a clue about the learning engaged in by the maker-of-the-sign-as-learner. A teacher could focus on how the interests of her or his students have engaged with the teacher's interest as expressed through the (curricular) materials that they have presented in lessons. For example, if students in a school science lesson have been asked to produce a concept map of 'blood-circulation', then the concept map can be read as one kind of evidence of the students' interests (Kress et al., 2001). The students' concept maps can be used to ask what elements of the teacher's work are included in the students' concept maps: Do they focus on all the organs involved or only the heart and the lungs, the entities of blood, or on the means of fighting disease? Do the students represent blood circulation as a quasi-narrative—a kind of flow-chart, even though it is a spatial display—or do they see it as a means of showing relations between the scientific entities in other ways, hierarchically, for instance? In such a conception of the assessment of learning, 'error', for instance, has a different place in the process of assessment.

There is, however, a more profound way of seeing the process of semiosis (of making meaning) as a process of learning. In making a representation a person is making a new sign out of what they want to signify, with existing signifier materials. The sign-maker chooses the signifier that is most apt for being the vehicle to represent that which they wish to signify. However, there is never an exact fit, but it is the best possible fit of meaning and form. In the gap between what they meant to mean and what they have to use to mean it exists the possibility of the new; a sign that not only had not been made before, but a sign that wrenches their meaning in unpredictable directions. That lack of fit, and that wrenching, change not only the externally made sign, but also the inwardly made sign in its relations to other signs inwardly held. The new state of all signs now marks the effect of sign-making as meaning.

In reading, the task is also to make signs. However, this time the process is inverted. The process starts not from a person wanting to signify to the world outside, but from their wanting to represent signs in the world outside (made by some other) to their inner self. A person receives a sign, in the material form of its signifier, in which it was realised. She or he takes the shape of the signifier as an apt indication of what was signified, and forms from that a hypothesis of what the signified is. But the readers' hypothesis about the likely, plausible, apt, signified is based on *their* interest. It, too, forms a new sign. The new sign itself and in its relation to all the signs inwardly held, changes their inner state of signs. That, too, represents learning.

In other words, the hypotheses that people make about the signs that they receive are based on their interests, just as much as they are in the outward making of the sign. A new sign has been made in each case; and the new sign, whether outwardly made or inwardly made, changes the inner inventory of potential sign material, and potential of signifier material. A sign outwardly made changes the cultural resource for making meaning. The potential of the cultural resource has been changed by the sign-maker's action (even if in infinitesimally slight ways). A sign inwardly made changes the sign-maker's inwardly held resources, both in this sign and in its interaction with all other signs in their inner resource. The sign-maker's potential for meaning is changed. That change to a person's inner resource, both through representation to the outer world and through representation to their inner world, through interpretation, can be thought of as learning.

Mode

Modes (of representation) carry the meanings of material affordance shaped by generations of the work of people in their social lives. Over time this gives rise to a resource with regularities shaped by 'convention', understood by members of a culture, and useable therefore by them for representation and communication. In making meanings as messages, members of a culture have available and make use of many modes at the same time. The modes of language (speech and writing) are often central, but need not be present for meanings to be made. For instance, people use images, gesture, and space as a means for communication, whether developed into a fully articulated mode or less so.

Materiality

Materiality refers to what a culture provides as materials for making meaning. Materiality is everywhere and always physiological and semiotic. Cultures select materials, which are drawn into meaning-making. All cultures have drawn on the human ability to make an infinitely varied range of sounds in order to make meaning, turning sound into a full means for representation (although not all have access to these cultural resources). Cultures have also used the facility to make marks on surfaces for the purposes of representation, and many cultures have developed that into full means of representing. But the range of materials is not exhausted by sound in the air (as in the mode of music, speech, or sound-effect) and light on surfaces (as in the mode of photography, or contemporary painting). Cultures make use of a vast range of materials (e.g. stone, wood, metal, plastic, straw, bone) all of which have inherent qualities or *affordances,* that suggest cultural/semiotic use: 'hardness' for durability and strength; 'scarcity' for value; 'intensity' (of sound or colour or texture) for salience and prominence of whatever kind; 'three-dimensionality' for forms of realism, and so on.

The inherent qualities of the material offer semiotic affordances that are selected by an individual or a culture for making meanings. Over time, the constant making of signs with a specific material leads to the shaping of a resource with understood regularities; and at that point the resource seems to attain grammar-like qualities. The purposes that a group has, for frequent or even constant communication, or in representation where communication is back-grounded, will determine what cultural, semiotic uses the material is put to, and consequently will determine the amount of cultural/social work which is put into the material to become mode. However, materiality always remains a potent factor in meaning, partly because of the remaining effect of affordance, and perhaps in part because human bodies through the 'senses' interact with materials in distinct ways. Colour affects bodies differently to smell, and sound differently to touch, even before culture has done its work.

Modal Affordance

The affordance of a mode can at one level be understood as what it is possible to express and represent readily, easily, with a mode, given its materiality and given the cultural and social history of that mode. Where a mode 'comes from' in its history of cultural work, its *provenance,* is understood by members of that culture, and becomes a part of its affordance. We can ask about graphic marks on a two-dimensional surface, and whether it is possible to express and represent with them what it is possible to represent with the sounds of speech in time. But we also must ask about the shapes of those marks, the type of font, and what meanings adhere to it. Or, analysing it differently, we can ask what image is best for, and what words and their arrangements are best for. Modal affordance has a physical, material side (the material features of mode), and it has a social, cultural, historical side (what has been done in the past with this material, and how the meanings made in the past affect what can be done with a mode).

Logics of Modes

The Logics of modes refers to what (deep) orientation to the world is necessarily and inevitably embedded in the resources for representation. The sounds of speech happen in time, and this sequence in time shapes what can be done with (speech) sounds. The logic of time as sequence is unavoidable for speech: one sound has to be uttered after another (with some qualification), one word after another, one syntactic and textual element after another. This sequence is an affordance: it produces the possibilities for putting things first or last, or somewhere else in a sequence. The mode of speech is governed by the logic of time. (Still) images are governed by the logic of space and simultaneity. A sign-maker has to display what she or he wishes to show in the space available for their representation—a wall, a slate, a page, a bit of bark, etc. All the elements that the sign-maker wishes to display have to be simultaneously present, and their relations in meaning have to be spatially indicated: close to or far away, below or above, centrally or marginal.

Functional Specialisation of Modes

Functional specialisation of modes is a feature of multimodal representation: it is an effect both of the affordances of modes (i.e., this mode is better for representing this), and of design decisions in relation to the audience. The specialisation of modes is also a longer term effect of cultural valuation: if a culture values a mode highly much work will inevitably go into its elaboration, through its constant use by members of a social group. Its constant use in relation to specific purposes will make it elaborate in relation to those domains, in lexis as in syntax as in sound.

Functional Load of Modes

Functional load of modes is related to, yet distinct and (independently variable) from, functional specialisation. The former refers specifically to the use of a mode in a particular occasion of communication: whether in a message or in interaction, most of the informational load is carried by speech, or by image, or by a 3D model, or by two modes conjointly (Jewitt et al., 2000). So on a contemporary textbook page, curricular content (depending on the school subject at issue) might be carried by writing or by image, or might be distributed evenly between the two. General framing might similarly be carried by one mode or another. In an English as a Second Language textbook, for instance information on adverbs, or on verbs of motion, might be carried both by words and by image. 'On' or 'under' might be shown in an image, and exemplified in an accompanying sentence: 'the book is under the table', and so on. Here the two modes share the functional load, but differentially: the image shows what is meant (the signified), while the sentence shows how to mean it (the signifier). On a science textbook page, information about the curriculum might be carried in images alone, while pedagogic framing (such as, 'we did this last time; do this now; this is the best way to do it') might be carried by writing.

The Facilities of the Media

The facilities of the media are the parallel to the affordances of the mode, and answer to the same type of question: What is it readily and easily possible to do with this medium? The book has, during the era of moveable type, been organised by the affordances of the mode of writing. This has shaped ways of thinking about the book and the page in all sorts of ways. Image could and did appear on the page, but the page was the domain of the logic of writing; when image appeared there, it did so subordinated to its logic. Now the screen is a dominant medium; and the screen is the site of the image and of its logic. When writing appears on the screen, it does so subordinated to the logic of the image, and over time we suggest that the effect of that 'reversal' will have far-reaching effects on the organisation of communication, not just on the screen but also on the page, and on the mode of writing. More recently the book and the page are coming to be once more a site of image, an effect of the organisation of the screen spilling back onto the organisation of the page. Now writing is often subordinated to image even on the page.

Even now, multimodality is much more readily achieved with the screen of new communication and information technologies than it is with the book. But there are other significant differences in 'facilities'. The recent history of the book in the West is governed by its shaping through the culturally and socially dominant mode of writing: that had become its culturally and socially given affordance. The book can accommodate sound only with great difficulty, as in some books for children; and moving image is not possible to produce on the page of the book. On the screen, by contrast, moving and still image can occur together with speech and writing, and music and soundtrack can accompany all these. It is the possibilities for action, and the 'reach' of the possibilities of action, that are changed dramatically by the shift from book to screen. With the book the reader cannot write back, and the reader cannot modify the text in any way other than in inner interpretation. The facilities of new information and communication technologies afford the potential for readers to modify some texts. On the screen of the PlayStation, for example, the player influences the shaping of the text in a significant way: no two games played are ever likely to be the 'same' games as texts. Above all, the reader can be a producer and a disseminator of her or his texts with the new screens.

Learning and Multimodal Design

Design refers to how people make use of the resources that are available at a given moment in a specific communicational environment to realise their interests as makers of a message/text. We make a distinction between design versus competence to signal a shift both in theories of representation, of communication, and of learning, as well as a shift in practices themselves. The era of the nineteenth century nation-state, of the economy of mass industrialised production, and of mass societies focussed on the ideal of competence. Competence recognises that there are established practices, and it makes them appear as convention expressed as rules. The desired goal, whether of education systems, of learning theories, as well as of many institutions, is to produce competence as rules in social individuals in relation to the set of practices that are at issue.

In an era of profound and rapid change, neither the goal of competence nor the (imagined) reality behind that goal are any longer serviceable and sustainable. For a while, through the 1970s and 80s, competence was replaced by critique; that is, not simply the "mastery" of a set of rules, but the ability to uncover the interested use of the rules. Critique asked the question in whose interest, and for whose benefit, both about the practices and the rules. In asking that question, the aim of those who asked was to bring the system into crisis, and produce the possibilities of conditions for change. However, critique necessarily acts on what has already happened, on past performance, and on the effect of the (past) agendas of others. If the aim is to act productively in periods of rapid change, and in one's own interest, then design must replace competence and critique as the essential goal of educational practice, of theories of learning, and of theories of representation much more generally.

Design incorporates aims inherent in competence and critique because in the social semiotic theory of multimodal communication, the affordances of the modes are well understood by the maker of the message, as are the assumptions that she or he act in their interests in social environments. It is an assumption of the theory that representation and communication are always interested, so that, for instance, there could be no such term as bias, which does take uninterested communication as the norm.

The views of learning presented in this volume are, in different ways, the result of the joint effect of a social semiotic view of representation, and the acceptance of multimodality as a feature of all representation and communication. We hope you will find this volume a useful contribution to re-thinking learning as a multimodal process.

References

Halliday, M. (1978) *Language as a Social Semiotic*. London: Edward Arnold.
Hodge, R. and Kress, G.R. (1988) *Social Semiotics*. Cambridge, United Kingdom: Polity Press.
Jewitt, C., Kress, G.R., Ogborn, J. and Tsatsarelis, C. (2000) 'Teaching and learning: beyond language' in *Teaching Education*, 11 (3), pp. 327–341.
Kress, G.R. (2003) *Literacy in the New Media Age*. London: Routledge.
Kress, G.R., Jewitt, C., Ogborn, J. and Tsatsarelis, C. (2001) *Multimodal Teaching and Learning: The Rhetorics of the Science Classroom*. London: Continuum Press.
Kress, G.R. and van Leeuwen, L. (2001) *Multimodal Discourse: The Modes and Media of Contemporary Communication*. London: Arnold.

Diane Mavers

COMMUNICATING MEANINGS THROUGH IMAGE COMPOSITION, SPATIAL ARRANGEMENT AND LINKS IN PRIMARY SCHOOL STUDENT MIND MAPS

This chapter explores how 9- and 10-year-olds have communicated with researchers through their mind maps. Their images, which predominantly represent objects, have been analytically condensed into key defining features or 'criterial attributes' in a way that communicates meanings effectively and economically. Interview data suggests that the perceptual, experiential and conceptual are interwoven in the semiosis of drawing. Varied detail in the same or similar items implies that differential representation is a consequence of meaning intention. The size and positioning of images on the page demonstrate how children have used spatial arrangement to organise and classify their nodes into 'families'. Links between images guide and assert directional control over the reader or invite exploration of non-hierarchical groupings. Children's spoken comments indicate that their choice, representation and arrangement of images in their mind maps are both a means of making meaning for themselves and of making themselves maximally understood by others. The spatiality of image on the page as against the linearity of writing affords particular possibilities in communication potential.

Outwardly communicated meaning-making entails some sort of complex socially and culturally shaped cognitive process where signifieds are given material forms (signifiers) to create signs. In composing communication texts children must make choices in how to go about 'bringing meaning into being' (Kress et al.,

2001, p. 70). Different forms of communication appear to be best suited to different purposes. Each does certain things well and other things less well. The communicator must decide on the most suitable means of conveying meaning according to the affordances of the mode or combination of modes, bearing in mind the available resources, the requirements of the task and the message's communicational charge. Choosing the most appropriate and effective means of representing and communicating meanings is dependent on knowledge of 'functional specialism' (Jewitt et al., 2000, p. 332) or which meanings the particular form communicates best. We select 'the most apt forms, the forms already most suited by virtue of their existing potentials, for the representation of our meanings' (Kress, 2000b, p. 155). Forms of communication privileged by the culture are explicitly taught whilst others are learned more or less informally as children are acculturated in their everyday engagement with the world. According to some, the predominance of written language in the curriculum signals a narrowing of the range of modes valued in school (Kenner, 2000; Millard and Marsh, 2001) with little formative feedback on images (Kress and van Leeuwen, 1996; Christensen and James, 2000). Yet the potentialities of drawing may enable new things to be communicated, or the 'same' things to be expressed in a different way.

In this chapter, I exemplify children's extraordinary skill in making meaning through the affordances of drawing. I examine how children have composed image-based mind maps and explore their apparent meaning intentions. My analysis is largely based on the methods developed by Kress and van Leeuwen (1996). Using baseline data from the English government (Department for Education and Skills) commissioned ImpaCT2 evaluation[1], I study three mind maps on the topic of 'Computers in My World' produced in June 2000. These are taken from one Year 5 class (9- to 10-year-olds) in a school in the Northwest of England. My interest originally arose from an analysis of Map A (Figure 2.1). The child's astonishing spatial organisation and linked arrangement prompted me to revisit the class set to study map composition more generally. Seven others showed similar characteristics to a greater or lesser extent. Those appearing in this chapter therefore represent one phenomenon of map structure evident in this class dataset (25) and elsewhere in the full pre-test sample (approximately 730 Key Stage Two submissions and more than 2,000 in total). On the other hand, whilst different drawing capabilities were apparent, any of the maps might have been chosen to exemplify the criterial attributes described below.

Some Background Information

These three maps have their context in the broader study for which they were generated. Adopting a phenomenographic approach, the ImpaCT2 team undertook content analysis with the aim of identifying qualitatively different ways in which technologies are experienced and can be understood (Mavers, Somekh and Restorick, 2002). In order to ensure some sort of consistency across the 60 participating schools, teacher research coordinators read out a scripted introduction and standardised instructions to the class. A time limit of 30 minutes was allowed for the mind mapping task in total with the final 5 minutes being spent either in writing a list of drawings or in labelling them. Four key messages appear to have had an impact on map composition and content:

1. The script made it explicit that the mind mapping task had been designed to enable the children to communicate their thinking with researchers. Implicitly, production for a specific adult audience indicated a need to communicate in ways that would be understood by these unknown others or 'just anybody' (interview response). The comment, 'When you're being asked to do something by someone not in school, then it's like different' implies consideration of readers beyond the school walls.

2. The scripted introduction to the task explained that the primary means of communication in the mind mapping was to be through drawing: 'Drawing is a useful way of communicating your ideas [. . .] We want you to tell us your ideas by drawing a mind map instead of writing'. Drawing rather than writing may have motivated the children or at least diminished the sense of the mind mapping as a formal school-like test. One child commented, 'It was a change from normal English and stuff' and another said, 'It was great doing it and it was a lot of fun just to keep adding stuff on'.

3. The instructions told the children that their mind maps would communicate information to the researchers through 'quick and simple' drawings that did not take too long to produce and did not need to be 'perfect'. Associated class discussion on signs, logos and icons in everyday life indicated the 'style' of the representations. The script also gave some hints about the nature of map content in that the children were prompted to think about types of computers, the places where they are used, how they are connected, the people who use them and why, and simple/complex computer systems. A practice map was undertaken, for example on the theme of holidays. As organisation and management of mind mapping in school was a responsibility of the teacher research coordinators, evidence of variations in discussion and examples given between schools was not gathered.

4. In describing how to go about composing the map, the instructions advised the children, 'You start with your first drawing and then you draw other things as they come to your mind. The order in which you do the drawings is not important but it is important that you draw lines between the drawings that you feel are linked. The idea is to draw all the things you want to tell people about and show how they are linked in your mind by drawing lines linking them'. Whilst linking images was made explicit, how they were linked was the individual child's decision. Like the Novak and Gowin (1984) concept maps, the ImpaCT2 maps have discrete nodes connected by links. However, the nodes are images rather than words in boxes and do not have

textual labels. In contrast, Buzan's (1993) mind maps have nodes (words or pictures) that radiate from a central item as branches. The majority of ImpaCT2 maps are linked rather than branched, yet they are more akin to Buzan's idea of 'radiant thinking'. Indeed, a number of children described their map's central node as the 'main thing' or 'really the first thing that came into my mind' and explained associations which led from one idea to the next (see Buzan, 1993), using terms such as 'goes off' and 'branched off'.

The original maps have been scanned and resized. Minor changes have been made to the wording of one map in order to anonymise it.

An interview with the child who created Map A (Figure 2.1) took place in March 2001[2]. One of a number undertaken within the project, the interview was conducted individually using Figure 2.3 predetermined open-ended questions. Copies of the children's maps were provided for reference. An aim was to give control to interviewees whilst recognising that any questioning may potentially prompt the unthought (Mavers, Somekh and Restorick, 2002). I also interviewed children from a different primary school whose maps showed like features in June 2001. The children's reflections on their maps, in addition to more impromptu and personalised questions, gave me a deeper understanding not only of their meaning intentions but also how they imbued their maps with meaning.

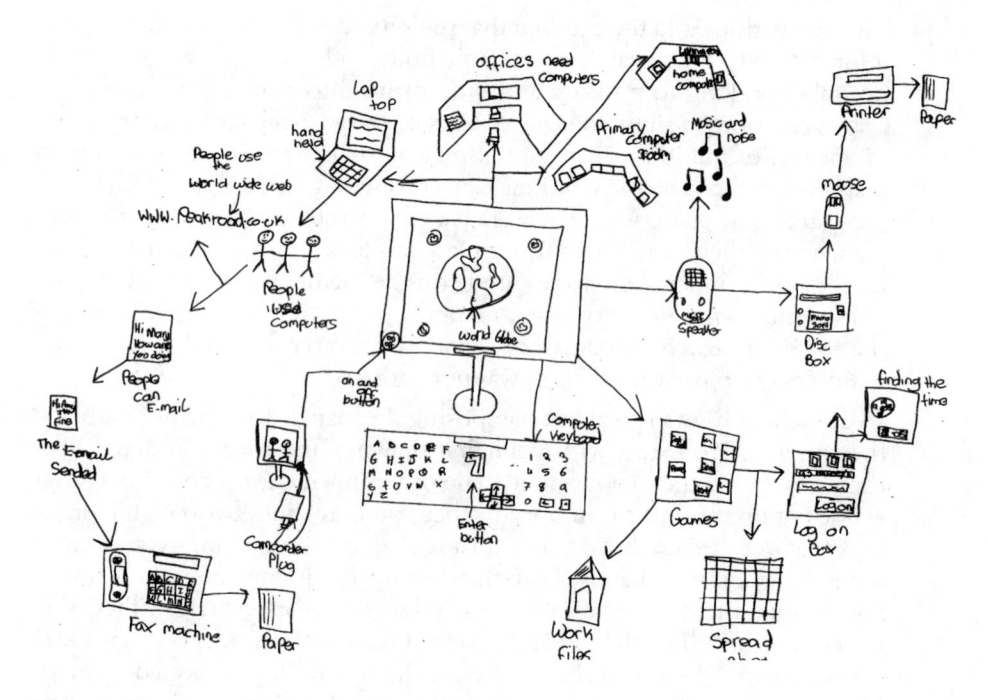

Figure 2.1

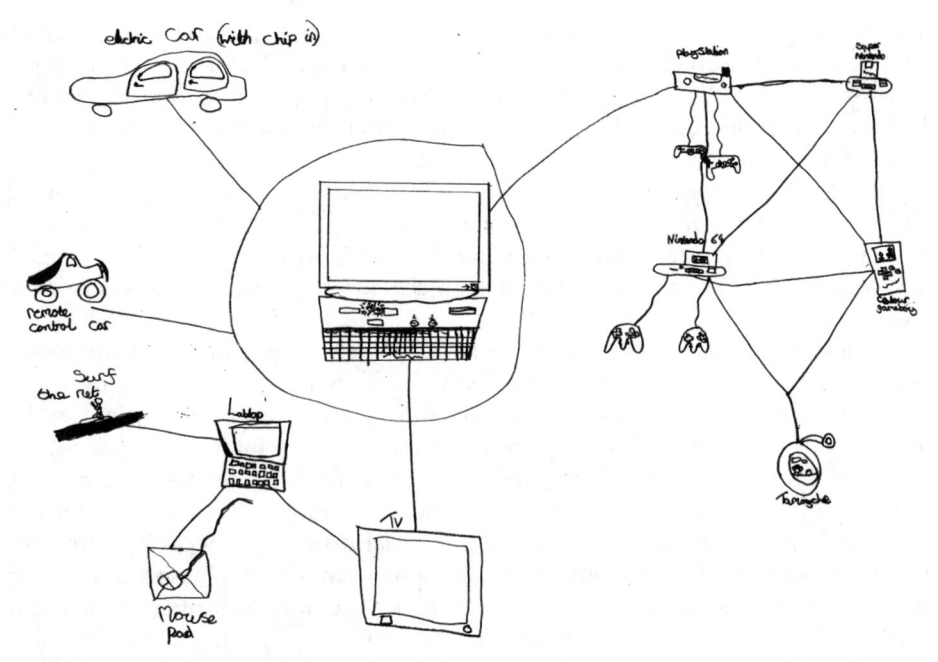

Figure 2.2

An associated 15-minute writing task, 'Telling an alien from another world about computer systems', was undertaken 7 to 10 days after the mind mapping. Again the children were requested to 'help the researchers', this time through imaginative writing on 'What would the "alien" need to know to understand computer systems in our world and what they can do?' Although the children were asked to write about their mind maps, the maps themselves were not returned to them. The instructions emphasised the importance of their own ideas and having 'fun', and told the children not to worry about spellings. Verbatim quotations replicate the spelling and punctuation of the handwritten texts.

Criterial Attributes

As task instructions stipulated the use of pencil, black pen or felt tip, the images are not coloured. The majority of nodes have been drawn as two-dimensional images from a frontal view and at eye level, although there are exceptions in Map A. The children's omission of shading was a design decision, as this was not mentioned in the script. Exclusion of background isolates items from their setting so that the maps achieve a diagrammatic rather than pictorial format. This gives an impression of the actual rather than the imagined and has the effect of raising modality. As far as more commonly represented images are concerned, we are able to see relatively uninterruptedly beyond combinations of shapes and lines to which particular objects children's pictures intend to represent. The images, drawn in a way that makes them clearly understood, are not simply reproductions of 'reality' but are socially and culturally mediated transformations of the world (Kress and van Leeuwen, 1996, pp. 8–11). Map A consists of nine items of technological equipment, three rooms, three people, eight resources accessible on computers, two sheets of paper and a representation of 'music and noise' (a total of 24 items). Map B has 11 objects, 10 of which are electronically controlled, plus a visual pun on surfing the net. The maps are therefore object rich with some extension to electronic resources and locations.

'Quick and simple' drawing may result in apparent minimalism, yet this belies the complexity of the analytical process of representation and communication. According to Kress and van Leeuwen (1996), interest in an object can be 'condensed' (p. 6) into its 'criterial characteristics' (ibid). Children make decisions about which aspects of an object, person or place are its key features and make it uniquely identifiable. These are their main defining characteristics (Kress and van Leeuwen, 1996, p. 11; Kress, 1997, p. 12) or criterial attributes. For example, the criterial attributes of the electronic games equipment in Map B (Figure 2.2) appear to be those things that portray individual objects' unique identifiers clearly and precisely. Overall shape and accurate detail, such as representations of buttons, handsets, wires, cards and screen display, work together within individual nodes to communicate key defining features.

In an interview, one child explained how his drawings were intended to afford maximal transparency to the reader. With regard to the controls in an electronic game image, he explained, 'They're like the clearest things that you see on them'. Another child, also alluding to the time constraints of the task, said, 'So I tried to make it as basic as possible but still be able to actually understand what it is'. Thus, criterial attributes are a means of communicating meanings economically but effectively and are bound up with consideration of the needs of the reader. This selection and representation of criterial attributes are preceded by a decision about which 'thing' should be drawn in the first place, for example 'I was looking for the most popular game thing there which probably everybody that's gone through town has seen it in the shop window' (interview). This demonstrates some sort of compromise in the context of task requirements between what suits the purposes of the producer and what will be maximally understood by the reader. It also implies an assumption of shared socio-cultural experience where it is expected that the reader will recognise images largely according to the producer's defining intentions.

When asked to explain how they knew how to compose their images, children's responses included, 'I've got pictures of them in my mind'; 'I can remember it from. . .'; 'They just really came into my head so I drew them all, all that I could remember about them' (child who created Map A); 'I knew what to do' ; and 'It just comes out'. Explanations of minute details in images demonstrated some children's intimate familiarity with games technologies in particular. This was not only to do with the shape and dimensions of features of the equipment; children also described items and explained operating instructions, often using the term control. One child said, 'You have to press some buttons that are arrows and two other buttons which are to shoot and jump, like Mario and everything, those type of games'. Despite their different shapes, the depicted games technologies in Map B are unified by control keys. This may indicate a thinking process something like 'games are about control and control is through buttons' (Kress, 1997, p. 12; Mavers, Pearson and Somekh, 2001, p. 11). Thus, whilst the electronic games images communicate that which has been visually perceived, their representation can be grounded in knowledge and understanding resulting from personal experience. Physical attributes and their function were interwoven in one child's description of small vertical lines in a Nintendo image, 'It's got little grids at the back, you know, to stop it heating up and fusing'. What the object looks like and what it does, therefore, are combined in the semiosis of the drawing. In this sense, the object, the using of the object and the concepts arising from that use are melded together in the image. Whilst some knowing was substantiated through ownership (self) and use (of technologies within the family or those of friends), in some cases children who had drawn images with accurate or careful detail accounted for their knowing by reference to consumer related media and social communication. For example, children justified how they 'know these things' (interview question), particularly games technologies, by seeing items and hearing about them on the television, in shops and in catalogues or magazines, 'Because it's just popular; everybody knows about them because like adverts [advertisments] and like everybody talks about them and things'. These culturally mediated subjective representations are therefore an amalgam of the individual's perceptual and/or experiential and/or conceptual and/or social world at a specific point in time, and represent some sort of polysemic image multifunctionality where these 'knowings' are inextricably, differentially and complexly interrelated.

Similarities and differences in representations of the same or similar objects in different nodes appear to be of significance. For example, the central nodes in Map A (Figure 2.1) contrast vividly with the child's representation of computers elsewhere in the map. In the detailed central monitor node, the screen is framed by a surround with a power button at the bottom left and stands on a plinth that comprises a stem and a circular base. The image alone communicates the child's memory of the physical features of a monitor, knowledge that it can be switched on and off and an implication that the screen displays visual information. This is substantiated by her writing where the child describes the screen as 'that is where all the imformation comes up'. The link between the monitor and the keyboard communicates something about how the separate items are connected, possibly one being related to the functionality of the other. Particular detail is given in the keyboard image. Apart from 't', all 26 letters of the alphabet are written in capitals (as on a keyboard) and in alphabetical order (unlike a keyboard, although few of us would be able to replicate the order of keys from memory). The child has also included each number beginning at '1' and ending on '0', again using left to right and top to bottom orientation. As well as awareness of the scope of English numeric and alphabetic systems and their presence on the keyboard, this also implies a knowing about their use for text input. The two symbols on the keys at the bottom right of the image appear to be '<' and '∧'. This may be shorthand for indicating her knowledge of a range of keys that provide characters for use in numerical formulae, punctuation or other presentational devices. Her inclusion of the enter key (specifically labelled) with the appropriate symbol (inverted) and the arrow keys shows further knowledge of the keyboard, possibly for functionality as command or control keys.

Other computer images are not given this detail. The laptop node shows the shape of the resource, that it is a single unit, its 'openability' (through use of perspective), its screen (with text squiggles) and the presence of a keyboard (minus characters). This reduced detail may indicate that the child knows something about laptops but is unable to provide more information. However, there might be an alternative explanation. Exclusion of detail may imply its redundancy, replicated features shown in the central nodes being deemed unnecessary. In the light of this given, the laptop's portability becomes the new.

The change in criterial focus between the central nodes and the laptop becomes even more manifest in the nodes that show location. Each of the three rooms (office, living room and 'primary computer room') has three-dimensional characteristics in that the three sides of the rooms are drawn as if the child were standing in the doorway. They are depicted as plans rather than pictures. Drawn from a high angle, this gives the reader a bird's-eye view of each room and enables the child to provide a plan of the number and positioning of computers. As readers, we infer contextually that the shapes in the rooms are intended to represent computers in line with the map's theme. Had the focus of the task been different one would expect different depictions of items to have been chosen. The conjoined squares representing the office computer may indicate a laptop, possibly supported by interview evidence, 'some people in businesses they have laptops'. The home computer(s) are squares inside squares, one possibly implying digital television, 'I've got the Internet on my television as well' (interview). The school computers are even less detailed (squares). The single office computer on the desk with the single chair suggests a different experience from the multiple computers in school that are not given tables or chairs. There may be a certain perception of the world of work (note also the use of squiggly lines in the item on the office wall, which implies a chart of some kind rather than a picture) compared with the world of school. Otherwise, the reduced detail of the computer systems may be to do with the constraints of the speed of production or space within the node. The technologies designated by simple shapes in the room plans therefore appear to have a specific function. They represent a 'fusion' (Kress and van Leeuwen, 1996, p. 51) or 'computerness' (Mavers, Pearson and Somekh, 2001, p. 13) where focal vision is on their existence, positioning and number in a particular setting rather than on their criterial attributes.

Contrasting levels of detail appear to be motivated by the child's key meaning intention for each node, its criterial focus. The detailed criterial attributes of items of computer equipment, as in the central nodes, communicate their main identifying features. Their reduced detail in nodes that are primarily locational is a shift in criterial detail that communicates a shift in focus. Different communication purposes therefore result in different representations of the same or similar items according to the particular function they are required to fulfil and the individual's particular meaning intention.

Spatial Organisation and Links

Whilst providing general guidance on map construction, the task instructions did not prescribe a specific format. The children had informational power over content and presentation, in what they chose to draw and how they went about their drawing. Located in the centre of the monitor in Map A is an image labelled 'world Globe'. The precise size and shape of the land masses appear to be either unfamiliar or unnecessary to communicate the meaning she intends, presumably the global. However, in the context of the map rather than as an isolated image, her meaning intention goes beyond this. In some sense the world is contained in the computer and the computer contains the world. Like lexis in writing, the globe image has significance in itself but situated meanings proliferate when it is drawn in relation to other images.

Sign-making in the choice and positioning of images in relation to others can communicate complex analogies and classifications (Kress and van Leeuwen, 1996). At the very heart of Map A, the two linked focal nodes (the monitor and keyboard) are enlarged. All surrounding nodes are of a similar size and broadly equidistant. This domination of the page through both size and positioning would appear to be significant and may have the function of assigning the central nodes status as a title (a statement about the focus of the map or the superordinate), formulating the central hub from which all other ideas (the subordinates) emanate. It is also an implied starting point for the reading of the map. Analysis of Map A reveals a use of space to organise 'Computers in My World' into four distinctly classified areas:

- *Items making up a computer system*
  Shown to the right of the central node and leading to the top right-hand corner of the page, these are the computer's physical components. The monitor and keyboard are linked to the speaker (with its 'Music and noise' association), a 'Disc Box' (not a box containing discs but the processing unit with on/off/ eject buttons or sockets for input devices, a rectangular, possibly CD, drive and a 'Microsoft' label), a mouse and a printer (with a paper association).

- *Locations of use*
  The home, office and school as designated locations of computer use are evident in the child's map (top centre), writing and interview. In the latter she

expands on her home experience to that in her extended family and at friends' homes and her personal experience of helping in the school office, visiting a pet shop and reference to her aunt in the police force.

- *Information and communication*

  The eight nodes to the left-hand side of the page identify use of computers for information and communication. This includes the web (note the correct components, order and use of 'dots' in the school web address), email (here for personal/social purposes), fax (the telephone link being explained in the interview as denoting oral communication and paper-based information transmission, as implied in the linked adjacent node) and video (moving images).

- *Computer resources*

  To the bottom right of the map are resources available on a computer: games, 'Work files', a spreadsheet, 'Log on Box' and 'finding the time' (analogue and digital).

Her four classifications (items making up a computer system, locations of use, information and communication, and computer resources) might be summarised as the 'what', 'where', 'why' and 'how' of computer use.

The links tell us that connections between nodes are intended in some way. As labelling the lines between nodes was not a task requirement, reading of the links necessitates an inference, what the reader thinks might be meant. We only know that particular nodes are linked in some way, not the child's specific meaning intention of the perceived nature of the associations. There may be implied subtleties around 'links to' (e.g., physically), 'links with' (e.g., functionally or conceptually) and 'links between' (e.g., locationally).

However, the child also uses links as a further means of classification and directing the reader in the reading of her map. Apart from the conjoining of the central monitor and keyboard nodes, there are clear links to the 'computer resources' and 'items making up a computer system' sections. The uppermost link has branched connections to the locations of use and information and communication sections, the latter being the only area to have a return link (and this may be something to do with the camcorder plugging into the computer). A relatively equal size of and distance between the surrounding nodes seems to imply that there is no particular order in which the designated routes to the four classified areas should be followed. The map invites a non-hierarchical reading of the four classifications. It could be that previous experience prompted the use of arrowheads. Alternatively, it could be that the child wished her map to be read in a particular way, that the arrows deliberately guide the direction in which the images are to be sequentially viewed and interpreted within each classified area. Another child explained arrowheaded links as 'They tell you which way to go' and one said, 'If it was in India it would go that way'. Thus, the reader is given a choice with regard to the order in

Communicating Meanings 29

which the sub-classifications might be explored but is then intentionally led through that section. There are therefore alternative and preferred paths through the map.

This interpretation of the apparently deliberate structure of Map A examined in isolation is supported by the child's writing and interview comments. For example, of the three paragraphs of her writing, the first gives a description of the computer's material components (items making up a computer system), followed by a second on use of the computer for various purposes such as email and games (information and communication) and how this is done using CDs and saving files (computer resources), whilst the third focuses on places where computers are used 'in homes, in offices, in school and all round the world' (locations of use). When asked why she joined the nodes as she did, the child replied, 'It was in sections. And then like on this half I've done what you can find on the computer like the keyboard and the speaker and all that; that one just went off there. And then I've done where you can find computers. And then saying how emails work because I've done a laptop and then world wide web and then emails and then going on to fax machines. And then what you can find in computers, like you can find the spreadsheets and work files and games and all that'. Despite the linearity of written

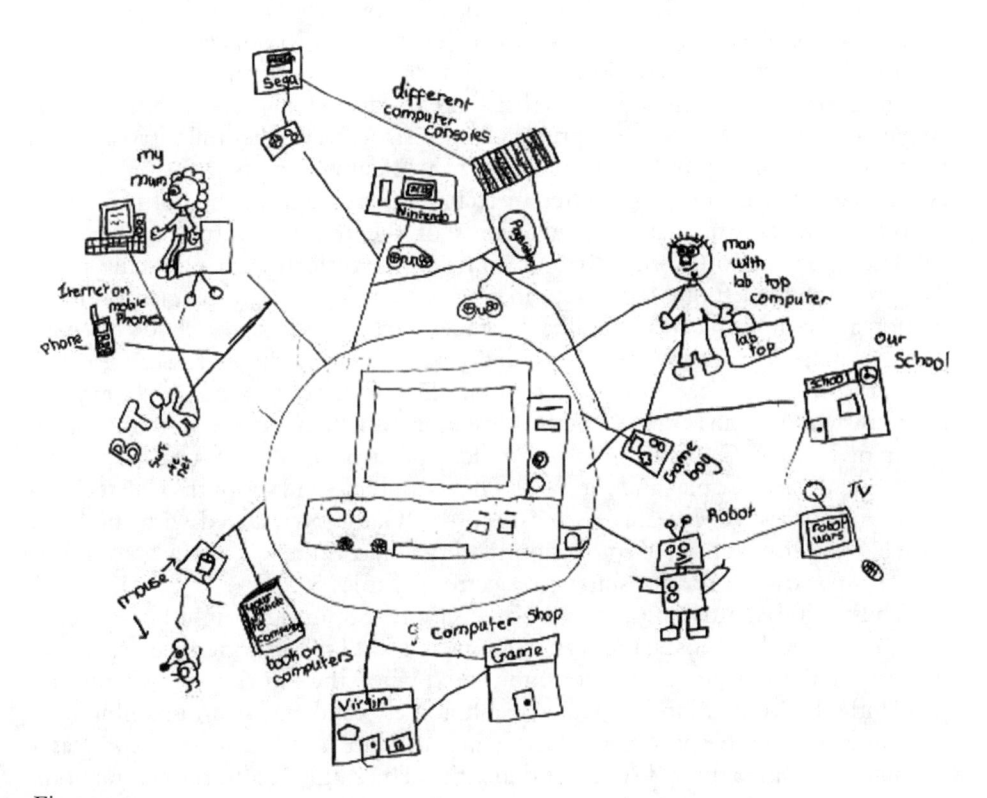

Figure 2.3

and spoken language (in this instance), the variant order in which the categories are presented in the oral and written forms substantiates her apparently egalitarian intentions which the map is able to communicate so effectively. Notwithstanding the 9-month gap between the drawing/writing and interviewing, the child's lucid explanation of the structure indicates that her map has remained 'readable' (and arguably her current view) even after such a time lapse.

Some links suggest a more definite reading path whilst others give the reader freedom to explore in different directions within and across groupings. Absence of arrowheads in Maps B and C reduces the prescription of directionality. Similarly, the framing of the central nodes implies exit at any point of its circularity. In Map C the reader can choose the order in which to explore the eight linked nodes or groups of nodes. Branched links to the four groups at the top, left and bottom of the map also give the reader choice. Similarly, the interconnections within the electronic games group in Map B give the reader freedom to explore in any direction, with the exception of the lowest node. This is linked only to the 'Nintendo 64' and 'Colour Gameboy'. Within this grouping, the child appears to have selected and positioned items carefully to create a reading path leading the reader from the more to the less well known ('PlayStation' to 'Tamogche') (see Kress and van Leeuwen, 1996, pp. 203–211; Jewitt and Oyamo, 2001, pp. 147–149). This shows sensitivity to a reader who may not be as knowledgeable as the producer.

On some occasions, juxtaposition and linkage take on an authoritative role in bringing together dissimilar images that share like functional, operational or locational (or experiential or conceptual) characteristics. The dissimilarity of items making up classifications forces the reader to work at making meaning, as in Map A. Similarly, the grouping of different technological items to the bottom left of Map B is not self-explanatory. The 'toyness' of the 'remote control car' seems to validate its separation from electronic control of an 'electric car with chip in it'. The group to the left of Map C appears to represent use of technologies for information and communication. Online resources are the focus of the child's opening sentence in her writing, 'A computer can do many different things you can use it to go on the internet. That means you can send E-mails/letters to different countries as far away as Ostralia [sic]'. Other sub-categories, which are not so immediately apparent in Map C, may be, for example, operational or peripheral tools (the mouse on the mouse mat and the 'book on computers') and shops that sell technological resources. A separate classification, the 'Game boy' linked with the 'man with lab [sic] top computer' implies portability whereas the link to the games console group shows its relationship with electronic games.

Whilst criterial attributes, spatial organisation and linkage might be separated out for analytical purposes, they can combine in a kind of semiotic alliance. Classificatory thinking is powerfully communicated when they work together interdependently. In Maps B and C games technologies stand out as an unambiguous grouping. The white space around the games in Map B and their positioning as a separate entity give them distance and identity. The single link to the central node strengthens the discreteness of this classification. When asked, 'Why have you joined them up in this way?' one child replied, 'Because they're all the same equipment, they've got the same purpose or something, to be made, and they're all computers really, so they're a family or something, something like that. That's why I joined them all up'. Linked groupings of games sharing criterial attributes and positioned together as a 'family' were explained in one interview as 'Well I was just linking them together to give a clearer view to somebody that's reading it, to say that these are all games and they're linked together. So the Nintendo is a game but the PlayStation 2, if I connect it to it, they will see that it is a game but it's a different type of make. Somebody could think that's a video player, couldn't they, if they didn't know what it was? That's why I linked them together so if you know what one is, a game, if you link them together, the rest of them must be games'. Likenesses and distinctions in the criterial attributes of these objects draw them together as a classified group yet differentiate them from one another. One child explained grouped games as 'Because, like, they're the same things almost' and another said, 'They would see the difference in the controls and that'. These families are not necessarily exhaustive and may be exemplars of the type. For example, one child commented, 'And there's a lot more but they're the basic ones that everybody knows'. The child who created Map A did not draw specific electronic games equipment. Rather, she identifies 'types' of games using words in boxes (e.g., 'football', 'races', 'space' and 'text'). A transfer to 'text squiggles' appears to imply that other games are available but the child either does not have the time or the knowledge to add more. It is rather like a visual etcetera.

Spatial arrangement appears to have been both the result of a pre-considered design and intrinsic to the process of map production, and was not something that was retrospectively superimposed. Children's statements such as 'I've put them in order like that, it's more neater to me' and 'So really, I used these to try and organise what I was going to actually use it for and just so that I could understand' imply that the positioning of nodes on the page and links between images aided thinking processes as organisational tools. Representation can therefore be a means of making sense for oneself as well as for others.

Conclusions

The children appear to have drawn in such a way as to make themselves maximally understood. For this reason, they have tried to make their images precise, clear and immediately recognisable, to be transparently readable. The nature of the drawing is of itself intensely meaningful. The children have shown the reader the criterial attributes of specific items or exemplifications of the type that they have deliberately selected out for representation and which convey what is important to the individual at this time, in this context and for this purpose.

A task requirement, linguistic labelling is used to 'anchor' (Barthes, 1977, p. 38) image definition (e.g., the 'Camcorder Plug' in Map A) and extends to processes and functionality (e.g., 'People can E-mail' and 'The E-mail sended' in Map A).

One child's comment, 'because if you didn't put them there, they wouldn't know what it was', suggests benefits to clarity. Actually, for the most part, the nodes would be largely recognisable without them. The children's subsequent writing mainly defined and described equipment, how to make things happen and what can be done with computers. For example, the child who created Map B wrote 'A computer is a kind of big metal box [. . .] It has something called a keyboard. When you touch a button it shows up on the screen [. . .] it can let you play games and write letters'. Their spoken words tended to focus on the functional, experiential and actional. Language is able to make explicit movement and processes which the static image does by inference (which is culturally dependent).

The mind maps are not just illustrations; they are communicators of analytical thinking. These image-based maps have enabled the children to communicate succinctly and effectively that which would not have been so easy with words. The spatiality of the page as against the linearity of language in speech and writing affords particular possibilities in communication potential. The ways in which images have been framed, positioned on the page and related to one another through links communicate salience, classify constituents into 'families' and provide reading paths. The children have used size, spacing, distancing and positioning to separate groupings but also to put nodes into a relationship with one another. They have created links to invite non-hierarchical exploration of 'families', sometimes with predetermined directionality, sometimes with non-linearity, guiding or exerting control over the reader to a greater or lesser extent. These are not accidental but suffused with meanings, meanings that are created with communicational and interpretational intentionality. There appears to be an assumption that, through shared cultural conventions, the reader will at least recognise preferred meanings.

The maps also provide an insight into children's representational practices and capabilities. The communicational landscape is changing (Street, 1998; Goodwyn, 1998; Kress, 2000a). Expanding communication possibilities in new and relatively new technologies are extending the communicative potentials open to children and the spectrum of semiotic resources available to them. Maximising on the modal potentialities of the visual, these children have used drawing effectively, economically and skilfully to communicate with researchers. Their choices and compositions (the 'what' and 'how') are bound up with their perceptions of modal affordance. The children have used the functional specialisms of drawing to realise particular meanings. Their use of the page demonstrates an intelligent visual literacy where they have conveyed aspects of their knowing and complexities of their thinking with precision and clarity.

Notes

1. Acknowledgements to my ImpaCT2 colleagues, Bridget Somekh (Manchester Metropolitan University), Colin Harrison, Tony Fisher and Kaye Hawe (University of

Nottingham), Peter Scrimshaw and Cathy Lewin (Open University) and to Helen Brown (Becta) for their kind agreement to allow me to use this data.
2. Interviews with a small number of children whose maps held particular interest for the ImpaCT2 evaluation's focus did not include the children who created Maps B and C. In my research into multimodality, I analyse the data for quite different purposes.

References

Barthes, R. (1977) *Image, Music, Text* (S. Heath, Trans.). London: Fontana Press.
Buzan, T. (1993) *The Mind Map Book: Radiant Thinking—The Major Evolution in Human Thought*. London: BBC Books.
Christensen, P. and James, A. (2000) 'Childhood Diversity and Commonality: Some Methodological Insights'. In P. Christensen and A. James (Eds.), *Research with Children: Perspectives and Practices*. London: Falmer Press.
Goodwyn, A. (1998) 'Adapting to the Textual Landscape: Bringing Print and Visual Texts Together in the Classroom'. In A. Goodwyn (Ed.), *Literary and Media Texts in Secondary English: New Approaches*. London: Cassell.
Jewitt, C., Kress, G.R., Ogborn, J. and Tsatsarelis, C. (2000) 'Teaching and Learning: Beyond Language', *Teaching Education. 11(3)*, pp. 327–341.
Jewitt, C. and Oyamo, R. (2001) 'Visual Meaning: A Social Semiotic Approach'. In T. van Leeuwen and C. Jewitt (Eds.), *Handbook of Visual Analysis*. London: Sage Publications.
Kenner, C. (2000) 'Recipes, Alphabets and I_U: A Four Year Old Explores the Visual Potential of Literacy', *Early Years, 20(2)*, pp. 68–79.
Kress, G.R. (1997) *Before Writing: Rethinking the Paths to Literacy*. London: Routledge.
Kress, G.R. (2000a) 'A Curriculum for the Future', *Cambridge Journal of Education, 30(1)*, pp. 133–145.
Kress, G.R. (2000b) 'Design and Transformation: New Theories of Meaning'. In B. Cope and M. Kalantzis (Eds.), *Multiliteracies: Literacy Learning and the Design of Social Futures*. London: Routledge.
Kress, G.R., Jewitt, C., Ogborn, J. and Tsatsarelis, C. (2001), *Multimodal Teaching and Learning: The Rhetorics of the Science Classroom*. London: Continuum.
Kress, G.R. and van Leeuwen, T. (1996) *Reading Images: The Grammar of Visual Design*, London: Routledge.
Millard, E. and Marsh, J. (2001) 'Words with Pictures: The Role of Visual Literacy in Writing and its Implication for Schooling', *Reading, 35(2)*, pp. 54–61.
Mavers, D., Pearson, M. and Somekh, B. (2001) *Exploring the Development of Children's Understandings of Digital Technologies 1999–2001*. Paper presented at the Cultures of Learning Conference, University of Bristol, United Kingdom, April 2001.
Mavers, D., Somekh, B. and Restorick, J. (2002) 'Interpreting the Externalised Images of Pupils' Conceptions of ICT: Methods for the Analysis of Concept Maps', *Computers and Education, 38*, pp. 187–207.
Novak, J. D. and Gowin, D. B. (1984) *Learning How to Learn*. New York: Cambridge University Press.
Street, B. (1998) 'New Literacies in Theory and Practice: What Are the Implications for Language in Education?', *Linguistics and Education, 10(1)*, pp. 1–24.

Carey Jewitt

3

COMPUTER-MEDIATED LEARNING: THE MULTIMODAL CONSTRUCTION OF MATHEMATICAL ENTITIES ON SCREEN

> *Educationalists who avoid asking questions of the epistemological significance and implications of their practices involving the new information and communication technologies do so at their peril*
> —Lea and Nicoll, 2002:8

This chapter explores the role of a range of representational modes (organised, regular means of representation and communication) in two students' construction of the entity[1] 'bounce' using Playground, a computer programming system designed for the use of children (ages four years old and over) to build computer games. The students' interaction with the resources of the screen suggest the need to look beyond language and to re-think learning as a multimodal accomplishment. The analysis centres on the impact of modes (including still image, gesture, posture, speech, animated movement and writing) on the emergence of the mathematical concept of bounce. I suggest that the choice of representational modes in the design of a programme is central to the engagement of the user with the programme. Modes (e. g., image and writing) provide the maker of an application and the user of it with different features for making meaning and for engaging with aspects of programming. Through a detailed multimodal analysis of the students' design process I show that the modal resources each makes available to the user realises the entity 'bounce' in quite different ways. I conclude that a multimodal approach can offer new insights into understanding the learning potentials of computer programming applications such as Playground.

Multimodality and Computer-Mediated Learning

Computer-based applications are frequently discussed as being effective tools for learning. However, the question remains of how the move from traditional technologies of teaching and learning to computer-based technologies actually impact on (re-shape) the practices of learning.

When a learner sits alone in front of a computer and engages with the resources on screen there is more going on than the interaction of that individual with the screen. Their activity is the complex outcome of their interaction: of the learner with other people, tools, and the cultural and institutional rules and norms of the community within which they are situated (Russell, 2002). With this complex web of activity in mind, we can think about learning as one complex result of interactions with others mediated by tools in culture. The computer is one such tool, and the *effect of tool mediation* is one way to understand the complexity of the relationship between the learner, the screen, and the content of 'what is to be learnt' in the move from page to screen.

The affordances of computer-based applications that are explored are often superficial, focusing on attractiveness as a motivating tool rather than the affordances of the medium as a pedagogic tool. The computer, like any other technological tool used in teaching (e. g., over-head projector, blackboard, or pen and paper), does not itself bring about '*improvements*' in learning. Nonetheless, all technologies, old and new, change the mediation of learning in particular ways. Research on the use of computers in schools shows that student engagement with computers mediates the re-organisation of interactions among teachers and pupils in ways that create new learning environments. Computer-mediated learning re-shapes literacy practices, for instance, and school activity more broadly, in ways that offer students the potential to construct themselves differently as learners (Morgan et al., 2002). The re-mediation of learning in virtual learning environments has been shown to impact on the notion of communities of learners, the norms and rules of these communities, and the division of labour within them, as people take on different roles (Russell, 2002).

Understanding the impact of the computer as a 'mediating tool' is central to understanding computer-mediated learning (Saljo, 1999). A change in tools, from pen and paper to computer application, for example, 're-mediates' the interaction between the learner and the object of study. Much of the work on how computers re-mediate learning focuses on how computers bring forth different kinds of talk between learners. The focus is on how the computer reconfigures the social relations between learners rather than on how the computer as a tool re-mediates the content of what is to be learnt. While speech and writing remain important communicative modes in computer-mediated learning environments, they are not the only (or the primary) representational modes on screen. (Nor are speech and writing necessarily the dominant modes in traditional classroom teaching and learning, as my work with Gunther Kress and others on the science classroom and the English classroom shows [Kress et al., 2001, Jewitt, 2002].)

The multimodal features of computer applications like Playground raise a number of questions about learning. The semiotic potentials made available via a multimodal text, whatever its technology, contribute to the shaping of what students can 'do with it'—how they can 'design meaning'. In order to understand the game-building practices of students engaged with Playground, a better understanding is required of the kinds of meaning-making resources these applications provide. In short, there is a need to understand what it is that students are working with and how these multimodal resources might contribute to the shaping of the learner, the learning environment, and what it is that is to be learnt.

This chapter focuses on how the design of the multimodal resources of Playground (i. e., animated movement, sound effect, still image, speech, and writing) might re-organise or re-mediate the ways in which students learn (produce knowledge). More specifically, it explores how two students' conception of 'bounce' develops as an emergent mathematical concept through engaging with Playground. I suggest that the students' understanding of 'bounce' is shaped (mediated) by the multimodal semiotic resources of Playground, as well as the students' everyday knowledge and experiences that they bring to their interaction.

Designing a Game

The chapter focuses on two students, Emily and Rachel[2] (age seven years), who build a game from scratch using a limited set of eight animagadgets (animagadgets are collections of ready-made pieces of code, or 'behaviours'). Initially, the students were given worksheets that directed them to explore the functionality of the animagadgets. They turned each animagadget on and watched the behaviours while discussing them with each other and with the researcher. They mapped out their game through talk, drawing and writing. The students were encouraged to be specific about what the game would do, and how the components (behaviours) would make the game work. Finally, the children were asked to draw a picture and to write the rules of the game.

The two students made the game over three one-hour sessions. In the first session the game is designed on paper and then visually on screen. In the second session the students concentrate on one aspect of programming—making the bullets bounce. In the third session the students program the 'blow-up behaviour' on the bullets and complete the game. In a fourth session the game was shared and re-designed with students in Sweden (see Noss et al., 2002, for a discussion of collaborative game design).

Designing the Game on Paper

The students' representation of bounce through the medium of pen and paper described below differs from the traditional design of bounce in a maths textbook; it

PICTURE OF MY GAME

THE RULES IN MY GAME

~~I want the~~ The little figure will move around the place and when the alien finally catches it. It make an expolshan noise and the bombs go sidways by arows and then then is or you touch the bags it goes diffrent way and when you touch the bar it makes a nois.

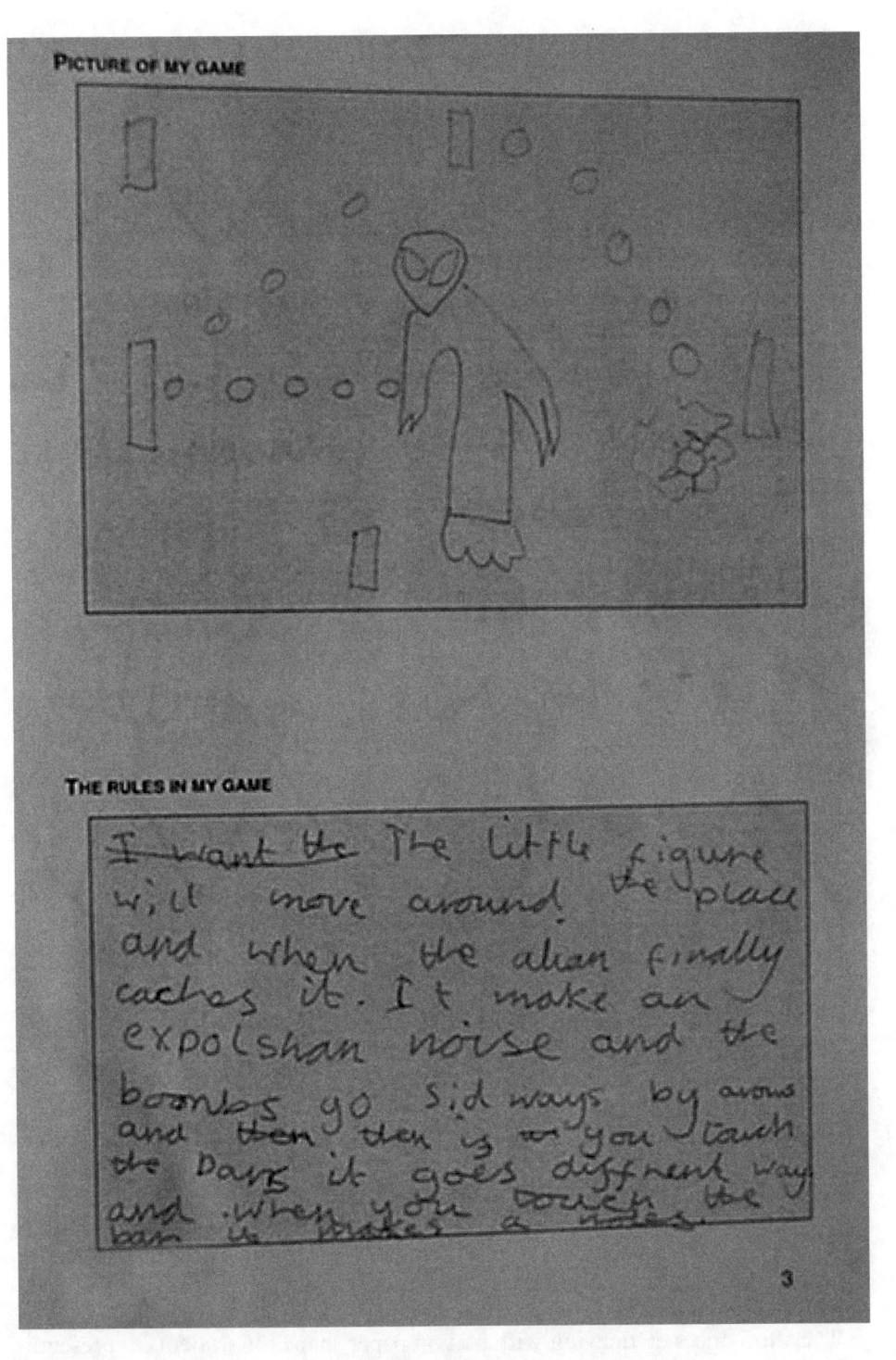

Figure 3.1. Emily and Rachel's completed worksheet for initial game design

38   MULTIMODAL LITERACY

is already shaped by the centrality of the demands of the screen. The students' design of the game on paper is shown in Figure 3.1.

Analysis of students' writing shows that the sequential affordances of writing realise the entity 'rule' as a narrative in which the elements of the game are named—the alien, the little figure, the bombs, the 'place', and the 'bars'. Through writing, the students represent the game as a sequence of events and actional relations between named elements.

> The little figure will move around the place and when the alian finally caches it. It makes an expolshan noise and the bombs go sidways by arows and then if you touch the barrs it goes different ways and when you touch the bar it makes a noies.

The entity 'bounce' is realised through the interaction of these elements but it is not foregrounded. The alien and the bombs are represented as agentive—they 'catch' or 'go' and 'touch', and the agency of the user 'you' is merged with that of the bombs to personify them, for example '. . . you touch them. . .'. This highlights the inactivity of the bars beyond the 'reaction/response' as the goal of the action of the bomb (and the user). The students' use of the mode of writing foregrounds the little figure and its movement (in the theme structure of the first sentence) and the combination of the descriptive adjective 'little' and the vague 'move around the place' suggest the little figure is the weaker element in the game. The use of 'catch' and the sequence of the sentence indicates that the role of the players is that of the everyday game-genre of catch/tag (which exists both on- and off-screen).

The entity bounce is linguistically represented as 'the bombs go sidways by arrows and then if you [the bomb] touch the bars it goes different ways. . .'. 'Bounce' is represented as a matter of movement and change of direction when something is touched. The modal affordances of writing do not demand that what causes the change in movement, the user, the bomb or the bars be made explicit.

The resources of drawing offer different representational affordances than those of writing, and these 'demand' a different representational commitment of the students. In drawing, the students are 'forced' to depict the size, shape and features of the elements of the game—the alien, the little figure, the bombs. They are required to visually 'fill in' the words 'little figure'—it becomes a little animal (not much bigger than a bullet), with two legs, two arms, two big ears, a head and a body. The spatial affordances of image require these relations to be newly specified. Through their use of compositional resources, size and detail, the students visually increase the power difference between the little figure and the alien. The alien is central in the drawing via its compositional position in the centre of the design space, its size (it is about eight times bigger than the little figure), and detail—specifically the inclusion of human-like features (eyes). The alien is visually represented as acting on the little figure via the vector [3] of the bullets emanating from it.

The affordances of drawing with pen on paper shape the students' representation of movement and noise. Through their drawing they visually extend the written entity bounce. They draw on the genre of time-lapse images, as the visual trace of a sequence of movement over time, to represent the movement of the bullets/bombs. They represent 'explosion' in a visual cartoon genre of 'effect'—the shaking of a near space around the little figure by a wiggly line around the form. Through these visual resources the entity bounce is visually represented as 'ricochet'. The direction of the movement of the bombs/bullets is realised spatially in relation to the static bars, the alien, and the little figure.

The student's drawing and writing on the worksheet is not the game itself; rather, it is the student's externalisation of the notion of game which is incited by her understanding of the potentials and genre expectations/experience of Playground, and games for screen more generally—that is, the potentials of animated movement, sound effect, 'catching', and destroying. The student's drawing is as an idealised account of the outcome of the game—the bullet comes from the alien, ricochets off a barrier, then off another, and hits the little figure which explodes. The affordances of pen and paper both enable and constrain the design of the game and the student's interaction with these affordances brings forth different elements of the game, ideas of 'bounce' and notions of game itself. The student then designs her game with the resources of Playground.

Designing the Game on Screen

Even though the initial design on paper was designed with screen and Playground in mind, the move to Playground demands a transformation of the students' notion of the game spatially and modally. Playground brings with it the potential for temporal sequences of movement across/within the space of the screen, which realise visual rhythms, and the illusion of three-dimensionality. The students are required to move the initial design from the boundaried flat page to open multi-dimensionality of the screen. They move from the affordances of written word and static line drawing to the affordances of colour, ready-made images, animated movement and sound effect. The students have to transform/formalise the shape of bounce /rule as written in language (and image) to the multimodal Playground system.

The affordances of Playground demand that the students re-specify the generalised elements of their game design on pen and paper. The visual design of the game (the visual design of the elements and their spatial relations) in session one is not 'merely' a matter of decoration: it is the design of the game narrative itself (Figure 3.2).

The 'little figure' needs to be fully depicted and the students select an image of a little dog from the Playground 'notebook' of images. The alien selected from the notebook is green, smaller, and more monster-like (less human). The bombs are transformed now into small white bullets. The background of the game named in the writing as 'place' and represented in the drawing as a grey rectangle (screen) is represented by an image of the planet Jupiter. And the frame of the

Figure 3.2. Closeup of the initial game designed in Playground

game is transformed from a rectangle to a circle. Through their engagement with (and selection from) the visual resources of Playground, the students create a strong visual game narrative that is emergent in the design on paper. A 'stranger/outsider' (the little dog) visits a planet where the (native) alien defends his territory. This narrative is expressed in Emily's spoken narrative at this stage of the design:

> I want there to be little bars where if you hit it, it [the ball] goes another way and another way and another way and I want there to be another little creature that he tries to kill.

The visual design of this game narrative in Playground brings forth the students' ambiguities about the movement of the game elements in the second game-design session. These are present in the paper and pen design of the game; however the modal affordances of Playground—in particular the potential for animated movement—'demand' that these be resolved. The students designed the visual frame of the game (and through it, defined the game narrative) and moved on to consider the movement of the elements. Interestingly, the move from the page to screen ups the stakes for the little figure who, instead of being caught, will now be killed, reflecting a change in game genre from the genre of board game to the genre of adventure/action game on the screen.

The programming function and affordance of Playground demands that the students specify (select) the action and movement of each game element. The students select the 'shoot in four directions' animagadget for the behaviour of the green alien; the initial movement of the alien in the written narrative of the game-design is transformed in Playground into "fires bullets". The vague movement of the "little doggy . . . around the place" is now specified as moving left to right in a straight line by the students' choice of the animagadget 'move left and right with shift and control'. In order for an object to have functionality in Playground the user needs to put a 'behaviour' (a ready-made piece of programming code) on the back of the object. This demands that the user decide what game element is going to 'have' the behaviour. In this way the resources of Playground foreground the agency of an object in the game-design process, and raises the question 'what objects have agency'—an issue that is present but not required to be resolved in the pen and paper game-design.

The students play the game and realise that the bullets do not move in the way that they want them to move, and Emily says, "but we need to make that [the bullet] bounce". The students have drawn the movement of the bullet, described it in their writing and talk, and traced it on the computer screen with their fingers. However, this is the first time that Emily has used the word "bounce" in the process of designing the game. Her specification of the movement in this way may be brought forth by the classification of movement in the Playground environment, one of which is 'bouncing'. As Emily discusses the behaviour 'bounce' she renames the object "ball". The student's engagement with the mode of speech forces her into lexicalising the general notion of 'movement'; and this brings forth a change in semantic field that then selects the object of discussion.

The Design of 'Bounce'

The remainder of this chapter focuses on how the students' concept of bounce develops through their interaction with the resources of Playground, each other and the researcher[4].

In session two of the game-design, the students program the bouncing movement of the bullets. The session consists of six framed activities, punctuated by the students playing the game.

Frames of activity in Session Two of the game-design

Play game
- Plan the movement of the bullets and the position of the sticks.
- Make the sticks and position them on the game.

- Read the bounce animagadget.
- Attach the bounce behaviour to the sticks.

Play game
- Attach the bounce behaviour to the bullets.

Play game
- Realise and specify the problem with the bounce.

Planning through Gesture and Speech

The two students play the game, and the bullets do not move in the way that they had wanted. The two students stop playing the game and begin to plan the movement of the balls visually through their gestures on the screen and their talk.

Three points emerge from a multimodal analysis of this interaction that are important in relation to what unfolds in the session as they program the bouncing behaviour. First, the two students' initial talk and gesture is strongly co-ordinated—they appear to have a shared vision of how they imagine the bullet moving: The bullet moves from the alien to the left stick, and then to the top-right stick. However, at this point the students stop acting in unison and two alternative versions of the movement of the bullet emerge (that they are alternative versions of events is indicated by the break in the co-ordination of their activity). The students' gestures with the screen are represented in Figure 3.3.

Rachel traces the bullet moving in a *vertical* line down to the bottom-right stick and from there in a *horizontal* line to the dog, and wiggles the pen to indicate either somewhere in that area or a generalised 'other place'. Rachel is working with the entity 'bounce' as a generalised concept of movement as going from one place to another.

Emily appears to be working with the entity 'bounce' as a specific (and more specialised) kind of movement. Holding her finger on the top-right stick is a gestural sign of her realisation of 'bounce' as a particular kind of movement. Emily understands that a bullet could not move in a perpendicular line from the top-right to the bottom-right stick (as gestured by Rachel). In order to 'imagine' the movement of the bullet Emily gesturally traces an 'imagined' stick to the right of the alien. This 'gestural overlay' adds another stick to the visual design of the game, which in turn enables her to imagine the bullet bouncing from the top-right stick to the bottom-right stick, and then off past the dog.

The second point to emerge from this multimodal analysis is the students' uncertainty about what it is that 'produces' the bounce. Just as their two accounts start similarly, they end similarly, with a faltering tone of voice, and lexical vagueness (R:'whatever', E: 'try to' and 'or something'), and gestural vagueness (R wiggles her pen, E slowly trails her finger off the edge of the screen). This is perhaps the students' gestural articulation of uncertainty about how the movement of a

Table 3.1. Students Planning the Movement of Bullets

Time	Person	Speech	Gesture with screen
12. 21. 00	E	Good	presses 'up' arrow key—alien fires ball
			presses 'left' arrow key—alien fires ball
			which moves through the stick
		but *we need to make that*	points finger at left stick on screen
		bounce, and *that*—	points to "little doggy"
		ooh *good* we can see the eye	points at image of 'Jupiter's eye' on screen
	I	so what's the next thing you all want to do?	
	R	Well	
		The bullet *shoots*	points with pen at alien
		to *there*	points with pen at left stick
	E	to *that*	points with finger at left stick
	R	to *there*	points with pen at top-right stick
	E	to bounce *up to there*	points with finger at top-right stick, keeps finger there
	R	and then *that*	still pointing at top-right stick
		bounces to *there*	points with pen at bottom-right stick
		and then to *the dog*	points with pen at dog
		or *whatever*.	wiggles pen in small circle
	E	or	takes finger off top-right stick
		no, or should we put *one there*	traces a short vertical line ('stick') with finger on screen on the right side of the alien
		so that,	alien
		so that could	
		bounce to there	with finger traces line on screen from alien to the right-bottom stick
		which could try to bounce to *there*	
		or *something like that*	traces finger past the dog and slowly off the bottom-left of the screen
12. 21. 40			

Rachel   Emily

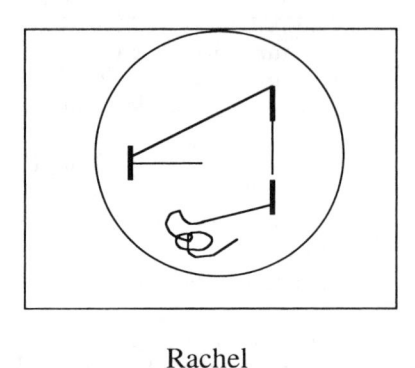

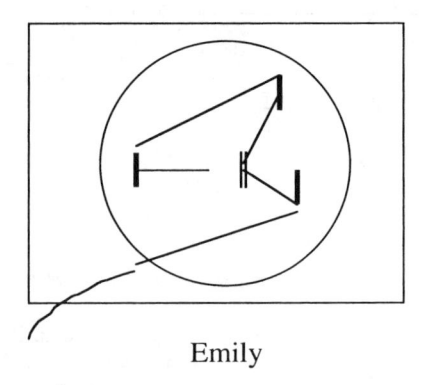

Figure 3.3. A 'map' of the student's gestural overlay on the screen

bullet would come to an end if the dog is not hit by it: would the ball keep bouncing, or go off screen? This is itself an uncertainty of what is *producing the bounce*—the ball or the something that is hit by the ball.

Thirdly, the students' lack of clarity about what it is that is producing the 'bounce' (the stick or the imagined bullets) is expressed in their spoken and gestural accounts. I want to suggest that the *invisibility,* the visual absence, of the bullets at this stage of the design is what proves to be problematic for the students as they move from this imagined account of the movement of the balls to programming it within Playground.

The students' gestural overlay with the screen leads them to 'calculate' where the ball will bounce, as does Emily's suggestion that they need to place some horizontal sticks on the planet.

Through their gesture with the screen itself the students create a space for making meaning which enables them to bring together their everyday knowledge of bounce and the Playground system. This space created by the gestures of the students on the screen serves to connect the students' activity, their imagined game (the trajectory of bullet), and the Playground program. The space is one in which the students can display their intentions without having to engage with the constraints of the program. This space is produced through the gaze and gesture of the students and is a space focused on outcomes—like a visual/gestural blueprint. In this space the vagueness of their gestures realises their recognition of a problem.

The Entity 'Bounce' within Playground

The students select the bounce animagadget from the Playground notebook. The entity 'bounce' is represented on the animagadget in three modes:

- The mode of writing—the word 'Bouncing'
- The mode of still image—two images of a spring and an image of a ball

- The mode of animated movement—three animated sequences, one of a spring moving up and down between two bars, another of a spring moving sideways between two bars, and a third sequence of a ball moving at angles within a square.

These three modal representations provide different resources for the students' construction of the entity 'bounce'. The writing names and classifies the movement 'bounce' in everyday terms. The static image of a spring brings forth (or specifies) certain meaning potentials of bounce and at the same time visually dismisses others. The image realises the potentials of 'bounce' as a mechanical regular ordered entity, rather than as an organic, unpredictable bouncing (like that of a rabbit). The animated sequences of the springs moving regularly between two bars, and the ball contained within the square, work to give meaning to the entity 'bounce' in the context of the Playground programme. The children's everyday experience of 'bounce' as a general uncontrolled movement (as Rachel attributed earlier), such as a highly bouncy ball, is excluded from the Playground entity bounce. The resources of image, animated movement, and writing work together to define 'bouncing' within the mathematical paradigm of the system.

In Playground, behaviours (ready-made pieces of program code) have two 'sides': the default side, called the 'action state', shows an animated and highly realistic visual representation of the behaviour; the other side, called the 'edit state', and this reveals the programming code and a written explanation of the behaviour. The behaviour can be selected and 'flipped' to move between the 'action-state' and the 'edit-state'. The two students first look at the bouncing animagadget in the

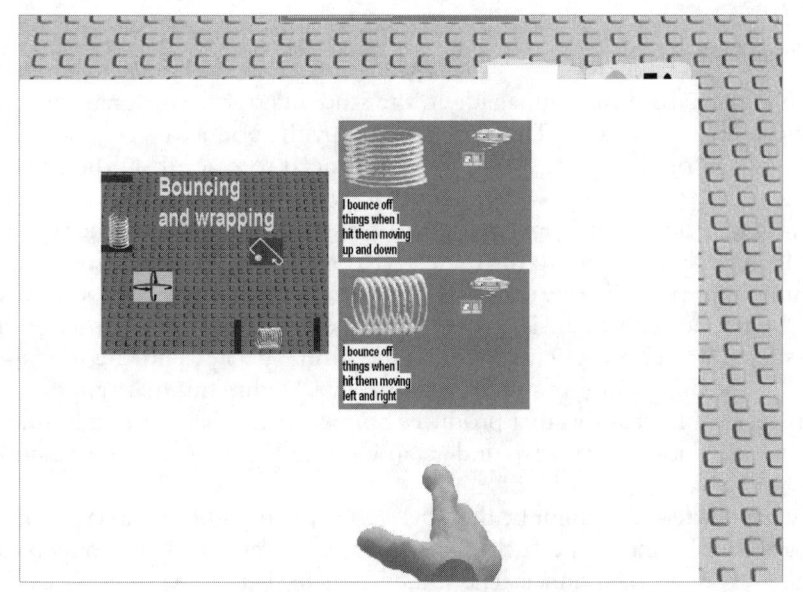

Figure 3.4. The bounce animagadget: action state and edit state

'action-state'. They select the two spring behaviours and 'flip' them over to look at the representation of bounce in the 'edit-state'.

In the representation of bounce in the 'edit-state' the mode of animated movement is removed, and the movement is instead described in the mode of writing and the mode of static image (although the image of the robot in the code represents a generalised potential for action). The entity bounce is represented in the 'edit-state' as two texts, one related to direction and the other to movement. Each text consists of a static image and writing. The text on the left represents movement; it includes the small image of a robot program, a written description—'I bounce off things when I hit them moving left and right', and the image of the spring. The text on the right represents direction, and includes the small image of a robot program, a written description—'I go up', and the image of an upward arrow. The use of 'I' in the written mode reflects the system requirement of Playground that a 'behaviour' (ready-made piece of program code) be attached to an object. In turn, it suggests that behaviour is a property *belonging* to an object. In programming, the work of the student is to specify which game-object the 'I' refers to. In this case, the students have to name the object to which the bounce behaviour should be attached.

The multimodal representation of 'bounce' on the animagadget specifies (and demonstrates) the multiple meanings of bounce within the Playground, and introduces the notion of agency. As discussed earlier, the students have not resolved the question of agency within their earlier design of the game. The students' interaction with the affordances of the Playground now requires them to do so.

Attaching Bounce

Once they have read the animagadget, the students start to program the bounce behaviour into their game. They select and copy the bounce behaviour (by copying the image of the springs) and they then need to place it on the back of an object.

In fact, in order for the game to work as the students intend it to they need to attach the bounce behaviour to the bullets. (Knowing this, the researcher persuades the students to program one stick.) The confusion of the students about where to place the bounce behaviour is, I want to suggest, the outcome of their everyday understanding (and experiences) of bounce and 'agency', and the modal affordances of the programming system, at this point. Within this there appears to be a confusion about 'what it is that produces bounce' and 'what it is that bounces'. In other words, students appear to understand something bouncing as a 'response' to something else.

In everyday terms it might be the 'sticks' that are thought to 'carry' the property of producing bounce—the sticks interrupt the movement of the bullets and in doing so 'produce' the bounce. The students are likely to have experience of a ball bouncing differently on different surfaces, from which they may deduce (correctly)

Computer-Mediated Learning 47

Table 3.2. Students' Initial Decision of Where to Attach the Bounce Behaviour

Time	Person	Speech	Gesture with screen
12. 43 30	E		Emily uses 'wandy' tool to copy the images of the springs—'pointing at the sticks' R copies a fifth spring
	I	where are you going to put that?	
	R	on the back of the sticks	
	I	so what will the sticks do?	
	R	so when the bullets sort of hit the sticks they'll bounce off. But we want them to.	R copies a sixth spring R points at springs on screen
	E	*those are clones*	
	R	go diagonally	
	I	okay	
12. 43 50			

that bounce is connected with a surface. I want to suggest it is the students' everyday experiences that bring the 'sticks' into the realm of programming bounce. Further, I want to suggest that the students' use of bounce in their everyday talk, their semantic field of 'bounce', does not 'fit' easily with the semantic field of bullet. As shown earlier, the word 'bounce' brought forth the students' transformation of the object from a bullet to a ball: bullets are hard, they do not 'have' bounce. It is this everyday understanding of bounce as a quality rather than a specific kind of movement that opens up the potential for the sticks to be what makes them bounce. This ambiguity of agency can persist in the multimodal representation of the entity bounce as a mathematical entity in the Playground behaviour 'action-state' (Figure 3.4). In the 'action-state' an image of a spring is shown moving (bouncing) between two 'bars'. When the students took the spring out of the animagadget notebook it moved in a straight line. Reading this behaviour from an everyday perspective, it is perhaps easy to understand the thinking that led the students to program the bouncing behaviour onto the 'sticks' in their game.

Table 3.3. Students Play Game and Re-think Where to Attach Bounce Behaviour

Time	Person	Speech	Gesture with screen
12. 46. 28			E finishes programming stick and flips it over to 'action-state'.
	E	Done it!	
	R	Oh yeah	
	I	So let's put that on now and let's *try it, test it out, before we do all the work on all the others*	E 'picks up' the stick and moves it across the screen to the game
	E	*okay*	She positions the stick on the *game*. As she 'lets go of' the stick the bammer tool* 'runs' onto screen and hammers the stick. The stick bounces and moves off screen.
	R	That wasn't supposed to go bouncing	
	E	What happened?	
	I	What happened?	
	R	No! that's supposed to stay STILL, and we are supposed to put that sense on the back of the BULLETS!	
12. 46. 55			

*Bammer is a Playground tool in the form of an animated mouse character with a hammer. Its function is to join elements within the playground system.

Modally, at this point in the game-design the students are working visually. The representation of the entity bounce is visual—the bounce is *in* the image of the spring and they are looking at the game to decide where to 'attach' the bounce. The 'sticks' (bars) are visible on screen; however, the bullets are not visible—they are only visible when the game is being played. In this visual mode of working, the system did not make the bullets available as a potential object that the students could specify as the object that the 'I bounce. . .' refers to. In short, when working in a visual mode, agency depends on visual presence.

Playing the Game

It was the visual experience of playing the game that led the students to realise their mistake and how to rectify it. The students programmed the sticks to bounce, placed them on the game and then played the game and the sticks bounced off.

Through their engagement with the playground system the students worked out their ambiguities about agency that were not challenged or required to be resolved by the design on paper through drawing/image and talk.

Making the Bullets Bounce

The students realised that in order for the game to work as they intended they needed to program the bounce onto the bullets. The bullets (as mentioned earlier) are not visible except when playing the game, and Rachel asks in frustrated and plaintive tones, "Where are we going to get a bullet?" Emily realises that the bullets are 'in' the alien.

The process of finding and re-programming the bullets is shown in Figure 3.5. The student flips over the alien object to find the behaviour that is attached to it ('I fire in four directions'). She then has to deconstruct this behaviour into its four 'directional' behaviours. Working with the behaviour 'I fire a white bullet to the left when you press the left arrow', the student selects and deconstructs elements of the code by removing the white bullet from the object box of the program code. She then flips over the white bullet object and changes the program code by adding the bounce behaviour to the bullet. Repeating these steps in reverse she reconstructs the code. The student visually interacts with the screen and physically manipulates the mouse and keys. Apart from her spoken appeal to the tools of the system (e. g., 'I need dusty, dusty, dusty, quickly dusty' or 'ok, F,F,F,F.'), there is little talk involved in the programming.

The researcher intervenes as the student is about to replace the bullet (with the bouncing behaviour attached) on the back of the alien object and asks her what bullet she has changed to bounce off things. The students both realise that they have to "do it on every single one". After expressing their dismay Emily realises how they can do this quickly: "oh I know, you can just copy the other bullet and put it on". The students then program each of the four bullets to bounce.

50 MULTIMODAL LITERACY

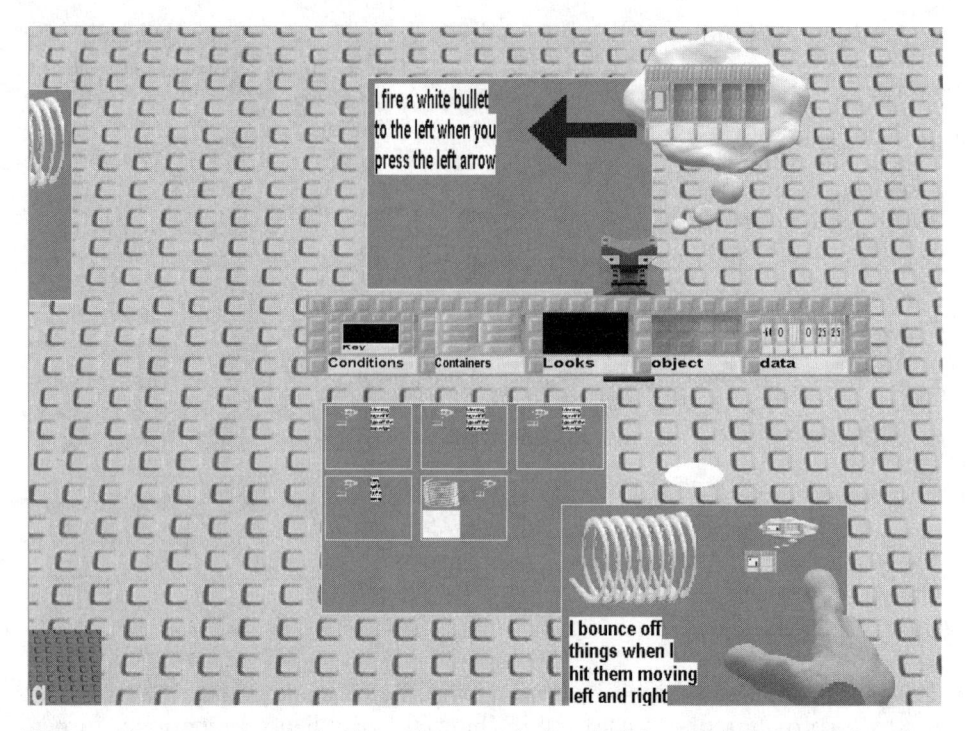

Figure 3.5. Programming the bullets to bounce: placing the 'I bounce left and right' on the bullet that fires left

I want to suggest that the students' ease in undertaking this programming process is in part due to the merger of the game as a narrative and the multimodal affordances of Playground at this point in the game-design. At this stage of programming the bullet and its context in the game-narrative are visible—in other words, it is the alien that fires the bullets. The visual grammar of the Playground system, in the form of the strip of the program boxes held by the robot, visually and lexically names the object as a bullet. This visual representation of the game narrative offers a potential to bring together the semantic field of 'bullet' and 'bounce' (bullets as game).

The Angle of Bounce

After programming the bullets to bounce, the students played the game. The intention is for the bullets to travel left, right, up and down. As the students press the arrow keys the bullets that the alien fires travel diagonally. The students comment on the movement of the bullets: Rachel says, "No, its supposed to go to there . . . the left's supposed to go that way". At this point she returns to gestural overlay on the screen to show the intended movement of the bullets. The researcher intervened at this point and asked "When you looked at the spring there were two beha-

Table 3.4. Discussing the Angle of Bounce

Time	Person	Speech	Gesture with screen
14.15.50	I	So let me, *what happens if you have something that says I move left* *And I move up* What direction if you move up and left at the same time do you end up going?	Puts hand on edge table, then just right index finger moves finger along edge to the left holds hand flat, Moves right hand vertical (diagonally) in front of her puts hands in lap
	R	I don't know	
	I	*Let's say your finger's right here* yeah	Picks up pen and holds it on paper on the table, scribbles a dot (position)
	R	*If I go left*	
	I	That's that way	Draws/moves hand to left
	R	*But if I go up also* what direction will I be going?	
	I	If I do them at the same time I'd be going yeah	Moves pen upwards Moves pen jerkily in small movements left and up, holds pen (i. e., diagonally)
	R	Which is what direction?	
	I	Diagonally	Stops moving pen but holds stretched-out position
	E	Yeah! [laughter]	
	I	So why is the ball, let's see if that's right, *try one of the balls*	Lets go of pen
		Ohh, heh [laughter]	E Presses the arrow keys, alien fires bullet
	E	So what can we do?	
14 16 54	I	Change it	

viours on the back of it? One said I bounce up and the other said what?... I go left, do you remember that? I go left".

Through playing the game the students realised there was a problem with the movement of the balls. The researcher prompted the students through her gesture, talk, and use of visualisation to think about the behaviours they have put on the bullets. The researcher's gestural enactment of the movement of the bullets prompted the students to understand the movement of the bullets in the game as the product of their programming. The researcher's use of gesture, which in contrast to the students is on paper and the table surface rather than the screen, created a different kind of 'idealised space' for the game-design. That is, the researcher's gestures suggested the need to think about movement (in this case, the angle of movement) outside of the Playground environment.

Discussion

The move from page to screen changes the available modes for meaning making. Analysis of the students' interaction with the Playground and one another shows that learning and mode are connected. The modal resources they worked with foregrounded aspects of the entity bounce in specific ways, which in turn shaped the students construction of the entity bounce. The configuration and arrangement of modes in Playground, the *multimodal design* of the system, shaped potentials for constructing the entity bounce. Some elements were visually made available and foregrounded, and not others. Semantic meanings brought to bear on the construction of the entity through the choice of words. The designed relationship between the modes of image and animated movement brought forth the students' different potentials for thinking about the entity bounce.

The students' engagement with the multimodal resources available in Playground serve to reshape entities, in this case the entity 'bounce'. The design of these modes within Playground requires students to formalise and increasingly specify the entity bounce within mathematical terms. As the modes for representing bounce increase, the entity became increasingly complex.

The multimodal affordances and design in Playground require the students to engage with specific kinds of imaginative work. The students' interaction with the multimodal resources of Playground brings forth new ideas for the game design, the process of engaging with the system reshapes the students notion (and genre) of game. The expressions of 'movement' made available via writing in the initial design of the game are not immediately transferable in the move from page to screen and the availability of animated movement as a representational resource. The modal affordances of Playground require the ambiguities afforded by image and writing to be resolved: How will the object move? In what direction will it move? How fast will it move? Under what conditions? What object 'has' the bounce? Through the process of addressing these questions that are raised by the demands of the Playground system, the concept of bounce is transformed from an everyday concept to a mathematical concept. The multimodal resources of Playground serve to highlight (make salient), to specify the entity bounce in mathematical terms, angle of movement, direction, agency, and the spatial/boundaries of movement. The affordances of the system demand that essentially mathematical questions and problems be solved in order for the game to be built—for the narrative of the game to cohere. Through the design of the modes in Playground, maths is naturalised within the Playground and the students are engaged in the process of math via game building. The multimodal character of Playground and the semiotic features of the screen as compared with the page bring about changes in the practices of game and mathematics. The user's task is to select and order the elements of bounce that are made available to them in order to make sense of the representation of the entity bounce on screen.

These changes can be understood as the move from a matter of interpretation to a matter of design. The students' design of the game is an outcome of the modal affordances of the resources of Playground, their interactions with the researcher, their everyday experiences/understanding of bounce, their original idea, and their game playing (and palpable disappointments with programming through this). Through their interaction with the spatial dimensions of the screen (a resource of Playground), the students create spaces for different kinds of activity. Through gesture on the screen they create an 'imagined space overlaying the screen' in which the students 'place' things where they want them and imagine their movement. This 'planning space' 'connects' the students and the Playground in terms of an imagined game. The students' use of the screen as a space serves to delineate between the practices involved in making a game (the practices of constructing objects and code) and those of playing a game.

Through this modal reconfiguration of potentials for meaning the learner is repositioned from being a re-producer of knowledge to being a producer of knowledge. Playground is realised within a highly sensory animated cartoon/game genre. This enables the user to work with principles of the game and via the mediating tools of the program (e. g., the robots, Wandy, Bammer) to engage with mathematical concepts. The user is engaged in the iterative work of transforming her or his understanding and experiences of the everyday into the mathematical (and vice versa)—both 'versions' of rules are enabled to 'co-exist' within the system. We suggest that the genre of computer-based learning environments brings forth (provides the potentials for) different genres of engagement with them (Jewitt, 2002).

Conclusion

The transformation of pedagogy and knowledge from page to screen offers teachers and learners access to different representational and communicational resources. Many of these are not language based. To summarise, this example shows how the designer's choice of representational mode re-mediates learning. The choice of representational mode shapes curriculum entities (in this case, the entity 'bounce') in different ways. The representational modes and their configurations on screen also shape the learning environment itself, and the position of the learner to the object of study.

Multimodality offers a way to think about the computer as a tool that takes account of the full range of representational resources modes on screen, and the interactions with screen and other people in the learning context. Multimodality offers a way of exploring the re-mediating effect of computer mediated learning and, in turn, re-thinking learning beyond language.

Acknowledgments

The Playground project was supported by the European Commission Directorate-General XIII under the ESPRIT programme (Project 29329: Playground). I would like to thank the Playground project team (Ross Adamson, Celia Hoyles, Sarah Lowe and Richard Noss) for our discussions of multimodality and screen and access to the data used in this chapter.

Notes

1. I use entity to refer to 'things to think about and think with' (see Ogborn et. al, 1996)
2. The students' names have been changed to annonymise the data.
3. A vector is a line, often diagonal, that connects objects or participants in an image. The vector expresses a dynamic, 'doing' or 'happening' kind of relation.
4. I would like to thank the Playground Project team for allowing me to use this data.

References

Jewitt, C. (2002) 'The Multimodal Reshaping of School English' in *Visual Communication*, 1(2).
Kress, G.R., Jewitt, C., Ogborn, J., and Tsatsarelis, C. (2001) *Multimodal Teaching and Learning: The Rhetorics of the Science Classroom*. London: Continuum Press.
Lea, M., and Nicoll, K. (Eds.) (2002) *Distributed Learning: Social and Cultural Approaches to Practice*. London: Falmer Press.
Morgan, W., Russell, A., and Ryan, M. (2002) 'Informed Opportunism: Teaching for Learning in Uncertain Contexts of Distributed Education' in Lea, M., and Nicoll, K. (Eds.) (2002) *Distributed Learning: Social and Cultural Approaches to Practice*. London: Falmer Press.
Noss, R., Hoyles, C., Gurtner, J. Adamson, R. and Lowe, S. (2002) 'Face to Face and On-line Collaboration'. Submitted to special issue of *International Journal of Continuing Engineering Education and Lifelong Learning*.
Ogborn, J., Kress, G.R., Martins, T. and McGuillicuddy, K. (1996) *Explanation in the Science Classroom*. Milton Keynes: Open University Press.

Russell, D. (2002) 'Looking beyond the Interface: Activity Theory and Distributed Learning', in Lea, M., and Nicoll, K. (Eds.) (2002) *Distributed Learning: Social and Cultural Approaches to Practice*. London: Falmer Press.

Saljo, R. (1999) 'Learning as the Use of Tools: A Sociocultural Perspective on the Human-Technology Link' in Littlejon, K. and Light, P. *Learning with Computers: Analyzing Productive Interaction*. London: Falmer Press.

Andrew Burn and David Parker   4

TIGER'S BIG PLAN: MULTIMODALITY AND THE MOVING IMAGE

Here is an image of Anansi the spider, from one of the cycle of African folk-tales about the spider-man trickster. It is a single frame from a short (about five minutes long) animated film made by 10- and 11-year-old children and their teacher in a primary school in Cambridge, United Kingdom, in collaboration with teachers from a specialist media school, a Film Education Officer from a partner cinema, a professional animator from the British Film Institute, and a composer-in-residence (see Figure 4.1).

The conception of this project is, we want to argue, multimodal: the architects of the project and the children working on it are imagining a final production in which speech, music and animated film blend. Our purpose, in this chapter, is to explore how this blending works, both in terms of the social and technological processes of design and production, and in the final film and how we might read it. As a framework to think about these processes, we will adopt what Kress and van Leeuwen propose as strata of semiotic production: *discourse, design, production, distribution* (2001). We will develop the idea of the moving image as a specific mode—the *kineikonic*—and identify some of the principles through which it integrates other communicative modes through the design of time and space, and the use of a wide variety of media and tools. We will use this theory to analyse a short section of the film of *Anansi and the Firefly;* and will also explore how a school curriculum leading to moving image production needs to be, itself, multimodal.

The film is a transformation of a Ghanaian folk-tale. It tells the story of how Anansi, the trickster spider, goes out with Firefly to collect eggs. While Firefly lights the way, Anansi takes all the eggs for himself, leaving Firefly to return home with none. However, Anansi now cannot see to find his way home, and has to stop for help at Tiger's house. In order to convince Tiger to take him in, he gives him the eggs for dinner. To present himself as unselfish, Anansi refuses any eggs at dinner,

Figure 4.1. Anansi screen-grab

secretly planning to steal any remaining eggs and eat them during the night. Tiger's suspicions are aroused, and he conceals a live lobster in the pot of eggs, covering it with eggshells. When Anansi goes to steal the eggs during the night, the lobster pinches him. Tiger shouts out, hearing Anansi's cry of pain; Anansi pretends it is only dog-fleas biting him. Tiger pretends to be outraged; and Anansi is driven from the house, disgraced and devoid of eggs.

Discourse: Mischief, Africanness, and Pedagogy

This image comes with certain cultural properties. It imports a notion of Anansi from the provenance of the African oral narratives, trailing discursive threads to do with trickiness and irreverence, an off-the-peg metaphor for our disobedient instincts, or, if we are children, for our endless desire to outwit the adult world, its rules and its humourlessness. There are two interrelated discourses at work here, perhaps. One is child-oriented, and is a discourse of childhood mischief, realised in different ways in different cultures and different historical moments, and a perennial topic of folk-tales. The other, more adult-generated, is a curricular discourse of multiculturalism, here reflected in the choice of a Ghanaian folk-tale as the basis of an animation made by a group of mostly white children in the United Kingdom.

As it is a picture, the child recreating Anansi here must make quite specific decisions about what he looks like. What resources have been used to make these decisions? We want to suggest three important factors. Firstly, the child could reach for images of 'Africanness', garnered from film or television, perhaps. The image, however, suggests nothing of this. Indeed, the landscapes the children have drawn behind Anansi are clearly European pine-forests. Though this is an African story, it is easier to stick with familiar images, which may duck the representational issue, rendering the Africanness of the story invisible; but may on the other hand avoid an embarrassingly stereotypical image of Africa. Already, the image has a complex relation to the provenance of the narrative on the one hand, and of the visual resources used to present it on the other.

Secondly, the child who drew the picture has made some decisions about colours. It may be no coincidence that the red and blue of the spider, along with the elaborate web, are elements of the design of Marvel's comic strip superhero, Spiderman, familiar to children as a TV cartoon packaged within children's magazine programme formats, now also a live action movie.

Thirdly, if the colours are those of Spiderman, the bulbous eyes with pinpoint pupils and the rotund body are reminiscent of the *Simpsons* and *South Park*, and the humorous characterisation associated with them, as well as the discourse of mischief and irreverence in which Anansi is rooted.

This image of Anansi, then, is on the one hand completely original—it exists absolutely for the first time. On the other hand, all the decisions in its making are framed by the discourses within which the children are working, and the genres that most typically express these discourses in their experience: the folk-tale, the comic strip, and the animated cartoon.

The discourse framing this act of transformation is pedagogic—it represents a set of beliefs about what is to be learnt and how the learning might best be organised. It also represents an approach to the question of how modes of communication can be organised in the curriculum.

This pedagogy has a double content. The subject matter of Anansi is important for cultural reasons: the secondary school involved in the project has a weblink with a school in Ghana, through a curricular programme organised in collaboration with Comic Relief, an aid charity in the United Kingdom; and Day Chocolate, a Fair Trade chocolate manufacturer partly owned by a Ghanaian cocoa-farmers' co-operative. However, the pedagogy here is also intended to promote a broad notion of literacy which encompasses the moving image. Though the moving image often becomes part of a wider definition of literacy through the notion of 'visual literacy' (cf. Raney, 1997), it is conceived of by the educators and professional artists in this project as multimodal (though they have not used that term). In other words, the design and production processes experienced by the children as an integrated series of activities have been organised through a pedagogic division of labour, involving media specialists, a film education specialist, the head of English from the secondary school, the head of art, a professional composer, and a professional animator.

For the educators, then, the development of the project follows the contours of the typical structure of moving image production: a period of specialised work on the different modes to be employed in the film, followed by a period of assembly in which these modes are brought together to make the moving image text. The experience of the children, on the other hand, is of all the different processes, as the project works to overcome the more usual monomodal way in which the curriculum is conceived, where print stories, film and music are experienced and made by children in quite separate curriculum slots, with no systematic regard for how such modes interact in almost every part of our cultural lives. As a result, and unlike the film industry, the children experience the full range of multimodal and multimedial engagement as they make their film.

Design: The Kineikonic Mode

The moving image is an integrative, combinatorial assemblage of modes, which has posed theoretical problems throughout its history. Its broad features have never been in doubt—that it consists of the combination of moving image and sound on the one hand—what Eisenstein called *vertical montage* (Eisenstein, 1968)—and of the combined practices of filming and editing on the other, which serve to frame the representation and to assemble it in a series of juxtapositions. We will regard this set of practices as a mode in its own right, the mode of the moving image, partly because filming and editing offer what is, in effect, a grammar within which sound and image are re-made, partly because this set of practices has been regarded since its inception as a kind of language. The terms often employed to describe these practices are *filmic* and *cinematic*. These are confusing terms (for Metz, for instance, they mean quite distinct things, as we shall see), and both evoke cinema rather than other forms of the moving image. We will introduce a new term for the mode of the moving image, then—the *kineikonic*, from the Greek words for *move* and *image*.

In the mid-1970s, the French film theorist Christian Metz made a distinction (Metz, 1974) between film language as *filmic*, by which he meant the whole assemblage of codes of language, gesture, music, filming and editing; and *cinematic*, by which he meant strictly those structures produced by the processes of filming and editing, and around which he built his theory of film language.

Our kineikonic mode combines the two aspects of Metz's distinction. It refers to how all the elements of the moving image are assembled, but includes the particular conventions afforded by the practices of filming and editing. This mode uses a range of semiotic resources to make the moving image, integrating them into the spatiotemporal flow by (re)designing and producing them within the spatial frame and the temporal sequence of the film. In other words, the kineikonic mode is distinguished by its relation between the grammar of filming and editing, and what Metz and others have called the *pro-filmic*—those elements of the moving image that have been made, as it were, before the camera got there. We will distinguish further, however, between the *pro-filmic* (communicative acts made for film) and the *pre-filmic* (communicative acts not made for film, but later incorporated into it, such as an event that is filmed as a piece of news footage).

What does the choice of the kineikonic mode mean for the educators and children engaged in this project? We need to look back at the beginning of the process: Like many moving image projects, this one began with storyboarding. Two points are clear in this practice: firstly, that the modes of written language and still visual design are employed as notations for the moving image that is to be; and secondly, that the eventual moving image has to be imagined by the child-designers in order for them to make any sense of this notation. If they cannot adequately imagine the moving image they are designing, the notation will become incoherent, or even slide into a quite different mode, such as the comic strip, which in some ways it resembles. Two particular difficulties children have experienced in previous years of this project (which is in its fourth year at the time of writing) at the stage of storyboard design are in framing the shot in each drawing. They showed a tendency to draw everything in long shot, as if needing to see whole figures against backgrounds all the time. The convention of the closeup, with its selective indications of salient detail and its implications of social proximity, needed to be explicitly taught. The other difficulty, not overcome in this film, is that of drawing low-angle shots, because of the technical difficulty of drawing foreshortened images. As we shall see, this difficulty with visual design can be overcome by saying something similar in another mode.

At the storyboard stage, the other key mode in play was writing, as a way of notating the dialogue and voiceover. For the children, the writing of the script involves cutting it up into groups of words, clauses or sentences, the decision hinging on which groups of words will go with which shot. Already, then, *design* means to articulate image and word.

The notation of movement on a storyboard is—can only be—minimal. Though movement and duration are criterial to the kineikonic mode, in the early stages of design they remain largely in the heads of the designers. The next stage of this animation moves more decisively towards the design of movement. It involves making drawn bits to be animated. The decision facing the children here is: which bits will move, and therefore need to be drawn separately? The head of art working with the children says, in a talk at a seminar in the later stages of the project, that he has never done this before—never worked with children to draw exploded versions of animals, with separate legs, mouths, eyes, eyelids, torsos. For him, as for the children, this movement from design into production is a new multimodal inflection of art—the mode of visual design orientated towards the kineikonic mode.

The production of the image as a set of exploded bits opens up another stage of the kineikonic mode, for which the design becomes a set of resources.

Designing and Producing Time

The animation of the disaggregated images, now scanned onto a computer network as digital resources within the animation software package, 'The Complete Animator', is largely about the design and production of movement. As the name suggests, this is a dedicated animation package which allows for a high degree of control over the production process (for an exploration of how children use this software, see Parker and Sefton-Green, 2000). The design of the software interface—the way the varied production options are communicated in an interactive, audio-visual manner—offers a set of iconic resource available to the kineikonic mode. For example, the fact that Complete Animator allows externally produced images to be imported as a 'stamp' brings together the resources the children design themselves for potential movement—disaggregated objects, the drawn mouths, limbs, eyes, and eyelids mentioned above—and the ability to use the principles of stop-frame animation to make up the first stages of the moving image grammar (Figure 4.2). The main difficulty facing the children in the design of the temporal axis of their film is in imagining how the accumulation of still frames and the repositioning of visual objects on each frame will result in variables in movement such as smoothness, speed, and direction.

As they make their animated sequences, the children come out in groups to record their music tracks with the composer on the project. They have previously composed and practised these pieces, and now bring their instruments to perform them, although the composition has been provisional and not notated, and is subject to further improvisation now as they think about the animation that will accompany it. These decisions of production as design add emotional inflections to the piece: warning, reassuring, darkening, lightening. They are produced in short syntagmatic clusters, roughly equivalent to short segments of the action in the film. Recorded on DAT tape, they again become digital resources for the next stage of production.

Finally, in the process of editing, the syntagmatic groupings of image and sound undergo a further reordering. The editing is done on a non-linear (digital) editing system called Media 100. Such a system brings another set of tools into play, making possible forms of digital inscription to produce the moving image in new ways, which we have described in more detail elsewhere (Burn & Parker, 2001). Unlike the animation package, in which the children work 'directly' with the images using digital tools for positioning, sizing, rotating and so on, in the editing programme sound and footage are represented in two ways. One is an edit window, which shows both sound and image as they will be in the final film. The other is the timeline, where groups of image, sound or graphics appear as coloured strips of image and sound, and in many ways are assembled as a series of graphic representations, using graphic waveforms, colour-coding, and horizontal and vertical alignment as cues for the composition of the piece (Figure 4.2).

62 MULTIMODAL LITERACY

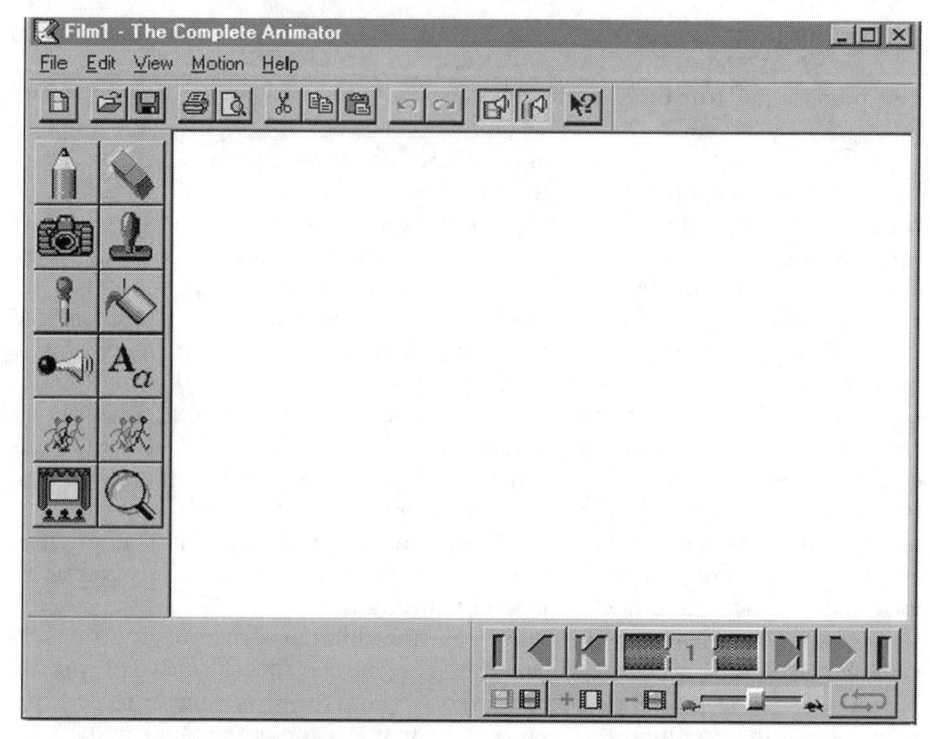

Figure 4.2. The interfaces of The Complete Animator and Media 100

Both of these inscriptional technologies—the animation package and the editing package—gesture both forwards and backwards in the history of the kineikonic mode, offering a configuration of tools and semiotic resources unique to a particular historical moment. One the one hand, they offer the children an audiovisual interface which is structured around metaphors of older material processes of moving image production. The animation package mimics the cell-frame structure of traditional animation, as well as offering tools that are metaphors of the cell-frame production process, such as "in-betweening". The editing package offers visual metaphors of the physical processes of editing film, in which strips of celluloid are represented by strips of image and sound on the timeline. On the other hand, the plasticity and provisionality of digital media mean that, where the physical properties of cell painting or celluloid recording meant that any action was impossible to undo, now such actions are in principle provisional, and can be undone and redone indefinitely. This principle is obviously valuable to educational practices, where making mistakes and redoing actions are important features of learning (cf. Burn and Reed, 1999). However, it is not only children who use these technologies, of course. Digital media mean that professional editors can also take more risks in editing 'on the fly', without needing the painstaking calculations in setting up part of an edit that were so necessary in the days of analogue video or traditional film editing, when they only had one chance to get it right.

Perhaps most important of all, what was originally very much a technology of assembly, to do with 'post-production', has shifted in terms of Kress and van Leeuwen's scheme of semiotic strata towards design. Digital editing is a medium of production and design, in which the functions of assembly are fused with the functions of composition: aspects of the soundtrack which were originally carried out at an earlier stage; aspects of visual design such as colour, brightness, cross-zooming, which formerly belonged either to filming or to physical treatments such as dyeing; and the integration of semiotic resources that have only existed in digital form, such as computer-generated images, synthespians and new kinds of transition effects.

Tiger's Soliloquy: Grouping, Boundary, Conjunction

In this section, we will analyse a short sequence of the film (Figure 4.3), to see how sections of the image and soundtracks are grouped, how the groups are articulated, and how this tells the story. In particular, we want to see how the different modes are articulated: how they *complement*, *reiterate*, *anticipate* and *contradict* each other.

In order to do this, we will sometimes reduce the complexity of syntagmatic articulation to a simpler principle—that of *grouping*. This is simply to see the wood for the trees, so to speak, as we expect to see groupings of different kinds made within modes, between modes, and within symbolic representations of the process of production, such as the timeline of the editing package. Where such groupings can be described using established systems of analysis (as in the lexicogrammatical structure of the clause, or the intonational patterns of spoken language, or the rhythmic structure of music), we will refer to these. However, some groupings in the kineikonic mode have much sparser histories of description: groups of gestures, groups of lights, groups of actors, groups of objects-to-be-animated, groups of image and sound on an editing timeline. We want to retain, for the moment at least, some sense of parity between all these syntagmatic bundles, even if it is at the expense of the detail of those which have hitherto been most 'visible'.

We will also refer to two related principles: *boundary* and *conjunction*. Simply put, if a group is made by the principle of what gets included, then an inevitable corollary is the principle that establishes the limit or edge of the group, and what this edge comes to mean, whether it is the frame of a picture, the silence between two musical phrases, the pause between two pieces of speech, or the cut between two shots in a film. Similarly, as is already apparent, the boundary is always going to lead to some kind of conjunction with an adjacent grouping. In the moving image, a new significance is added by the principle of conjunction—the significance of the frame when juxtaposed with the next frame, which is the principle at the heart of Eisenstein's *montage* (Eisenstein, 1968); or the significance of the mobile frame which moves within the shot, discussed at length by Bordwell and Thompson (2001).

In the diachronic axis of the visual track, the most obvious conjunctions are those between shots, called transitions. These offer a quite specific grammar of cuts, wipes, dissolves, and so on, familiar to anyone who has used a digital editing package. The transition, which constructs the distinctive disjunctive structure of the moving image, always has, in narrative films, a spatial meaning (we have moved to a different position) and temporal meaning (there has been no gap in time; or there has been a gap in time).

At the same time, however, boundaries at the edges of speech, music and sound—pauses, hesitations, silences, breaks—will delimit, fragment and conjoin the meanings made in these modes, in patterns which will complement those of the image track rather than being identical with it. Though we are used to analysing film by shot segmentation, and though visual shots make up an important signifying layer, it is necessary to consider how other layers in the kineikonic mix may work through different rhythms.

We want to look at this in terms of three overarching functions of any form of communication (Kress et al., 2001, p. 13): *ideational* (how some aspect of the world is represented); *interpersonal* (how the film constructs imagined relationships between text and spectator); and *textual* (how the text is composed as a coherent message).

Ideational

In this first part of the sequence in Figure 4.3, who is doing what? The answer is complex. As far as the overall sequence is concerned, Tiger is talking, and we infer his image, perhaps, from the sound of his voice, which we recognise. The sound of his voice, in other words, only works if the spectator's act of interpretation produces a new sign, combining the speech with the memory of Tiger's appearance from earlier shots. At the same time, this is a double narrative—Tiger as part of the larger story, and Tiger as narrator of this section, which is both a memory and a plan for the future. The first shot, then, in terms of the image track, represents the cub eating eggs: a single action, grouped into a sequence of three—the eating movement is repeated three times.

In the speech track, the voiceover has two groups for the three in the image track. The two groups do not represent the cub at all, but make the eggs the subject of the first clause: 'All the eggs are gone'. Clearly it is the disappearance of the eggs that is important rather than who has eaten them, teaching us that the cub is simply an exemplary instance of egg-eating. Shots 2 and 4 reinforce this emphasis, presenting a visual equivalent of the deleted agency of Tiger's first clause: it is the disappearance of the eggs that is important, rather than who has eaten them.

The second group tells us Tiger's feelings about the egg-supper: 'What a feast!'

The unworried enthusiasm in Tiger's voice (partly achieved by the words themselves, partly by the material signifier of the mildly excited tone of voice of the

Tiger's Big Plan 65

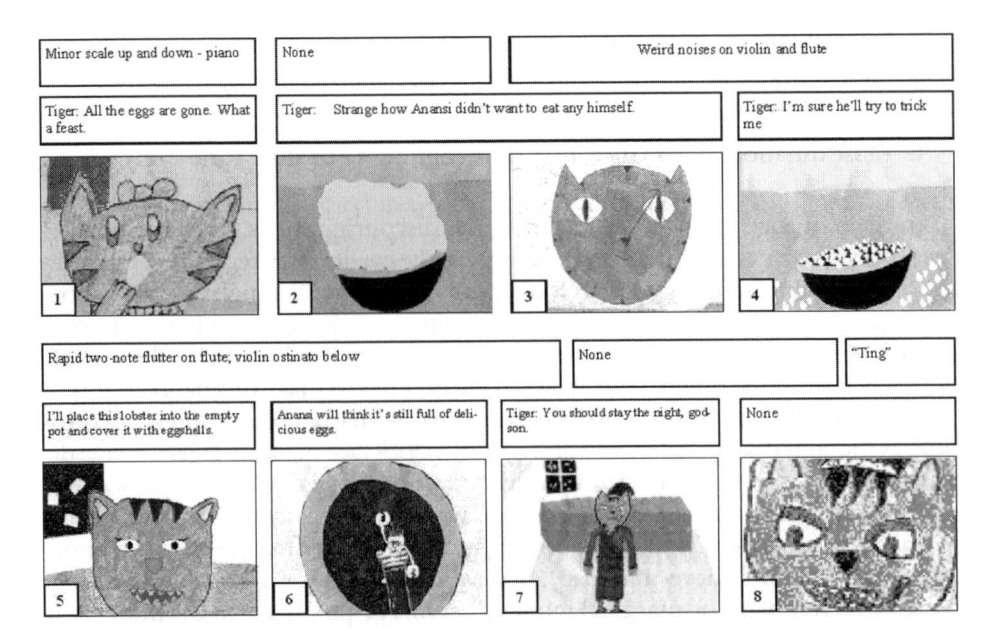

Minor scale up and down - piano	None	Weird noises on violin and flute	
Tiger: All the eggs are gone. What a feast.	Tiger: Strange how Anansi didn't want to eat any himself.	Tiger: I'm sure he'll try to trick me	
1	2	3	4

Rapid two-note flutter on flute; violin ostinato below		None	"Ting"
I'll place this lobster into the empty pot and cover it with eggshells.	Anansi will think it's still full of delicious eggs.	Tiger: You should stay the night, god-son.	None
5	6	7	8

Figure 4.3. The kineikonic mode: a short sequence

child doing the voice characterisation) is significant because of its contrast with the dawning suspicion in the next clause/shot group. This contrastive structure, which works to heighten the suspicious tone of the next section, is also related to the music track. The initial shot/sound group has coinciding boundaries for the speech, image and music tracks. While the image shows the cub enjoying the eggs, and the speech shows Tiger innocently enthusing over the meal, the musical phrase consists of a rising and falling minor scale on a piano. Its function is to introduce a sinister note of warning, *anticipating* the suspicion in the following speech, and *contradicting* the image and speech groups with which it is conjoined.

The other images in the sequence represent other projections of Tiger's mental act. If the cub represents the immediate past—the delicious dinner—the lobster (shot 6) represents the future—Tiger's plan to place the lobster in the pot to punish Anansi. However, the complex temporal design of this sequence—Tiger's voice-over in the 'present' tense of the overall story, the dinner in the past, and the lobster in the future—is constructed through a complex multimodal interweaving of speech, image and music.

Temporality is constructed in all moving image narrative sequences using five possible time relations which have been categorised and used within film semiotics (Chatman, 1978):

1. Summary duration: the discourse takes less time than the events depicted.
2. Ellipsis duration: the discourse stops but we infer from subsequent shots that some time has passed.

sign production which Kress et al. propose (2001, p. 6). Finally, the temporal nuances of this sequence are overlaid by the vertical grouping of modes. It is worth remarking that, in the case of every visual shot, the grouping of temporal representations in image and speech is disjunctive rather than conjunctive—the times in the speech groups are most typically at odds with the time in the visual groups, the two tracks sliding over each other, syncopating, staggering, shunting around the past of the dinner, the present of Tiger's soliloquy, the future of his plan.

Interpersonal Function

For reasons of space, we will not examine this in detail. The text works to establish a particular relationship with the audience: that of confidant. This sequence is directly addressed to the audience, evoking the genre of the theatrical aside, which in the moving image is characterised by a direct gaze at the camera; by a closeup of the character's face, which augments the social proximity of the theatrical aside with actual proximity; and by a voiceover, which indicates in various ways that it represents the character's thoughts, spoken aloud to the audience. We can see that they are spoken aloud in shot 5, which is clearly not addressed to anyone in the story, but in which Tiger's lips move, and speech and image are grouped in one of the most common multimodal groupings of the moving image, lipsynching. The entire voiceover's interpersonal function is affected by this—it is the visual equivalent of the words 'Dear Spectator', and we hear the words as a dialogue with the audience. At the same time, our speculation about Tiger's trick and our sense of certainty about how these future events will pan out is coloured by the modality created by the music: anxiety, uncertainty, lack of closure.

The different modes offer other aspects of spectator position. We appear, for instance, to be on an equal level with Tiger, as the horizontal angle of the frame is level. However, this may be a question of what semiotic resources were really available to the children. They drew the characters from front, side and back—drawing them from different angles may have been beyond the resources of the students— and drawing a human figure from below requires a sophisticated ability to represent foreshortening, which is not easy. That the children's intentions may have been to make Tiger a powerful character, at least to a child audience, is perhaps shown in the choice of the material quality of Tiger's voice—a simulation of gruff adulthood, which is a sound-signifier in some ways equivalent to a low angle camera shot. These principles operate in different modes to construct the relation between text and spectator around spatial principles, placing us higher or lower (through angle), and further or closer (through shot distance—or through sounds that suggest distance, or through signifiers of social hierarchy, such as the gruff voice of Tiger, or his patriarchal location in the family group shown in the visual design of the animation). In the sequence immediately before the one upon which we focus, Tiger is shown in a family group, almost like a family portrait—he is central in the group, and taller than his wife, who in turn is taller than the child/cub.

Textual Function

The distribution of information throughout the sequence sees a similar interplay between the modes. In the voiceover (shot 5), which anticipates the lobster shot, there are two clauses: 'I'll place this LOBster into the empty pot/and cover it with the EGGshells.' The information marked as new by its tonic prominence is 'lobster' in the first clause and 'eggshells' in the second. By the time we see the lobster in the following shot, then, it's not new; though its appearance is. What's new is its comic appearance, with one claw waving over its head. The marked aspect, then, is this comical quality. Simultaneously, the voiceover is saying: 'Anansi will think it's still full of deLICIOUS eggs.' Here, the tonic prominence is placed on the second and third syllables of 'delicious'. Eggs are old news—we've been told about those in the previous section of the voiceover; the emphasis on 'delicious' implies the potency of the snare being laid for Anansi.

Anansi, as agent of the presumed conspiracy to eat the eggs in the night, is represented not in the image track at all, but purely in the spoken sequence. His visual absence both suggests the negative action that triggers Tiger's suspicion—he didn't eat the eggs at dinner—and allows Tiger to be foregrounded in the image track as the dominant character of this sequence. The spoken voiceover sometimes anticipates the information in the image track, as in the introduction of the lobster; and in the emphasising, again through tonic prominence, that ALL the eggs are gone in the voice-track for shot 1, whereas the eggs do not finally disappear on the image track till shot 4. Sometimes information is offered in one mode which contradicts that in another mode, for purposes of ambiguity (as in the uncertainty expressed in the music while Tiger is spelling out his plan); or for dramatic irony, as when the tooth glint and the "Ting!" contradict the apparent hospitality of Tiger's offer of a bed in the final shot, suggesting a much more sinister intention.

The composition of the groupings, boundaries and conjunctions within and across the modes also suggests which bits of information are most salient, offering hierarchies of significance. In shot 1, for instance, the large closeup and centrality of the cub on its own would make the cub indisputably the most salient item. As we have seen, however, the salience of this image is significantly reduced by the voiceover, in which the authority of Tiger's voice and the way in which the words and emphases in the tonal group are organised make ALL the eggs the most salient piece of information. Towards the end of the sequence, the importance of the 'Ting" sound accompanying the glint on Tiger's tooth is emphasised by the boundary of silence that surrounds it on the image track.

Constructing Time: Rhythm

The function of rhythm as an integrative principle in film is discussed by van Leeuwen, on whose work we draw (van Leeuwen, 1985; 1999). The rhythm of editing in the image track is mostly aligned with the representation of story time we have already discussed. Every transition signifies a temporal shift of one kind or another, and the overall effect is that of a rapid sequence of shots in which time is segmented, omitted, elided and compressed.

The rhythms of the speech tell a different story. Across the sequence, the rhythm of Tiger's voiceover is measured and even, and flows over the rapid breaks in the editing; while the tempo is fairly slow. If the edits—and the verb tenses—show rapid movements, fragmentations and inversions of time, the speech-rhythm suggests a thoughtful musing about Anansi's duplicity and the brewing of Tiger's plot.

The music, again, is performing quite specialised tasks. In the sequence immediately before the one we have analysed, its rhythms are quite at odds with both speech and the editing of the visual track. While the dinner is being set up, there is a two phrase piano sequence in triple time, which continues over two shots. Tiger then makes the offer of eggs to Anansi, the refusal of which sparks off Tiger's suspicions. This break is not marked in the visual sequence, nor in the rhythm of Tiger's speech. It is marked only by the music, where the phrase in triple time stops abruptly, and a sinister two note (a minor third) sequence, changing the triple time to double time, and the major key of the first sequence to a minor. This sequence continues across the next transition, so that where the editing breaks the rhythm to suggest the ellipsis, the music insists on the continuous rhythm of the threat and counterthreat implied between Tiger and Anansi. This sequence then gives way to the unmeasured time of the minor scale in shot 1 of the sequence we have discussed above, and finally to the even less well-defined rhythmic and melodic patterns of flute and violin.

The movement of rhythms in the music, then, is from triple time (suggesting here cheerful dance-like dinner), to sparse double time, suggesting possible imminent threat, to minor scale, suggesting the sinister significance of Anansi's refusal to eat the eggs; to the indeterminacy and lack of closure of the final sequences, suggesting the uncertainty of the future events. These rhythms are all to do with the play of insinuation and conspiracy which snakes through the sequence, and provide a sinuous undercurrent to the rapid fragmentation of the editing and its temporal representations; and the slow, musing rhythms of Tiger's speech.

Finally, there are many kinds of spatial rhythm—we will mention just one, which has to do with signalling life—literally, a rhythm of animation, which functions simply to keep the characters animated, even when they are not doing anything particularly important. This consists of a regular blinking of all the characters, made up of animated eyelid graphics; and of slight movements of Tiger's head when he is talking. These are background rhythms, just keeping the animation on the boil.

Conclusion: Multimodal Pedagogies and the Kineikonic Mix

The teaching and learning of the kineikonic mode is an explicit objective of this project. One thing we have not made clear, however, is that only some aspects of this multimodal venture become part of the conscious design of the animation, and are explicitly taught and learnt. These include narrative conventions, the words and grammar of the speech track, the music, and the visual conventions of the moving image, as well as the specific visual and auditory repertoires offered by the two software packages. However, some aspects of the design may be less conscious. These may be because the children designing the piece make unconscious associations that determine how certain semiotic resources are imported (for instance, the colours reminiscent of Spiderman). Elsewhere, it may be because both children and teachers are less aware of some of the semiotic resources they use than others (a good example would be the tonal patterns of speech, which clearly contribute to the meanings of the sequence, but are almost certainly not consciously designed). The question with these, as with other features of the kineikonic mode, which we have tried to make visible in this chapter, is whether they can then be drawn more consciously into the design process in the future.

The design of an animated film by 10-year-old children is a collaborative and creative venture that embraces a range of processes, each deploying particular tools and other resources in different ways at different stages. We have attempted to show how the creation of a moving image text is simultaneously multimodal and yet governed by a single overarching mode that we call kineikonic. In the sequence of shots analysed above we have attempted to show how this kineikonic mode acts as a kind of mixing board through which different combinations of image, music, sound and speech can create a narrative experience, like spun colours blurring into white, in the synthesised narrative perceived by the spectator. In design, however, as in the disaggregative work of analysis, the significations of character, location and event are revealed as transformatively shuttled between the modes.

Our understanding of moving image, therefore, allows for a fully realised grammar of the moving image at every level. Unlike the grammar proposed by Metz, in which there could be no proper grammar of film below the level of the shot sequence, the kineikonic grammar used here can accommodate both spatial visual design at the level of the single frame (particularly important in animation); the spatiotemporal articulations of the shot and sequence; and the different affordances of the modes which Metz recognised in his notion of a 'filmic language', which assembled the different elements of film, but which he was not able to conceive of within a single semiotic framework.

For us, this is an urgent task, because the use of the kineikonic mode, though a century old for film theorists and the texts they describe, is newly deployed by schoolchildren, teachers and community artists, who have only had access to these resources in a widely distributed way since the recent advent of digital technologies. We need a new way to describe this kind of curricular vision and practice: a coming-together of communicative specialisms in an effort to create the moving image with children in a break with the monomodal pedagogies of the past.

Acknowledgments

We would like to acknowledge the work of: Newnham Croft Primary School, Cambridge, United Kingdom; Parkside Community College, Cambridge, United Kingdom; Trish Sheil, Film Education Officer, Cambridge Film Consortium; Louise Spraggon, Animation Officer, British Film Institute; and Andrew Lovatt, composer-in-residence on the project.

References

Bordwell, D. and Thompson, K. (2001) *Film Art* (6th ed.). New York: McGraw Hill.
Burn, A. and Reed, K. (1999), 'Digi-teens: Media Literacies and Digital Technologies in the Secondary Classroom, *English in Education* 33.3, NATE (National Association of Teachers of English).
Burn, A. and Parker, D. (2001), 'Making Your Mark: Digital Inscription, Animation, and a New Visual Semiotic', *Education, Communication & Information*, Vol. 1, No. 2.
Chatman, S. (1978) *Story and Discourse: Narrative Structure in Fiction and Film*. Ithaca: Cornell University Press.
Eisenstein, S. (1968) *The Film Sense*, trans. J. Layda. London: Faber and Faber.
Kress, G.R. and van Leeuwen, T. (1996) *Reading Images: The Grammar of Visual Design*. London: Routledge.
Kress, G.R. and van Leeuwen, T. (2001) *Multimodal Discourses*. London: Arnold.
Kress, G.R., Jewitt, C., Ogborn, J. and Tsatsarelis, C. (2001) *Multimodal Teaching and Learning: the Rhetorics of the Science Classroom*. London: Continuum.
Metz, C. (1974) *Film Language*. Chicago: University of Chicago Press.
Parker, D. and Sefton-Green, J. (2000) *Edit-Play*. London: bfi.
Raney, K. (1997) *Visual Literacy: Issues and Debates; A Report on the Research Project 'Framing Visual and Verbal Experience.'* London: Middlesex University.
van Leeuwen, T. (1985) 'Rhythmic Structure of the Film Text', in T. van Dijk (ed.), *Discourse and Communication*. Berlin: de Gruyter.
van Leeuwen, T. (1999) *Speech, Music, Sound*. London: Macmillan.

Gemma Moss 5

PUTTING THE TEXT BACK INTO PRACTICE: JUNIOR-AGE NON-FICTION AS OBJECTS OF DESIGN

In this chapter I consider the potential relationship between ethnography and multimodality as ways of understanding reading as a situated social practice, and argue for the aptness of the literacy event as the means of bringing these two perspectives into play. The chapter puts, side by side, ethnographic observation of literacy events in school settings and analysis of the texts involved in these events, considered in the light of shifts in the contemporary design of junior-age non-fiction.

Browsing Non-fiction Texts in Informal Contexts

Extract 1: School 4

Mitchel:	Yeah, there it is, there's an atom bomb
Terry:	Where's an atom bomb?
Mitchel:	There/ atom bomb// That's a V2 rocket.
Terry:	Yeah, I know.
Mitchel:	That's a doodle, that's an AK-47, MP-5, M-16 and there's a doodle bomb

:

Terry:	Hang on, what's that then?
Mitchel:	That?
Terry:	Yeah.

Mitchel:	That is (. . .)
Terry:	No that.
Mitchel:	Oh that is a spy plane.
Terry:	Oh, oh yeah, a spy plane.
Interviewer:	How do you know that, Mitchel?
Mitchel:	Because spy planes are, have not got any like big missiles and stuff, they just fly over the base (. . . .).
Terry:	Do you know, I've got this game called [Desert Rat Army].

[Terry goes on to discuss the role of spy planes in his computer game. Mitchel knows the game and joins in too]

The two boys in the extract above have been flicking through the pages of *In the Beginning: The Nearly Complete History of Almost Everything*, by Brian Delf and Richard Platt. Described on the dust jacket in these terms: "From cave to skyscraper, from candle to lightbulb, here in one superbly illustrated volume is the story of how almost everything began", the book is organised as a kind of thematic encyclopedia, which runs though the history of human development in different areas by arranging in chronological order on each page a sequence of images and accompanying text on the given theme. In the transcript above, the boys have paused to discuss some of the items that appear on pages 28–29, a double-page spread on the development of weapons (Delf and Platt, 1995).

Over the years I have collected a lot of conversations that look like this, particularly from boys perusing non-fiction together in this kind of informal context. Such data have been gathered as part of a series of interlinked research projects that might most easily be characterised as ethnographies of reading, in which the main unit of analysis has been the literacy event, though the precise focus for data collection has varied from children's use of a range of media texts in informal settings, to the place for reading in the junior school curriculum[1] (Moss, 1993a; 1993b; 1996; 2000a). In the case of the literacy event above, this formed part of an interview in which two nine-year-old boys, whom I had observed reading a range of non-fiction texts during quiet reading time in their classroom, brought some of those same texts with them to the interview, talked about them and also did what they often did in class—flipped through them, whilst they talked to each other as much as to me.

What for me characterises this kind of conversation is the way in which the talk flows round the text. On the one hand, the text is a necessary resource. It acts as a prompt for the talk, whilst the participants pause over one part of the text or another. But at the same time the text does not wholly constrain or indeed prefigure what gets said. In this kind of event, these readers do not feel they have to stick too precisely to its contents. Other reference points, other sources of relevant information can be invoked too. In these respects, the text enables the participants to announce what they already know about the subject at hand.

In the example quoted above, the book under discussion had been brought to the interview by Mitchel. I had watched him using it in class, often looking at it

Putting the Text Back into Practice 75

alone during quiet reading time. Although the book was too large to fit into his tray and I never saw it in the class library, which was mainly stocked with fiction and picture books, he could always find it when he wanted it, somewhere around the classroom. In many ways he treated it as his personal property, though it could not be borrowed or taken home. (At that time, the non-fiction stock that the school owned was lodged in the central school library for reference purposes, and for use in topic work if a class needed it.) This sense of ownership comes across in the extract above. Mitchel had been working his way through the pages, pausing only over certain ones. For him, this included those featuring dinosaurs, then anything to do with the army. When he stopped at the doublespread on weapons, he used the opportunity to offer a guided tour of the bits and pieces on the page that interested him, selecting just a few from the many to actually comment on. The nearest he got to reading any of the text aloud was when he said "that's an AK-47, MP-5, M-16". These headings are used in the text to label a series of pictures of machine guns lined up one under the other on the page. Terry played the part of interested visitor, quizzing the guide for information, and sometimes appearing to check up on what the guide really knew:

Terry:	Hang on, what's that then?
Mitchel:	That?
Terry:	Yeah.
Mitchel:	That is (. . .)
Terry:	No that.
Mitchel:	Oh that is a spy plane.
Terry:	Oh, oh yeah, a spy plane.

One could say that the conversation is structured around the relative expertise participants can already muster about the contents of the text, as much as around the text itself. It is perfectly legitimate in this kind of context to use other sources of information, so when the conversation turned to spy planes, Terry turned to what he knew about them from playing a computer game at home. The talk drifted away from the immediate text in front of them towards this other source of shared knowledge. Neither of them had paid any attention to the writing immediately above and below the illustration which Mitchel had so authoritively announced was a spy plane. In fact, the heading placed immediately above the picture read *1943 Flying bomb*, whilst the accompanying paragraph tucked underneath went as follows:

Germany launched more than 8,500 flying bombs against London in 1944. Their engines stopped above the city, and the explosives crashed to the ground.

There is a discrepancy here between what the text asserts about itself and how the children in this instance 'read' it. Some would argue that, consequently, they are simply not reading the text at all.

The Salience of the Text in Reading Research

There is a strong tradition within conventional work on literacy that successful reading, in one way or another, reproduces a given text; it is a kind of getting to grips with what is already there. Those who get the best marks at reading do so for reading aloud without deviating from the script; or for answering questions about it which show that their version of the text agrees with their examiners'. Everyone can concur on the accuracy of what has been done, as the text provides the given yardstick against which the performance can be judged. From this perspective, the kind of talk about the text produced by the speakers above simply does not measure up. If this were a comprehension test, too much of this text is being ignored; not enough is being accurately reproduced. Whatever else this kind of conversation is about, it would not count as reading. (Oakhill and Beard, 1995). The account I have given above for the boys' motivation and investment in what they are doing, and the way in which their talk is structured, would be pushed to one side.

By contrast, ethnographies of reading do not use the text and what it contains as the central reference point against which to measure what readers do. Instead the analytic focus is upon the event itself, the socially structured moment when reading takes place (Heath, 1983; Barton, 1994; Street, 1993; Baynham, 1995). For from an ethnographic perspective, it is the interactions between participants in the literacy event that will both establish and steer what the text will mean (Maybin and Moss, 1993). This is how reading becomes culturally and socially shaped in relation to, for instance, community membership, the repertoire of communicative strategies which participants bring to that event, or the institutional or social setting in which the event takes place. All of this has the effect of backgrounding the text itself. Indeed, it is comparatively rare for this kind of study of reading to reproduce the text around which a given literacy event revolves, at the same time as it produces the talk; or even necessarily make such a text identifiable through close referencing (Dombey, 1992; see also Barker, 1989). Where texts are reproduced wholesale in this kind of research, they are much more likely to be those that participants have written (see, for instance, Barton and Hamilton, 1998). So far my analysis of the literacy event, reproduced in Extract 1, fits this pattern. I have used the discursive interactions between the boys to guide my analysis of 'what counts as reading' here (Heap, 1991), without judging or measuring what they do against the text that is the object of their conversation. Below, I will go on to argue that understanding the nature of the text they are perusing, and its affordances and resistances as a multimodal object (Kress, 1998), gives new insights into what is happening in this event and its place in a larger textual economy. This presupposes building the text back into the analysis, but in a new way.

Being a Non-fiction Reader in School: Selection with a Purpose

The version of non-fiction reading most actively promoted in schools can be characterised as 'reading with a purpose'. This kind of reading is taught as an organised hunt for knowledge in which children identify at the outset what they want to know, then go out to find that information and bring it back to a context where they can present what they have found.

Often referred to as information retrieval, this kind of practice has a long history within the junior school curriculum. Sometimes conflated with library skills, in which children learn to use the library classification system to find the books as well as the bits of information they contain, in the British context such an approach to non-fiction is most immediately associated with the EXEL project which sets out to identify, support and promote a range of strategies that work in this way (Wray and Lewis, 1997). They include skimming and scanning, as a means of processing the written language; and what has become known as the EXIT model, where children learn to direct their search in a carefully staged sequence of pre-, during and post-reading activities. The assumption is that these strategies fit on to and in many ways express what good readers already do with non-fiction texts. Teaching prescribes the strategies, which are enacted in classrooms, thus confirming that this is indeed how non-fiction books are read. A kind of virtuous circle is built in which 'good' non-fiction texts are deemed to be those that both allow and encourage readers to behave in this way. Publishers, particularly those with strong links to the education market, then meet these needs by picking up on these criteria and producing the texts to match. There is a circularity to the imagination here, in which the model of reading produces a context in which that model will be put into place, thereby necessitating a kind of text that will fulfill these same requirements, thus confirming the model.

A real-life version of the kind of encounter between text and reader which the information retrieval model predicts might look something like this:

Extract 2: School 3

Daniel: I'll read it to you the different types.
Types of gladiator. Not all gladiators had the same weapons and armour. There were different classes of fighter depending on their size strength and skill. Large strong men trained to become Marmarillos or Samnites
I'll just show you [pause] this is a Samnite there [pause] um armour here [. . .] he's having his armour up his arm large helmet shorter shields and leg armour [. . .] OK? right he's the most powerful [. . .]
Such men used thick used short thick swords and huge rectangular shields and leg and armguards. The Marmarillos [. . .] the Marmarillos [. . .]
The only difference between these two, um the only difference between a Marmarillo and a Samnite was their helmet. If you look at a Samnite's one [. . .] this is a Marmarillo's is not it [pointing to a picture of a helmet] [. . .] right [. . .]
The Samnites' helmet had a crest and a tuft full of feathers on the top. Such helmets were as much for decoration as protection, as the visors sometimes made it difficult for the gladiators to see clearly. The Retiarii and the Thracian gladiators were lightly-armed and used speed and agility [. . .] The Retiari like the smaller gladiator on page 4

Wait a minute, wait a minute, wait a mi[nute [pause] weird oh no so that is a Re-tiari that's a Retiari gladiator right um ah right um...
Thracian gladiators were lightly armoured and used speed and agility to defeat stronger men. The Retiari like the smaller gladiator on page four fought with a net a trident and a dagger.

[Italics represent passages from the text as they were read aloud. The text in use is Steel, A. (1988).]

Here the speaker treats the text as a source of information. The information can be presented to someone else by reading it aloud. At the same time, reading aloud can be put on hold to allow for some diversions away from the written text, in the first instance here for additional explication, which happens around the accompanying pictures. Later the reader makes a voyage into other parts of the text for a bit of judicious cross-referencing. This looks like purposeful reading that fulfills all its objectives. The reader clearly has a topic in mind—how to distinguish between different kinds of gladiators—and pursues that topic in relation to the text in a variety of different ways, building up a kind of conceptual understanding which looks entirely portable. The chances are that later, he will be able to draw on what has happened here to enunciate the differences between Murmillos (pronounced Marmarillos in the extract above) and Samnites, or more accurately identify Retiarii. From the perspective of information retrieval, this reader looks like he's reading well, whereas the first pair looked like they were reading poorly. Of course, the ease of passing this kind of judgement is one reason why ethnographies of reading, working from participants' perspectives, will not allow the text in to simply act as judge and jury over the value of any one performance.

The Text as a Multimodal Object of Design

How might the concept of multimodality help at this juncture? In studying texts, multimodality expands the analytic object beyond the written language or the visual representation which traditionally has been seen as carrying the meaning of the text, to the highly specific material realisation of language or image in a specific case. The assumption is that always such a material realisation will necessitate the use of many modes. In this instance the texts I am interested in are junior-age non-fiction books. From a multimodal perspective the physical constitution of these books as material objects, the kinds of paper they use, their size, how they are packaged together (stapled, perfect bound), the way in which they absorb the ink which carries the writing or image, the way in which the text will be laid up on the surface of the page, are all elements which play their part in determining how these objects will be read and what we take them to mean. Each mode has its own meaning potential. In any given text, 'the consequences of using the possibilities of a different material mode . . . bring about a difference in meaning' (Kress, 1998, p. 4). The possibilities represented by each mode may or may not be realised, and can be exploited in different ways. The analytic endeavour is both to understand that potential — the affordances and resistances that any mode offers — and the use that is made of those multimodal resources in the specific case. In the first instance, I want to think about this from the point of view of text design and the way in which different approaches to text design reconstitute the text as a different kind of object for reading. The texts I consider here are all junior-age non-fiction.

Non-fiction and the Rise of the Double-spread

Some years ago, I and my son bought a second-hand copy of *The Hamlyn Junior Encyclopedia of Nature,* originally published in 1974 (Moore, 1974). Organised around air, water and land as habitats for different kinds of living things, coverage of a particular topic can and does begin almost anywhere on a given page and then, just as easily, spill over to the next. So, for instance, the section 'The Soil' begins halfway down the final column on the right-hand side of the book at p. 163, and continues over the page and on to the top of page 165, where the topic switches to Earthworms. Turn over the page and half way down, the topic changes again to Beetle larvae, and so on. This is quite different from the principles of design currently most widespread in non-fiction for this age group, where turning the page invariably means changing the topic, and the double-spread takes prime place as a way of organising the text.

In *The Hamlyn Junior Encyclopedia* the main body of writing, through which the naming of the current topic and its description happens, is presented in columns. Each page can accommodate two columns of print, alongside one narrow and one wide margin. Exactly how this space is used varies. In the first instance, the design seems to be guided by this potential of the page to be expressed as four vertical strips of varying widths. Whilst the width of the actual column of print remains constant, cropping its height and varying its starting point on the page then provides different options. Sometimes short columns of print march evenly across the bottom of facing pages, leaving a wide gutter margin and the rest of the page free to be filled with drawings (Ibid, pp. 176–177). Elsewhere, facing pages show different arrangements: here a short column of print, placed at the top of the page to the immediate left of a wide gutter margin, there a longer column of print placed at bottom left adjacent to a narrow gutter margin (Ibid, pp. 174–175). In each case, illustrations fill the spaces left behind[2].

This suggests a potential sequence to the design task. First the written text is assembled by laying it up into justified columns. Then the columns of print are broken up into appropriate chunks on the page, probably by the book designer, or editor, whoever is taking control of the final product at this stage. Next, book illustrators are commissioned to produce drawings to fill the remaining spaces. These are then captioned before the whole goes to the printers. The outcome is a book with plenty of illustrations, but one where the overall design remains firmly text-led: it is the logic of the written text which drives the reader's progress through the encyclopedia.

The written text determines the sequence in which topics change (see above), as well as guiding and constraining the illustrations that will be used, in terms of their size and position. The illustrations fill the space where the written text might have been. In this sense, as well as in relation to the actual design process, the illustrations follow the writing rather than vice versa (Kress and van Leeuwen, 1996). But in design terms, what the linear logic of the writing keeps on bumping up against is the spatial logic of the page. To take one example, on the page introducing the topic, 'Ants' (Moore, 1974, p. 154), the first column of print at the immediate top left ends a third of the way down with the words 'Try some meat of any'. The reader then has to wait to the start of the next column placed at bottom right of this page before finding 'kind: some fruit such as apple; some bread; some sugar and anything else you wish.' In between is a large continuous illustration running from bottom left to top right of the page showing different kinds of ants and their activities, effectively interrupting the sentence. My point here is not whether the typographical layout has been well or poorly executed, but rather that this moment of disjuncture neatly illustrates the two different design logics at work.

The logic of written text is primarily linear and sequential, unfolding as it must over time: the reader begins at the start of the sentence and reads on. From the point of view of traditional typography, disruption of this process is kept to a minimum through the rules of composition that printers employ. Type face, type size, leadings, letter spacing will all be carefully chosen 'to allow the eye to follow the line of type without strain . . . and easily travel back to pick up the next line' (Simon, 1945, p. 26) The printer's craft is precisely predicated upon managing these relationships well. 'Printing is the vehicle: legibility is the well-greased bearing that allows the wheels of sense to revolve without squealing', as Simon quotes approvingly from an earlier text (Meynell, 1933, quoted in Simon 1945, p. 26). The end of the line, turning over the page—these are points of potential disruption to the reading flow whose proper handling is explicitly addressed through craft rules. The way in which the sentence 'Try some meat of any kind; some fruit such as apple; some bread; some sugar and anything else you wish' has been broken up here would meet these rules, if it were simply a case of moving from one line to another, or turning over a page. What in this instance so disrupts the flow from one part of the sentence to the other is the placing of the illustration, which seems to demand attention in its own right. *The Hamlyn Junior Encyclopedia of Nature* is in effect trying to marry two different design worlds, whilst still working primarily from the written text. Under these circumstances, written text and illustration do not always make easy bedfellows.

Once text illustrations are no longer corralled off, and kept to a page of their own, but rather begin to be integrated with written text, they set new problems in terms of page design, even as they open up new possibilities. Kress and van Leeuwen argue that the technological means that increasingly facilitate these new ways of combining the verbal and the visual in effect make possible the production of texts which operate with new rules. In place of the strict linearity employed by print-dense texts, such texts develop a non-linear logic of their own, which precisely exploits the potential of the more diffuse spatial relationships between different objects placed on the same page. This in turn instigates new forms of reading by making available different kinds of reading pathways:

> [Non linear] composition sets up particular hierarchies of the movement of the hypothetical reader within and across their different elements. [In these texts] reading paths begin with the most salient element, from there move to the next most salient element, and so on. Their trajectories are not necessarily similar to that of the densely printed page, left-right and top-bottom, but may move in a circle . . . from the most salient element . . . to the text, and from the text back . . . again, in a circular fashion. Whether the reader only 'reads' the (image) and the headline, or also part or all of the verbal text, a complementarity, a to-and-fro between text and image, is guaranteed. (Kress and van Leeuwen, 1996, pp. 218–219)

The (linear) logics of time versus the (non-linear) logics of space construct different kinds of pathways through the text. The rise of the double-spread in the design of non-fiction precisely encourages this different kind of relationship between text and image in the given and finite space of the page.

Dorling Kindersley and the Design Logic of the Double-spread

In the British context, the publisher Dorling Kindersley (DK) has made its name through the adoption of the double-spread as the primary organising principle in the design of its non-fiction texts. The series *Eyewitness Guides* provides a good example of the DK approach. For purposes of comparison, I will turn to the Eyewitness Guide *Ancient Rome* (James, 1990). Constructed in large part around photographs of many of the Roman objects to be found in the collection of the British Museum, the book consists of a sequence of double-spread layouts in which each pair of facing pages does a separate topic. (The one exception is the topic of gladiatorial combat, which gets two double-spreads on consecutive pages with the main heading, 'Mortal combat', followed on the next double-spread by the sub-heading, 'Steel and claws'.) This immediately creates a very different organising principle for the text, as what can be said is already bounded at the outset by the space to say it in.

On each of the double-spreads, the pictures dominate. They occupy more space than the written text and are placed more centrally. Written text is present in the form of paragraphs and headings, which link to the objects on display. Paragraphs are sometimes right justified, sometimes left justified, but never both. Often the words flow around the shape of the picture to which they are linked. So a short paragraph headed 'Jewellery' on the double-spread titled 'The women of Rome' forms a half-moon shape as it follows the line of the necklace next to which it is laid (James, 1990, p. 19). Each paragraph operates as a self-sufficient unit. This means that the paragraphs can effectively be read in any order, and there is no need to carry the sense from one paragraph to another. Cohesion on the page is achieved through the thematic grouping of objects, and the descending order of salience established, for the paragraphs, through the use of variations in the point size and typeface in which the written text is laid up, and for the images, in relation to their size and prominence of position. On most of the double-spreads, the main heading and its accompanying paragraph are positioned towards the top left, but there is no necessity to start reading here. Instead, reading the page means making individual choices about where to start and what to jump to next.

In terms of the design process, the written text is no longer the given around which the rest of the book will be assembled. Rather, the finite space of the double-spread is the starting point. Writing the book is the act of assembling on any given page the 'right' mix of images and written text. This act is performed by the editor, or book designer, who commissions both the illustrations and the written text with this job in mind, but will make the final decisions about what gets in and what stays out, at the time of layout. In these respects alone, what Kress and van Leeuwen call the technology of inscription—that is, the means by which the text as material object is produced—has had a profound impact. The ability to manipulate written text around images, the fluidity of the potential locations for both on the page, so characteristic of DK's house style, depend upon computer technology, which in itself underpins this different approach to questions of design. The technology and design processes open up new possibilities, even whilst they may close others down.

The Move from Linear to Non-linear Composition in the Design of Non-fiction Texts

When they first produced their Eyewitness Guides, Dorling Kindersley (DK) were not publishing primarily for the school market, and indeed they remain outside the Education Publishers' Council (EPC), a body whose members must be able to demonstrate they are 'producing materials which can specifically be classified as publications for use in the course of instruction in school' (EPC, quoted in Attar, 1996). Instead DK targeted parents and children, whom they reached mainly by direct marketing. Later, as DK books increasingly found their way into schools, it was as a resource for individual reading, rather than as textbooks or topic books with a specific job to do on the curriculum. The increasing popularity of these kinds of texts have gradually led other non-fiction publishers to take up and apply some of the DK design principles. Examples of this kind can now be found in the stock of publishers such as Wayland, Franklin Watts and MacDonald Young Books, longstanding members of the EPC who have historically designed their output with the school market in mind. This looks like convergence on the same territory.

However, whilst the double-spread as a finite composite of words and images has now become ubiquitous (so much so that the *Hamlyn Junior Encyclopedia* looks increasingly quaint and difficult to navigate, precisely because it eschews this structure), substantial differences remain as to how this kind of page design is actually executed. Whilst accepting the organising discipline of the finite space of the page, many educational publishers continue to exercise their design choices differently. In effect, what this has led to is a heightening of the distinction between texts that augur work, and texts that augur play. The freedom to roam the text which the Eyewitness design style represents, through the potentially different reading pathways each page offers, and the contexts for reading with which they are associated, are not inevitable consequences of the move to the double spread.

Work Versus Play in the Design of Non-fiction Texts

To exemplify this point, I will turn to the Watts series, *How would you survive?*, and in particular, *How would you survive as an ancient Greek?* (MacDonald, 1995). Directly linked to the range of topics covered in the National Curriculum for History, and produced quite specifically to support classroom study at KS2, at first sight these texts seem to have a lot in common with the Eyewitness layout. True, they use illustration rather than photography, but the generic layout of the double-spreads which present a range of topics—On the farm; Your clothes; At war; Sports and games—seem to take the same approach to combining written text and image. Images take the central and dominant place on the page, with writing playing a more marginal part in directing the reader's attention. Writing is presented in short paragraphs, accompanying an image. There is a lead paragraph, establishing the topic which is signalled through the point size of heading and accompanying text.

But there are also substantial differences. On each of the main topic pages a strong marginal space is constructed, running from top left down the first page, across the bottom of the double-spread and then up to top right, by assembling a sequence of little illustrations and captions. The illustrations are sometimes enclosed by a rectangular box, the edges of which are aligned. Elsewhere on the page the left justification of the paragraph captions is aligned with the edges of the illustrations immediately above or below (MacDonald, 1995, p. 21), or with strong vertical elements formed within larger illustrations. (On pp. 22–23, the table leg where the potter works, and the collection of pots waiting to be fired at the kiln, line up with separate captions below.) Overall this has the effect of dividing the space available once again into a series of 'ghost' rectangular shapes in which the strongest element in the design is the virtual column, marching its invisible way across the page, top down, from left to right. On the one hand the pages adopt a design style that signals modernity; on the other hand the layout continues to struggle to impose a linear, and vertical sense of order on the potentially chaotic fluidity of the space. It is as if such books cannot quite give up the old order, whilst simultaneously trying to adapt to the new.

At a certain point in time, the design solution represented by the grid system, and demonstrated in the *Hamlyn Junior Encyclopedia,* offered the most efficacious way of integrating word and picture on the page. At one level, such an approach was clearly tied to the technological processes which then made it easier to manipulate print in rectangular blocks, thereby setting a horizon to what it was possible to do. Print technology has now altered, opening up new ways of manipulating writing and illustration on the page. But the old solution remains as a resource, a way of thinking about the disposition of space after other possibilities have opened up. Kress' point that 'the consequences of using the possibilities of a different material mode . . . bring about a difference in meaning' (Kress, 1998, p. 4) applies here. As a semiotic resource, the DK picture-led non-linear style of layout has become associated with the new as opposed to the old, and with play as opposed to work. When other publishers appropriate that style they can use it to signal play. When they employ design principles that are much closer to the grid system, then they can more strongly signal work. Both become options to be exploited. Indeed, Dorling Kindersley itself, in its current attempts to sell more directly into the school market, uses stronger horizontals and verticals in some of its publications that are clearly targeted in this way.

Work and Play in the Context of the Classroom: Going with and against the Grain of the Text

I now want to bring this discussion back to how these kinds of design distinctions in the text can feed into an ethnographic account of what children do as readers in given literacy events. To do so I turn to data collected on the Fact and Fiction research project, which was designed to study children's use of fiction and non-fiction texts in and out of school[3]. As a way of tracking how non-fiction texts were differentiated through use on the school curriculum, the Fact and Fiction project carefully documented which kinds of texts got into which kinds of contexts for which kinds of readers as part of the daily school routine (Moss, 1999). (In many respects, the regularities observed in this way became the starting point for the kind of exploration of text design outlined above.) The extracts with which this article began were collected on that project, and stem from two contrasting contexts for reading. What role does the text play in determining the shape of these events?

In Extract 1 two boys are browsing through a text which invites dipping in and out. The information that is presented is chunked into small units consisting of image, heading and paragraph. These are loosely aggregated on each double-page spread, to make a common theme. Each theme sits within a broader section. So the theme 'Energy' sits within a section of the text called 'Making, measuring, and recording' and as a double-page spread encompasses a series of smaller units headed variously 'Charcoal'; 'Solar Heating'; '1982 Wind power' and so on. The actual sequence of these units across the double-page is left to right, but in choosing which headings to quote here, I found myself working in the opposite direction. The reading path through the text is not constrained by a given order, and can be taken either in relation to the illustrations or the headings, or both. All of this means it is possible to edit a great deal of the text out, precisely in the way Mitchel does. In many ways, the boys in this literacy event work with the grain of the text. On the Fact and Fiction project data as a whole, observation of reading choices exercised in the classroom showed that such texts have a particular attraction for weaker boy readers. Part of the affordance these texts offer through the prominence of the pictures is the capacity for weaker readers to steer their way around them without recourse to the written text. At the same time, the small point size used for the writing prevents this kind of text from being pigeon-holed as 'easy reading'. For many boys, this seems important to their social standing in the larger group (Moss, 2000b). In this kind of context they can take the risk of being challenged over whether or not they can actually read the print, precisely because they already have something to say about the pictures.

Extract 1 shows text, context and readers, all pulling in the same direction. Extract 2 shows a different kind of relationship between these three elements. What I did not point out when I presented the transcript above is that it comes from a regular paired reading session during which Daniel, a Year 4 child, is expected to read with a Year 1 pupil from the infant school. They began this session by reading through the book she had brought with her, a collection of poems from a reading scheme. When they finished, he went over to the class library to get another book and came back with *A Roman Gladiator*. Much smaller than most non-fiction topic books, with relatively few pages, its size suggests a picture book. Linear rather than non-linear in design, each double-spread contains roughly a page of print forming a single textual unit, sub-divided into sequential paragraphs. Introducing this text into a paired reading session between a Year 4 and Year 3 child changes the nature of the literacy event. It allows Daniel to redefine their respective roles and under the guise of reading aloud, read for himself instead of for his partner. This becomes a one-way display in which Daniel pursues knowledge on his own account, making few concessions to his audience. In effect, the text re-orders this context and the part the readers can play within it by allowing the substitution of one kind of work for another. Its introduction here thereby puts this boy and this girl in their place.

Conventional work on literacy uses the text as the yardstick against which to measure the reader. Multimodality reconfigures the text by insisting that it is more than the language or even the image which it contains. Instead, we need to consider the text as a material object, the affordances and resistances of the stuff from which it is made, the particular combination of written text and image it synthesizes and co-ordinates on the given space of the page. In the act of reading, the reader re-makes the text, drawing on the possibilities each mode represents. But this is not to cede all rights to the reader, to make of each text what they will. There is a tension between the meaning potential of the text, the meaning potential of the context in which it will be read and the resources the reader brings to that exercise (Moss, 1999). The literacy event, conceptualised in relation to the text, context and reader, focuses on precisely this point and, I would argue, provides the means to study precisely how such tensions are resolved, as a socially situated act.

Notes

1. The research projects included the Informal Literacies project and the Negotiated Literacies project, funded respectively by the Institute of Education and the ESRC (Economic and Social Science Research Council), and later the Fact and Fiction research project.
2. Craft knowledge within the print industry codifies this particular approach to book design using the term the *grid system*.
3. The Fact and Fiction research project, conducted between 1996–1998 and funded by the ESRC, was a two-year study into boys' development as readers, which collected data in four U.K. primary schools. The research team included Dr. Gemma Moss and Dena Attar. To date, accounts of the project's findings include: Moss and Attar, 1999; Moss, 1999; Moss, 2000b.

References

Attar, D. (1996) *Quantitative Review: Summary of Sources and Data on Texts for Children, Production and Distribution at 27 November 1996*. Unpublished paper prepared for the Fact and Fiction project.

Barker, M. (1989) *Comics: Ideology, Power and the Critics*. Manchester: Manchester University Press.

Barton, D. (1994) *Literacy*. Oxford, United Kingdom: Blackwell.

Barton, D. and Hamilton, M. (1998) *Local Literacies: Reading and writing in one community*. London: Routledge.

Baynham, M. (1995) *Literacy Practices: Investigating Literacy in Social Contexts*. London: Longman.

Delf, B. and Platt, R. (1995) *In the Beginning . . . The Nearly Complete History of Almost Everything*. London: Dorling Kindersley.

Dombey, H. (1992) Lessons learnt at bed-time. In Kimberley, K., Meek, M. and Miller, J. (Eds.) *New Readings: Contributions to an Understanding of Literacy*.

James, S. (1990) *Eyewitness Guides: Ancient Rome*. London: Dorling Kindersley.

Kress, G.R. (1998) *Modes of Representation and Local Epistemologies: The Presentation of Science in Education*. London: Institute of Education.

Kress, G.R. (2000) Design and transformation: New theories of meaning. In Cope, B. and Kalantzis, M. (Eds.) *Multiliteracies: Literacy Learning and the Design of Social Futures*. London: Routledge.

Kress, G.R. and van Leeuwen, T. (1996) *Reading Images*. London: Routledge.

Heap, J. (1991) A situated perspective on what counts as reading. In Luke, A. and Baker, C. (Eds.) *Towards a Critical Sociology of Reading*. Amsterdam: John Benjamins.

Heath, S.B. (1983) *Ways with Words*. Cambridge, United Kingdom: Cambridge University Press.

MacDonald, F. (1995) *How Would you Survive as an Ancient Greek?* London: Watts.

Maybin, J. and Moss, G. (1993) Talk about texts: Reading as a social event. In *Journal of Research in Reading*. 16: 2. 138–147.

Meynell, F. (1933) *The Monotype Recorder*. 32: 3.

Moore, L. (1974) *The Hamlyn Junior Encyclopedia of Nature*. London: Hamlyn.

Moss, G. (1993a) Children Talk Horror Videos: Reading as a Social Performance. In *Australian Journal of Education*. 37: 2. 169–182.

Moss, G. (1993b) Girls Talk the Teen Romance: Four Reading Histories. In Buckingham, D. (Eds.) *Reading the Audience*. Manchester, United Kingdom: Manchester University Press.

Moss, G. (1996) Wie Jungen mit Wrestling umgehen. In Bachmair, B. and Kress, G.R. (Eds.) *Hollen-Inszenierung "Wrestling": Beitrage zur padagogischen Genreforschung*. Opladen. Germany: Leske and Budrich.

Moss, G. (1999) Texts in Context: Mapping Out the Gender Differentiation of the Reading Curriculum. In *Pedagogy, Culture and Society.* 7: 3. 507–522.

Moss, G. (2000a) Informal Literacies and Pedagogic Discourse. In *Linguistics and Education.* 11: 1. 47–64.

Moss, G. (2000b) Raising Boys' Attainment in Reading: Some Principles for Intervention. In *Reading*. 34: 3. 101–106.

Moss, G. and Attar, D. (1999) 'Boys and Literacy: Gendering the Reading Curriculum'. In J. Prosser (Ed) *School Culture*. London: Paul Chapman.

Oakhill, J and Beard, R. (1995) Guest editorial. In *Journal of Research in Reading*. Vol. 18:2 pp. 69–73.

Simon, O. (1945) *Introduction to Typography*. London: Faber and Faber.

Steel, A. (1988) *How They Lived: A Roman Gladiator*. Hove, United Kingdom: Wayland. p. 8.

Street, B (1993) *Cross-Cultural Approaches to Literacy.* Cambridge, United Kingdom: Cambridge University Press.

Wray. D. and Lewis. M. (1997) *Extending Literacy: Children Reading and Writing Non-Fiction*. London: Routledge.

Charmian Kenner 6

EMBODIED KNOWLEDGES: YOUNG CHILDREN'S ENGAGEMENT WITH THE ACT OF WRITING

The physical process of learning how to write has often been characterized merely as the acquisition of a mechanical skill. However, for young children the act of creating and positioning symbols carries considerable significance, and they are concerned with interpreting the meanings involved. This chapter will look at young children's bodily and cognitive engagement with script-learning as a multimodal process, involving particularly the visual and actional modes. The examples will be drawn from research with bilingual six-year-olds learning to write in Chinese, Arabic or Spanish (three writing systems with very different visual realizations) as well as in English. I shall argue that the teaching of handwriting promotes certain cultural patterns with regard to the writing process, spatiality and directionality, and that biliterate children therefore gain access to a variety of 'embodied knowledges' through their learning of different scripts. The chapter will also consider how individual children interpret and transform these available cultural meanings.

The Significance of the Act of Writing

The study of handwriting has traditionally been separated from research on how children learn to 'understand writing' and 'become writers'. The process of 'understanding writing' through script-learning is seen as a cognitive one, as children work out what individual symbols stand for and how a particular writing system operates. This area has largely been dominated by psycholinguistic theorists, although other researchers have taken a social semiotic approach by examining how children construct such concepts within particular cultural environments (see Harste, Woodward and Burke, 1984; Dyson, 1984; Kress, 1997; Kenner, 2000). The process of 'becoming a writer' through learning how to produce texts has been seen as both a cognitive and a cultural one, including knowledge of different genres (Kalantzis and Cope, 1993) and familiarity with the types of literacy event that take place in the child's community (Heath, 1983).

Discussions of psycholinguistic or sociolinguistic aspects of learning to write have rarely included the act of writing itself. However, work that has been done on handwriting contains some clues to its potential importance. A notable contribution has been made by Sassoon (1995), who takes a social approach in arguing that the act of writing is intensely personal, and the form in which it is carried out by each individual is a response to the human desire to 'make one's mark'. This personal response occurs within a cultural context, and Sassoon's examination of learning to write within different cultures shows how the form of individual handwriting actions is partly shaped by early experiences. She also discusses the ways in which different orthographies may have different expressive capacities, as well as requiring different writing postures and pen holds.

This wider understanding of the significance of handwriting underpins the literacy curriculum in France, where it is considered fundamental for one to become a culturally competent writer (Thomas, 1997). 'Le graphisme', the nearest English translation for which is 'the graphic act', is defined as 'un geste delicat' (a delicate movement) and 'un act complexe' (a complex action). The aim of 'le graphisme' is to develop children's visual and bodily awareness through a variety of activities, in art and physical education as well as in actions using pen and pencil; all of these are considered as preparation for the understanding and production of writing. Four-year-olds focus on particular aspects of works of art, such as pointillism in Seurat or lines in Picasso, and then try to recreate such patterns themselves. In physical education, children practise wavy movements with their whole body and make patterns with streamers in the air, before learning a new handwriting pattern involving a wavy motion. An activity such as placing coloured clothes pegs in sequence along the edges of a box is used to simultaneously develop pincer grip control and develop awareness of visual patterns.

Another example of the link perceived between the actional and visual modes in writing instruction is the 'kinaesthetic model' (Krampen, 1986, p. 109), in which the adult guides the child's hand. This is considered to help the transition from movement to form, giving physical information on shaping and direction, which supports the child's visual apprehension of the written symbols. Sassoon (1990, p. 52) also recommends using letters made from different materials such as clay and sandpaper, and encouraging children to scoop letter shapes out of soft materials such as cake icing and dough, to enhance 'kinaesthetic reinforcement'.

A Multimodal Analysis

A multimodal approach to the act of writing takes into account the multiplicity of means involved in the making of a sign. Rather than seeing 'meaning' as residing only in the compositional process of writing, with the production of written symbols as simply a mechanical 'scribing', multimodality gives equal prominence to these activities and argues that they are cognitively linked. The visual and actional aspects of the interpretation and production of written symbols are an integral part of conceptualizing 'what writing stands for'. Put another way, the cognitive understanding of writing is intimately linked with its visual and physical apprehension.

Young children have a particular capacity for what Kress (1997, p. 97) calls 'a multiple engagement with print'. In the relative freedom of their approach to meaning-making in general, 'children act multimodally, both in the things they use, the objects they make, and in the engagement of their bodies; there is no separation of body and mind' (ibid.). In coming to understand what writing symbolizes and how to produce it, they treat print as a complex semiotic system. As Kress also points out, the child has a choice as to which aspects of a multimodal system to focus on in her learning. Individual children tend to have their own paths into writing, highlighting different aspects at particular moments.

However, children's paths are also influenced by the important question of 'what is to hand' (ibid.). The child's environment offers particular constraints and possibilities with regard to the act of writing. The material provision (tools for writing, places to sit) affects what is possible, in conjunction with prevailing models of physical action (ways of holding the pen, ways of sitting) and the rules (if any) for enforcing these. The production of written symbols involves a number of different facets—the type of stroke to be used, directionality, shape, size, spatial orientation, placement on the page—and these will be culturally specified in the teaching experienced by the child.

It is from these features that children create their own repertoire of representational resources. For children learning different writing systems through culturally different pedagogies, we might expect that these repertoires will be expanded and become quite varied. The availability of a range of possibilities gives the child enhanced potential for multimodal experience and cognitive reflection. The result is a variety of 'embodied knowledges' relating to the ways in which the act of writing can be performed and interpreted.

This chapter will consider aspects of the 'embodied knowledges' formulated by six-year-old children growing up bilingually in South London. Each child was learning to write in English at primary school and in another writing system—either Chinese, Arabic or Spanish—at a supplementary Saturday school run by their language community. I shall first discuss certain characteristics of the act of writing as it was presented in each Saturday school, in comparison to children's experiences at English school. I shall then show how individual children interpreted these conventional meanings, both through their own writing and when teaching their writing systems to peers at primary school as part of the research project.

The Research Study

The project consisted of case studies of six children, all aged five (or just six) when the research began. Two were learning Chinese, two Arabic, and two Spanish—a girl and a boy in each case. Selina and Ming were learning to write in Chinese at the Lambeth Chinese Community School, Tala and Yazan were learning to write in Arabic at the Arabic Community School in Hounslow, and Sadhana and Brian were learning Spanish at the Latin American Saturday School. Each child attended a different English primary school, apart from Selina and Ming, who attended the same one.

Cantonese, Arabic or Spanish were also spoken in the children's homes, along with English, although in Ming's home most interaction took place in Hakka rather than Cantonese. All the children except Yazan had been born in London, and apart from Sadhana (who had no older siblings preceding her in the British educational system) they were fluent in a local dialect of English; Sadhana and Yazan were becoming so.

The children therefore lived their lives in two languages. Although they were receiving a greater amount of literacy instruction in English (five days a week) compared to their community language (one morning a week, with some support at home), they were encountering both writing systems simultaneously.

Over the course of one year, the children were visited at home, community language school and primary school. At home, interactions with siblings and parents around literacy were observed, and parents were interviewed about their children's literacy learning in both writing systems. At community language school and at primary school, classes were observed and teachers were interviewed concerning their teaching methods and the children's progress. In order to gain further insights into the children's thinking, they were asked to teach classmates at primary school how to write in Chinese, Arabic or Spanish, with the aid of materials from community language school. These peer teaching sessions gave children an opportunity to express ideas they had interiorised about different forms of written representation.

Key Concepts Taught at School

In this chapter I shall focus on several aspects concerning the act of writing as it was taught in each school: how symbols were built up individually and in sequence (which I have called 'the writing process'), how symbols were distributed within the frame of the page (which I have called 'spatiality'), and different levels of directionality (for the whole text, for the line and for the individual symbol). Table 6.1 summarises the characteristics of each writing system, and is discussed below.

92   MULTIMODAL LITERACY

Table 6.1. Characteristics of Each Writing System as Taught at School

School	Chinese	Arabic	Spanish	English
Writing process	analytic	synthetic	synthetic	analytic (print) synthetic (cursive)
Spatiality	centred	linear	linear	linear
Directionality (text)	right-left or left-right	right-left	left-right	left-right
Directionality (line)	vertical (top-bottom + right-left) or horizontal (left-right)	horizontal (right-left)	horizontal (left-right)	horizontal (left-right)
Directionality (symbol)	left-right top-bottom	mainly right-left top-bottom	mainly left-right top-bottom	mainly left-right top-bottom

The Writing Process

Observation at the Chinese school showed that the writing process was presented as 'analytic', which is defined for the purposes of this study as producing separate pen strokes in a particular pattern to create a unit. The unit under consideration here is the written Chinese character. Most characters stand for a particular concept, thus being similar to a word in English.

In Selina and Ming's Chinese classes, each character was built up from short separate strokes, as discrete segments combined in a particular order. The individual strokes were of particular lengths and placed at particular angles, and some were straight whilst others were curved. Basic stroke types were taught at the beginning of the first year in Chinese school. The children were then required to practise the sequence of strokes making up each character, and then practise the whole character many times, with the aim of memorizing it. A page from Selina's first-year exercise book, when she was five years old, shows this activity (Figure 6.1).

In this way, children were expected to produce characters that were correct to the last detail and could not be confused with any other character. The precise design of each stroke was discussed by the Saturday school teacher, who would write similar-looking but subtly different stroke patterns on the board and ask children to differentiate between these and the correct patterns.

At the Arabic school, the writing process was actionally and visually 'synthetic', which is defined here as using a continuous pen action to create a unit. The unit under consideration here is the word, made up of individual alphabetic letters.

Embodied Knowledges 93

Each alphabet letter was written as a flowing whole, and the flow continued as letters were joined to make words. Arabic script requires letters to be always joined together to the left, apart from six letters which are known as the 'stubborn' ones and cannot join in that direction. A line from Tala's exercise book, written at the age of six, demonstrates the 'joined-up' nature of Arabic writing (Figure 6.2).

In the Spanish school, the process could also be termed 'synthetic'. Each alphabet letter was practised in cursive form, in a flowing movement without the pen being lifted from the page. The teacher explained that this was a necessary preparation for joining letters together to form words, and that the ability to write fluidly depended on 'motricidad'—a key principle of teaching writing in Spanish. The nearest translation of this word in English would be 'motor skills', but the meaning seemed much richer, nearer to the French 'le graphisme', discussed at the beginning of this chapter.

As Brian and Sadhana's teacher described it, 'motricidad' is seen as an integral part of building a bodily disposition towards writing. She described how it could be developed through physical exercises, such as drawing large circles in the sand with a stick, although English playgrounds were sadly lacking in the materials (and the climate) suitable for performing these activities compared to her native Ecuador. However, she managed to integrate many aspects of 'motricidad' into the classroom sessions. Children were asked, for example, to hold a sheet of paper in

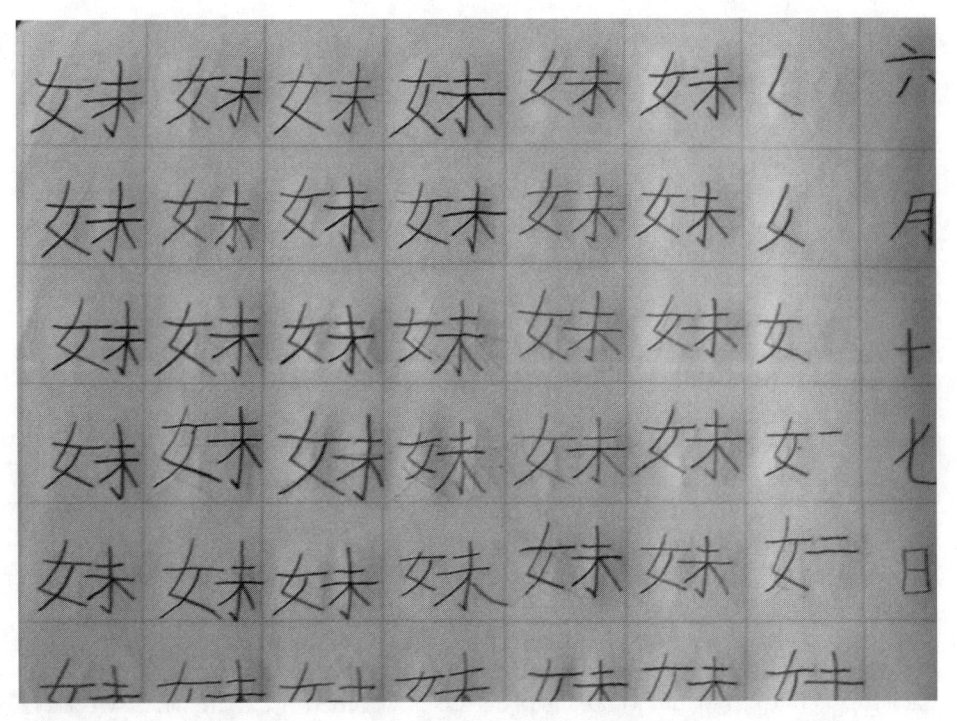

Figure 6.1

94 MULTIMODAL LITERACY

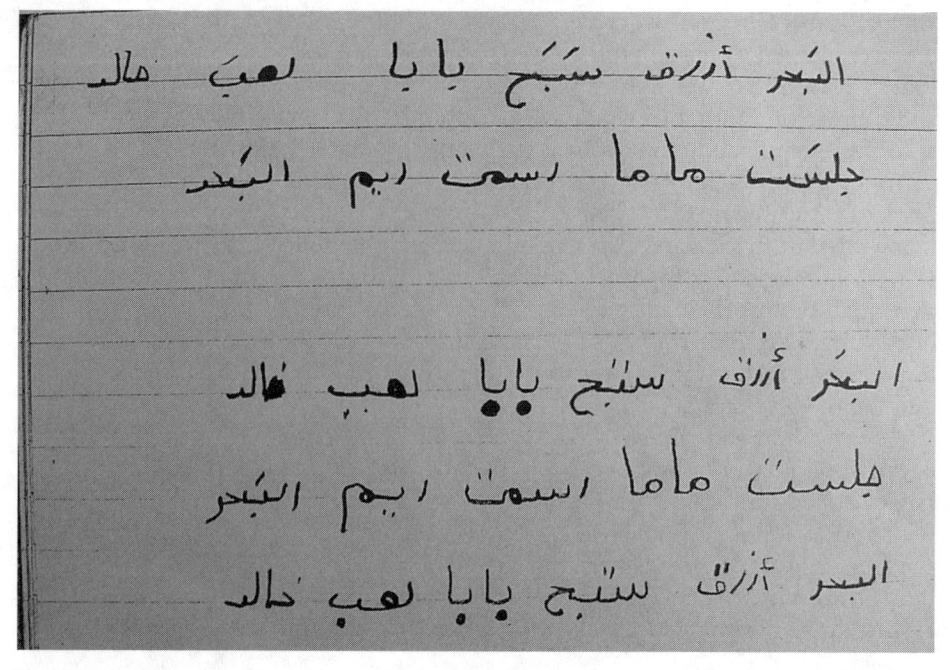

البَحرُ أَزرَقُ سَبَحَ بابا لَهِبَ خالِد
جَلَسَتْ ما ما رَسَمَتْ رِيمٌ البَحرُ

البَحرُ أَزرَقُ سَبَحَ بابا لَهِبَ خالِد
جَلَسَتْ ما ما رَسَمَتْ رِيمٌ البَحرُ
البَحرُ أَزرَقُ سَبَحَ بابا لَهِبَ خالِد

Figure 6.2

the air and tear it into narrow vertical strips, and then tear each of these into tiny pieces which could be individually picked up and made into mosaic alphabet letters. This required considerable visual and bodily co-ordination and dexterity. Another exercise for building strength and flexibility was the recitation of the rhyme 'Bate, que bate el chocolate' ('stir, stir the chocolate') about stirring a thick hot chocolate drink, accompanied by a circular movement of the wrist.

In the English primary schools, a more mixed process was observed. The cursive form of letters was taught in specific handwriting sessions, usually lasting about ten minutes and occurring no more than once a day. This could be seen as 'synthetic', as in Spanish, with a continuous hand movement. In Ming's English school the teacher emphasized 'for joined-up writing, don't take your pencil off the paper till you finish your letters' (see Figure 6.3 for an example of the worksheets involved). In some cases children were given exercises involving handwriting patterns that practised a flowing hand movement, such as a repeated chain of loops moving along the line. Similar exercises were to be found in the Spanish school materials, and also in the Arabic school (with slightly different patterns and of course a different directionality).

In the sessions on cursive writing in English school, there was a focus on where each letter would join to previous and following ones. As well as learning individual letters, children would join pairs of letters and sometimes write whole words in cursive. However, children were also seen to write in a 'print' style which was more 'analytic', involving separate strokes within some letters and no connections between letters in a word. This 'print' style was almost always used in activities other than the official handwriting sessions.

Whereas the teacher of Spanish considered that cursive writing should be taught from the beginning, the English primary school teachers were dealing with a period of change and flux in handwriting instruction. For a number of years before the introduction of a National Curriculum in the late 1980s, it was thought easier to teach children a print style initially, and cursive later (Sassoon, 1999). In some schools, handwriting was not taught at all since instruction in a particular style was seen as repressive, invoking ideas of control and uniformity. The National Curriculum set the aim of children being able to write clearly in cursive style by the age of seven, although children were still allowed to begin with print style. Schools therefore continue to employ a variety of styles and teaching methods. In Brian's English school, for example, cursive writing was not taught until children were eight years old. Meanwhile, in Selina's class, children were expected to be trying to join up their letters in all their written work—although the teacher's own handwriting showed a mixed style, using both print and cursive.

Spatiality

Ming was in the first-year class in Chinese school, and his teacher drew a grid on the board every time she wanted to present a new character. The stroke sequence was built up with each step being shown in one square of the grid, as seen in

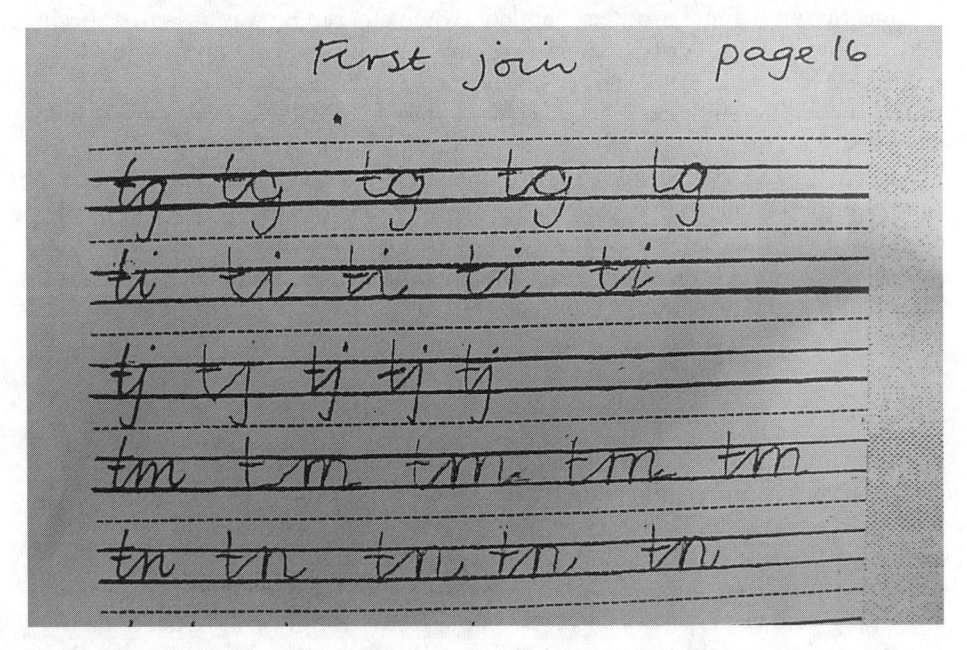

Figure 6.3

Figure 6.1. Each stroke was placed quite precisely with respect to the centre of the square, in order to occupy the correct space in relation to other strokes which would follow. In this way, as the writer proceeded through the complete sequence, a correctly written and harmoniously balanced character would result. On one occasion Ming's teacher used the slightly different technique of drawing dotted vertical lines on either side of a character, emphasizing explicitly 'make sure it's centred'.

In Selina's second-year class, the teacher was not seen to provide a grid when teaching characters, although the children's exercise books contained one. By this point, children were expected to be able to visualize the imaginary squares within which the teacher was placing her characters, and balance their own writing of strokes in their exercise books accordingly. In addition, the squares in the second-year exercise books were smaller than those in the first-year books, requiring the children to develop increased hand control and more detailed visual understanding in order to write characters on a smaller scale.

In Arabic school, Spanish school and English primary schools, children were encouraged to visualize and use the space on the page as linear rather than centred. This was particularly obvious when they were practising the writing of letters on lined worksheets. Most of the work in the Arabic and Spanish schools took place in this way, with children being provided with several lines on which to practise each letter or word. In the English schools, children were usually given lined paper for literacy work, but also given unlined paper for other subjects such as science, although they were still expected to write in a linear fashion.

Linearity was often set out as 'banded': when an exercise was designed specifically to promote handwriting, lines were provided in bands of three (as in Ming's English class, Figure 6.3). Brian's Spanish teacher explained to the children that the aim of these different lines was to keep the letters of equal size. For example, with the name 'Eduardo', the letters 'u', 'a', 'r' and 'o' should keep within the central band. For 'E' and 'd', the main part of the letter was to be placed in the central band, whilst 'the branch that goes higher' would reach into the top band. For a letter such as 'p' the 'branch' would reach down into the lower band. In Arabic school, letters were set out along one line only in workbooks for beginners, with three bands being provided as the balance of children's handwriting was expected to become more precise.

Directionality

Traditional Chinese texts are written from right to left, with characters placed in vertical columns proceeding from top to bottom and from right to left across the page. Ming and Selina's textbooks and exercise books were of this kind. Their teachers in Chinese school did not make explicit verbal comments about the directionality of text, but children were involved through visuality and physical action in opening their exercise books and text books from the right-hand side. The directionality of line was also demonstrated through action; when Ming's teacher drew grids on the board to teach a new character, she used a right-left direction. The children were then expected to follow her by starting to write at the top right-hand side of the page, going down each vertical column and moving to the next column on the left to continue practising the character.

Selina's second-year class was required to write longer passages of characters, and when they were using their textbooks as a model they would follow the right–left directionality of the columns. However, children were also shown how to create their own sentences, and in this case teachers wrote across the page horizontally from left to right in the modern style. Consequently, directionality at the page level was presented as a varied experience in the classroom.

When writing Chinese characters, each individual stroke is written from left to right or from top to bottom. The stroke-pattern used to build up each character also tends to be constructed from left to right and from top to bottom. Law et al. (1998) suggest that there is a psychomotor basis for this directionality, originating from the activity of calligraphy. The stroke directions were strictly observed by the Chinese school teachers and reinforced through verbal comments such as 'make sure you write from top to bottom, left to right'. Children would be asked to talk through the direction of the strokes as the teacher built up the character on the board. Even if a stroke looked correct, the teacher emphasized that it was wrong if it had been written in the wrong direction. On one occasion, Ming's teacher guided his hand to show him the correct sequence, saying 'this way' as she did so. In the second-year class, the teacher produced a possible stroke sequence for a character and asked the children if she had done the strokes in the correct order and direction.

In Arabic school, the most intensive teaching about directionality concerned the line. Whilst the right-left directionality of exercise books and textbooks was demonstrated by example only, teachers often made verbal comments to emphasise that writing on the page needed to be 'in Arabic—right to left, in English—left to right'. Recognising that their pupils were growing up in an Arabic-English biliterate environment in which this particular distinction was key, the teachers considered it their responsibility to help children remember the difference.

With regard to individual letters in Arabic, Yazan's teacher told the class that they needed to write from right to left and up to down. These were the general directions to keep in mind, and children were corrected if they were seen to be starting letters from the left or beginning from the bottom of a vertical stroke.

'Lateralidad' (directionality) was considered an important concept to teach in Spanish school, and a good deal of work was done on this through songs and games. Once again this was because of the principles of 'motricidad'; the teacher explained that the concept needed to be built up through physical activity as well as mental exercises. So games involving instructions such as 'touch your left eye' aimed to help children to clearly identify the left side of their body, and thus to more easily apprehend the difference between letters such as 'b' and 'd'.

The macro-directionality of text was emphasized by example in the reading of Spanish storybooks, and that of line was similarly demonstrated without verbal comment. As in the Chinese school, the most intensive instruction was concerning micro-directionality, which in Spanish involved the individual letter. When the letter 'o' was being taught in Brian's class, children were asked to trace it in the air and on the surface of the table, in bigger and smaller circles, and the action was reinforced by drawing pictures of snail shells in a spiraling motion. As the children traced or wrote the 'o', the teacher emphasized that this particular letter needed to go to the left, otherwise when children began to write 'a mano escrita' (in cursive) they would not be able to join it up to the next letter. Similarly, as children practised the letter 'm', they followed the verbal instructions of 'down, up . . .' and so on. Sometimes the instructions involved visual metaphors; the teacher described how to write the lower-case letter 'd' by telling children first to write 'la bombita' (the little bubble) and then 'el palito' (the little stick). They needed to join these together in the right way: 'if the little bubble is left open, an elegant little stick will fall from it'.

In the English schools, no explicit instructions about textual directionality and line directionality were observed. In handwriting lessons, precise verbal instructions were given about letter directionality, combined with a visual demonstration. For example (for the joining of 't' to 'o' in Ming's school), 'go straight down, it's straight round over the "o", give your "o" a little tail, then cross your "t"'. As in the Spanish school, the teacher might draw upon a visual metaphor: Brian's teacher was heard to say 'the letter "s" is a lovely easy letter to write—it's just like a snake'. In this way we can see how the action of the hand in inscribing the letter was closely connected with visual meaning.

Children's Interpretation of the Act of Writing

Here I will consider the ways in which children learning Chinese and Arabic as well as English (thus dealing with systems which differed substantially in embodied knowledges) presented and interpreted these differences when peer teaching and when producing their own writing. The focus is on Chinese and Arabic because the children learning Spanish were not found to emphasise aspects of the act of writing when peer teaching, perhaps because they did not perceive the writing process, spatiality or directionality in Spanish to be radically different from the way in which they were taught at English school. However, I would suggest that involvement over a long period of time with the Spanish school would add to those children's repertoires of representational resources, through continuation of the visual and actional experience discussed earlier, described by their teacher as 'motricidad'.

The Children Learning Chinese

AN ANALYTIC WRITING PROCESS

Both Selina and Ming presented Chinese characters to their English school classmates as each consisting of separate strokes built up in a particular sequence, in the way that they had been taught in Saturday school. Selina, whose mother also taught her at home with an emphasis on precision in each stroke, was strict with her 'pupils', rubbing out their efforts if these failed to reach her own high standards. Ming, who did not receive such a strongly framed input at home, was more flexible when peer teaching. However, he showed that he was aware of criteria such as the correct length, angle and balance of strokes when he made comments such as 'That one's very shorter', 'It's wonky and it's not straight', 'He did it nicely', and 'It looks neat'.

The children's highly developed memory for visual detail was demonstrated through Selina's ability to reproduce stroke sequences of over 15 steps, and Ming's awareness of the key differences in stroke pattern which differentiated two potentially similar characters. When teaching his classmate Roberto to write the character meaning 'six' (Figure 6.4), Ming suddenly became dissatisfied with his pupil's efforts. He complained that at various points Roberto's writing of the first vertical stroke was 'too long', and that the lower part of the character was wrong 'because it's next to each other' (the two strokes under the horizontal line were supposed to be farther apart). It turned out that these particular details were indeed salient in differentiating this character from the character meaning 'big'(Figure 6.5).

Ming was also explicitly aware of the bodily disposition engendered by becoming a writer of Chinese at his Saturday school, where the process of practising

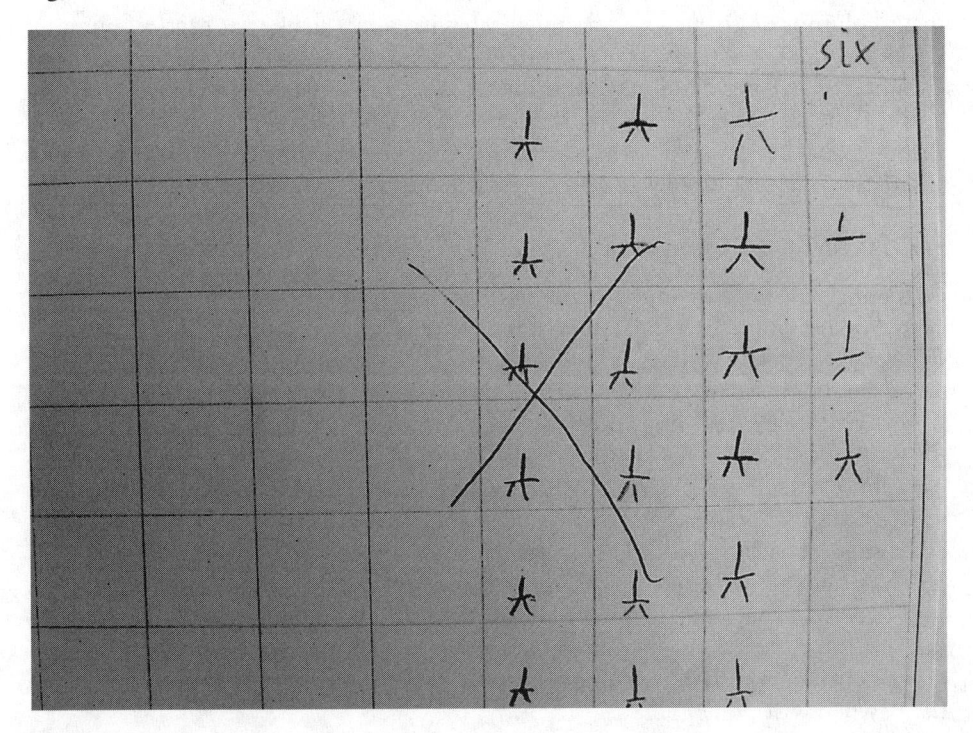

Figure 6.4

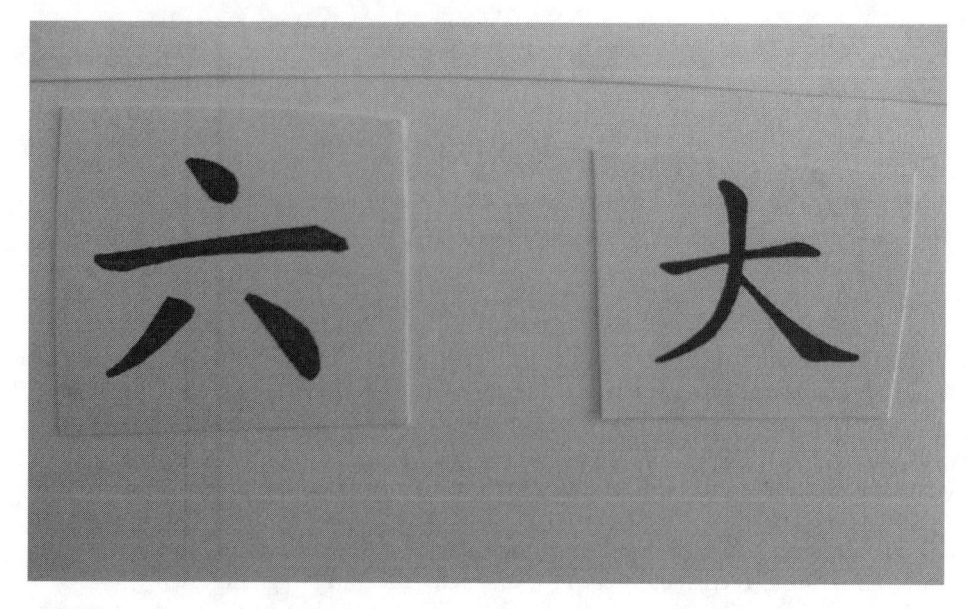

Figure 6.5

many columns of characters at a time (each with a neat stroke pattern) required intense and precise activity of the hand. When teaching his first pupil, Amina, he commented, 'If her hand gets tired, I'll do it'. Amina managed to finish an entire page of the character for 'seven', but sat back with a sigh of exhaustion. Part-way through another page of work she was seen to be shaking her wrist, and Ming asked, 'Is your hand tired?' and proceeded to finish that page on her behalf.

SPATIALITY

As mentioned above, Ming's teacher in the first year of Chinese school drew a grid on the board when teaching a new character, presenting each step of the stroke sequence in a separate square. Selina's teacher in the second-year class no longer used a grid on the board, although the children's exercise books still contained squared pages. When peer teaching, both children demonstrated how they saw the space for writing Chinese as consisting of squares within which to centre each character.

Selina presented characters to her 'pupils' on the board without providing a grid, since she was already able to visualise the squares. As she built up a new character, she placed each stroke in relation to the centre of the imaginary square, with an awareness of its position with regard to strokes yet to come. The result was a well-balanced character. Selina's English school classmates found it difficult to interpret this use of the space, since it differed substantially from the linear arrangement of English writing, but Selina was easily able to switch to a centred spatiality when writing Chinese.

Ming usually drew a grid when teaching his peers, but on one occasion he did not do so. I commented that he had also written the character much smaller than usual, and he explained that it was because of the boxes. When I said 'But you haven't done any boxes', he pointed out that the boxes were already there. Indeed, when I looked closely at the board there was a matrix of squares in the whiteboard material underneath the surface layer, invisible to most onlookers but visible to Ming because he was looking for them—to him, squares were part of the affordance of the page.

DIRECTIONALITY

Selina and Ming both emphasised text directionality as right to left, by handing their 'pupils' exercise books from the Chinese school and opening the books from the right. Typically, their English school classmates then began to write in the top left-hand corner of the page, whereupon they would be corrected by their 'teacher' rubbing out their writing, and pointing to the opposite corner or explicitly telling them 'you have to start here'. Once the 'pupil' had successfully completed the stroke sequence, Ming and Selina would indicate that they had to practise several columns of the whole character. This indication was usually given by the 'teacher' moving a finger across the page, from top to bottom and from right to left, showing the number of columns that needed to be filled. Selina was strict in ensuring that her classmate followed this vertical directionality, whereas Ming allowed occasional latitude but showed that he knew the conventions: for example, when Amina began to fill the squares horizontally, he commented 'she's going across!'

At the same time, both children were comfortable with using the left-right, horizontal directionality that is conventional in more modern Chinese text forms. Selina knew that Chinese New Year greetings could be written both in traditional vertical columns, as on the red paper banners which adorned her home at the time of celebration, and in horizontal lines. She read out one of the banners to her friend Ruby in a peer teaching session, and later made a New Year card in which she wrote the same message across the front from left to right. Ming liked to produce 'tests' for his 'pupils', featuring a set of squares running horizontally from left to right in which they had to demonstrate each step of the stroke sequence for a given character. Like Selina, Ming was accustomed to writing stroke sequences in this direction when doing similar tests at Chinese school.

The children thus demonstrated considerable flexibility in terms of directionality when writing, a flexibility which seems likely to have been engendered by dealing with such a variety of conventions within Chinese itself. Directionality seemed to be a highly varied and unproblematic concept for these young learners of a script which had several different principles of visual organisation. For example, Selina could also make use of vertical columns going from left to right when showing how to write a long stroke sequence on the board. A similar flexibility was shown by Ming's cousin, Ping, who was also his classmate at English school, when participating in a peer-teaching session with him. Although she attended a different Chinese school where exercise books used the horizontal left-right system, Ping adapted rapidly to the traditional system in Ming's exercise books and noticed when she had forgotten to start on the right after turning to a new page. She was also quick to realize that Hinh was using vertical columns rather than horizontal lines, and checked with him before she wrote, asking 'do you go downways or across?'

The Children Learning Arabic

A SYNTHETIC WRITING PROCESS

As Tala's brother Khalid commented, 'Arabic is always joined-up'. In their writing, Tala and Yazan showed an awareness of the continuous pen action used to join most alphabetic letters together and produce words, and also of the need to leave a gap within words after the few letters which did not join to the left.

Tala was able to explain to her peers at primary school which letters she used from the Arabic alphabet chart to construct her name, and how 'I joined them up'. When her 'pupils' had difficulty in perceiving how a word was constructed and in producing an accurate replica, Tala provided them with a 'join-the-dots' model as an aid to perception and action, just as her teacher used to do in the first year of Arabic school.

When demonstrating her brother's name to her classmates, she pointed out that there was a gap in the middle of the word. This is because the letter 'alif' (for the sound /a/) cannot join to the left, so 'Khalid' is written as a synthetic unit of 'Kha' followed by a gap before a second synthetic unit of 'lid'. Tala's explanation was as follows:

> 'Can I tell you something? You know this and this (pointing to each part of the word)—they're not actually together. They have to be split up. This (circling the first part) says 'Khal', and this (circling the second part) says 'lid'. 'Khal' is one word and 'lid' is another one word'.

Allowing for Tala's slight inaccuracy in joining the /l/ sound to 'Kha', she had clearly understood the principle of producing integrated units of letters whilst leaving a gap at certain necessary points. She made use of the term 'word' to try to explain the synthetic nature of the units to an audience not familiar with the Arabic writing system. Tala showed that she could apply the synthetic principle consistently, and knew which letters could join to the left and which could not, when writing words in Arabic which were new to her (such as the name of her friend at English school, Tina).

Yazan also wrote with a continuous 'synthetic' action when producing Arabic words in peer teaching sessions and when doing a 'spelling test' in Arabic at home with his sister Lana. Within this action, Yazan indicated the joins between individual letters with an awareness that the word was not simply one undifferentiated whole. When writing his name, Yazan knew where the gaps were sited.

SPATIALITY AND DIRECTIONALITY

Arabic uses a linear arrangement of the page, as does English, and Tala and Yazan tended to use a linear arrangement for their own writing in both Arabic and English, whether or not lines were actually provided on the paper. Both sometimes worked in columns, as when Tala gave tasks to her 'pupils' in which they had to practise versions of her model words, with the instruction 'copy it all the way down to here' and a mark at the bottom of the page where they could stop. Such columns were typical of practice in Arabic school too.

The main issues that called Yazan and Tala's attention when peer teaching concerned directionality. In the case of Yazan, his focus was on the whole text. When showing his Arabic school textbook to his English class, he was aware that they would expect the book to open at the other end. Pointing to the cover, he explained 'Not the end', and then turned the book over and said 'This is the end'. Returning to the cover, he emphasised 'This is the first'.

Tala was concerned both about text directionality and about directionality of the line. On one occasion when I was taking research notes in a peer teaching session, she insisted that I turn my notebook over, and then castigated me for beginning on the left-hand side of the page. She pointed to the right-hand corner and said 'Do it the Arabic way!' With her 'pupils', she was similarly strict: 'We don't start from there, we start from here!' (when they began from the left-hand rather than the right-hand side of the page). To help them remember, she sometimes provided an arrow at the right-hand side.

Yazan was initially less focused on line directionality, but during the year of the research project he showed awareness that it was an issue, asking me once at his English primary school 'Where do I start? I think it's here' (pointing to the right-hand side of the page, although he then began writing from the left). In my final visit to his Arabic classroom, I saw him self-correct: 'Oops! I always do it wrong way'.

The much greater quantity of English input, and the dominance of English in society, led to both Tala and Yazan sometimes writing Arabic with a left-right directionality. This was the reason for their Arabic teachers' constant reminders of 'English—left to right, Arabic—right to left'. However, they were both aware that there were two potentialities for directionality, and often made use of these in their texts.

Tala wrote on both 'front' and 'back' covers of her exercise book for Arabic school, because from her dual perspective both had the potential to be the front. Exercise books used by Yazan and his sister Lana at home started at both ends. For example, one began with the Arabic alphabet at the right-hand end and the English alphabet at the left-hand end. In another case, the 'English' cover of the exercise book contained Yazan's name in English, written by his sister. On the 'Arabic' cover, she had written his name in Arabic. Yazan showed a desire to experiment with line directionality, writing his name in English—but from right to left—immediately below.

On another occasion, I witnessed Yazan writing his sister's name, 'Lana Sibay', with 'Lana' written from right to left and 'Sibay' from left to right. This seemed a particularly deliberate kind of experimentation. As with the Chinese children, Tala and Yazan's varied experiences of the act of writing seemed to have engendered flexibility in the use of visual and actional modes.

A Note on Posture and Pen-hold

These issues were not seen to be dealt with explicitly in any of the schools observed as part of the project at the times when I was observing literacy learning. Exceptions were when Brian's primary school teacher reminded her pupils to 'sit up nice and straight so you can write, and tuck your chair in' and when Brian's Spanish school teacher demonstrated a pen-hold on one occasion to Brian. At all three Saturday schools and at all the primary schools, children were seated around tables and allowed to position their chairs and their hands in a variety of ways. Some of the Chinese children, for example, rested their heads on their arms on the surface of the table itself, thus looking sideways at the page, whilst concentrating hard on writing characters with the other hand.

Tala developed her own positioning of her body towards the page in order to write Arabic. She would turn the page through an angle of 90 degrees so that she appeared to be writing 'sideways'. This unusual but consistent posture may have derived from Tala's desire to be able to see more easily what she had produced as she was in the process of writing.

Children's experiences were therefore relatively varied and unconstrained, in comparison to the physical constraints that were supplied in the past (in Britain in the early 20th century, for example) by desks with benches attached, reinforced by the commands of teachers who ensured that an upright posture was maintained for writing. Under the circumstances observed in this project, children would still have been internalizing a body posture, though a somewhat more variable and individually chosen one.

At times when explicit instruction was given about posture, whether through verbal or actional modes, children demonstrated a recognition of this. For example, Brian was seen to be 'tucking his chair in' as a response to his teacher's instructions. And Selina, whose mother insisted on her sitting close to the table in an upright posture when writing Chinese at home, was observed to move her chair to a similar position at her primary school table and sit up straight on her own initiative.

With regard to pen-hold, some of the participants in the research showed an awareness of this. Tala told her 'pupils' in a peer teaching session that they were not holding the pen correctly. When I asked her how she had learned to hold the pen, she said she had taught herself. Both Brian's mother and his Spanish school teacher commented on the importance of training in holding the pen, with the desire to see this implemented in primary schools.

Sassoon (1993) argues that a comfortable posture and pen-hold are key to successful and pain-free writing, and need to be established for each individual with the advice of the teacher. She also points out that different writing systems are likely to require different pen-holds, because of the type of stroke and directionality involved. The attention paid to these issues by an approach such as 'le graphisme' in France, or 'la motricidad' in Latin America, could benefit children. This would not necessarily mean a return to the rigid discipline which the 'iron grip' of Victorian schooling aimed to instill—discipline in the schools observed in this project was being accomplished in other ways. If individual flexibility was allowed for, as Sassoon suggests, and teachers were able to help biliterate children to vary these aspects of the act of writing in each of their systems, children's representational resources could be expanded still further.

Conclusion

The act of writing has been seen as a lower-level skill, mechanical rather than mental. Such a view stems from a dualistic concept of mind and body, in which 'the cognitive' is characterised very narrowly. This chapter has argued, instead, that the act of writing has equal cognitive importance with other aspects of learning to write. Indeed, the visual and actional processes of producing written symbols are intimately linked with the processes of 'understanding writing' and 'becoming a writer'.

Research with children learning to write in different scripts highlights the ways in which familiarity with the act of writing constitutes a key aspect of children's representational resources. Young biliterate children have the opportunity to develop a flexible and comprehensive approach to the act of writing from an early age. The ability to take different angles on aspects such as the writing process, spatiality and directionality should enable children to design multimodal texts that take full advantage of the affordances of page and screen. On the screen, in particular, space is often conceptualised as non-linear, with texts having different visual arrangements and different directionalities. Children with a variety of 'embodied knowledges' will be particularly well placed to grasp the communicative possibilities of the future.

Acknowledgments

This research on which this chapter is based was supported by the Economic and Social Research Council (ESRC) via Award Number R000238456, 'Signs of Difference: How Children Learn to Write in Different Script Systems'. I would like to thank the families involved in the research project, and the following schools: Lambeth Chinese Community School, the Arabic Community School in Hounslow, the Latin American Saturday School, and Berkeley, Duncombe, Eveline Lowe, Richard Atkins and Wellington Primary Schools. Thanks also to Hayat Al-Khatib, Angel Tsai, Roy Kam and Gunther Kress for comments on a draft of this chapter.

References

Dyson, A.H. (1984) 'N Spell My Grandmama': Fostering Early Thinking about Print. *The Reading Teacher* 38: 262–71.

Harste, J.C., Woodward, V.A. and Burke, C.L. (1984) *Language Stories and Literacy Lessons*. London: Heinemann.

Heath, S.B. (1983) *Ways with Words*. Cambridge, United Kingdom: Cambridge University Press.

Kalantzis, M. and Cope, B. (Eds.) (1993) *The Powers of Literacy: A Genre Approach to Teaching Writing*. London: Falmer Press.

Kenner, C. (2000) *Home Pages: Literacy Links for Bilingual Children*. Stoke-on-Trent, United Kingdom: Trentham Books.

Krampen, M. (1986) On the Origins of Visual Literacy: Children's Drawings as Compositions of Graphemes. In M. Wrolstad and D. Fisher (Eds.) *Toward a New Understanding of Literacy*, pp. 80–111. New York: Praeger Publishers.

Kress, G.R. (1997) *Before Writing: Rethinking the Paths to Literacy*. London: Routledge.

Law, N., Ki, W., Chung, A., Ko, P., and Lam, H. (1998) Children's Stroke Sequence Errors in Writing Chinese Characters. In C. Leong and K. Tamaoka (Eds.) *Cognitive Processing of the Chinese and Japanese Characters*, pp. 113-138. The Netherlands: Kluwer Academic Publishers.

Sassoon, R. (1990) *Handwriting: The Way to Teach It*. Cheltenham, United Kingdom: Stanley Thornes Ltd.

Sassoon, R. (1993) *The Art and Science of Handwriting*. Oxford, United Kingdom: Intellect.

Sassoon, R. (1995) *The Acquisition of a Second Writing System*. Oxford, United Kingdom: Intellect.

Sassoon, R. (1999) *Handwriting of the Twentieth Century*. London: Routledge.

Thomas, F. (1997) *Une Question de Writing?* London: Teacher Training Authority.

Lesley Lancaster 7

BEGINNING AT THE BEGINNING: HOW A YOUNG CHILD CONSTRUCTS TIME MULTIMODALLY

This chapter will examine the key role that very young children's co-ordinated use of physical and bodily resources plays in their structuring of semiotic events. It will focus on how a concept of 'beginning and ending' is constructed by a two-year-old during sequences of activity involving making a greetings' card. A micro, multimodal description of the physical and bodily resources used in the mediation of these activities is used in the analysis. It will be shown that language, gaze and action are used in systematic configurations to construct the concept. It will discuss how during this process, gaze is used to link images of past experience with anticipation of future activity; and interpersonally to maintain the involvement and help of an interested adult. The chapter will discuss the significance of multimodal analysis in understanding the conceptual construction of very young children. Finally, the chapter will consider the degree to which this systematic co-ordination of physical, bodily modes in the mediation of meaning is a conscious, knowing process.

In this chapter I shall discuss the means by which very young children construct and operate systems of temporal structuring as resources for learning about how cultural practices like electronic communication and visual representation are organised. In the first part of the chapter I reflect on how the conception of time is socially and materially segmented, and the ways in which this is mediated through different physical and bodily modes. In the second part of the chapter, I consider evidence drawn from a case study of the activity of a 23-month old child around the kind of semiotic event that retains long-term educational significance, and which is associated with key cultural practices and systems of representation. The concern of this study is to describe and analyse not just the outcomes, but the *process* of the child's thinking as she structures a beginning and end to her activity. Central to all this is the interactive and affective setting in which it all takes place. This analysis of the proceedings derives from a micro level of description, with a time frame of only seconds. The multimodal descriptors are generated from a close interrogation of video data, showing that it is through the motivated and coordinated use of different bodily modes of expression that she is able to mediate the complex and abstract meanings involved.

Part One

A Sense of Time

An early memory, probably around the age of three, is of a children's radio programme which was turned on every weekday lunchtime. To begin with, it seemed that the announcer was addressing me directly: 'Are you sitting comfortably?' she would enquire as the signature tune faded, and then barely pausing for my reply would continue, 'Then now we'll begin'. Of course I soon got used to this introductory routine: its significance for me was quite quickly transformed from a question and a statement whose ideational content required some kind of consideration and thought, to a musical and linguistic routine whose principal purpose was to mark a break in the continuum of adult programmes and signify a salient point in the routine of the day.

Like a number of people, I think, I have a conscious memory of what time felt like when I was very young. A time span such as a day was experienced as moving very slowly, even though it was broken up by the regular iteration of social routines built up around basic needs such as eating, drinking and sleeping. The distance between significant and enjoyable annual events like festivities and holidays appeared to be almost interminable and unimaginably long. Indeed, this early perception that time moves slowly seemed to derive from the vista of potentially unconstructed time that lay between these keenly anticipated events: things that we 'look forward to'. Lakoff and Johnson (1999) point out that perception of time is based on the knowledge that it is segmentable: that our experience of time is relative to our experience of events. The radio programme was an event and resource that was used by those in my immediate social environment to add structure to an otherwise uneventful part of the day. Time, in this respect, was socially and materially constructed.

I am not just talking here about synchronic time: about a single point in a linear progression of time. In my example, the very act of pleasurable anticipation of listening to the radio could only take place if previous experiences of the event had been enjoyable. In this sense, past experience was incorporated into present experience; and arguably was also part of any future experiences, since the knowledge that it could be repeated inevitably informed perception of the present event. So although the programme itself can be said to begin when the signature tune starts, and to finish as it fades away, the boundaries of the event of which the programme is a part are distinctly fuzzy. This carrying of past experiences into present and into the anticipation of future involves the use of complex configurations of images: Damasio (1994) describes these as *recalled images:* 'Those images, which occur as you conjure up a remembrance of things past' (p. 97). Such images might comprise narrative memories: maybe the door bell rang just as the programme was about to start, setting in train a number of unexpected events; tactile memories as well: the physical feel of the radio knob as it was turned on; or affective memories: feelings of pleasurable excitement. These images are often a temporal composite, linking and combining salient features from different times and situations.

Listening to the radio was altogether a multimodal affair: incorporated were language and text, since it involved listening to the presenters talking and reading from a script, as well as stories that were written down; and then there was the music: the signature tune, music for the songs, and much hearty singing. This was mediated through the technology of the radio medium, the material object of the radio itself, and the acoustics of our dining room. The major tool used to orchestrate the procedure of these events was the human body: with gaze used to locate the radio, movement to move towards it, gesture to indicate intention of movement, action to turn the radio on, sound used to join in the songs and to produce language to communicate with others in the room, and so on: this is not an exhaustive list. Johnson (1987) reminds us that our bodily experience is a key factor in the way in which we structure concepts about time, 'bodily movement, manipulation of objects, and perceptual interactions involve recurring patterns without which our experience would be chaotic and incomprehensible.' (p. xix).

For a young child, understanding when an event begins and ends requires learning about how the segmentation of time is organised within a specific social group and community, and the specific cultural and bodily routines and practices involved: a set of dispositions transferable to new situations as they arise (Bourdieu, 1986, 1991). Whilst many of the instructional routines used in educational institutions do highlight when certain operations and activities are to start and end, the broader and more complex question of how cultures structure time is one that children have been actively addressing since infancy. Indeed children become skilled from a very early age at using all the resources available to them to construct their own systems of time segmentation. Weinberg and Tronick (1994) looked at how babies of six months old organise gaze, vocalisation, gesture and movement into intentional, 'multimodal configurations' that open and close distinct events, such as looking at their mothers, focusing on an object and actively protesting!

Constructing Events

The events that I have been discussing here are semiotic events informed by semiotic practices (Kress and van Leeuwen, 2001). Drawing parallels with the relationship between literacy events (Heath, 1983) and literacy practices (Scribner and Cole, 1981; Street, 1995), any particular semiotic event is informed by the wider ideological and cultural properties of linked semiotic practices. Bourdieu (1991) again points to the 'close correspondence between the uses of the body, of language and no doubt also of time' through which "choices" constitutive of a relationship with the economic and social world' (p. 89) are inculcated. In my example above, these would have included practices attached to the mode and genre of broadcasting, particularly as they pertained to broadcasting to young children at that point in the mid 20th century. Another domain drawn on would have been that of practices of parent-child interaction prevalent at that time. I think my construction of the event, could I go back and view it through 21st-century eyes, might have looked rather different from its latter-day equivalent. Then, the radio tended to be turned on only when it was to be listened to, rather than being on much of the time as would be likely to be now. There was a moment or two of absolute stillness and quiet, whilst waiting for the valves to warm up, making the anticipation of the start of the programme seem much more marked and sharply framed (see Goffman, 1986) than it might seem now. The bodily stillness and quietness would have been maintained once the programme started (apart from when being exhorted to join in), since there were then expectations about how children were to disport themselves when 'listening to a radio programme', which would be unlikely to apply now. In other words, social practice was realised in the event through characteristic modes and stances of physical behaviour (see also Nelson, 1985).

Part Two

Analytical Framework

BEGINNING AND ENDING EVENTS

In the second section of this chapter I am going to turn to evidence from the case study and look at how one very young child co-ordinates available semiotic resources in order to structure the starting and completion of the making of a card for her mother. A striking feature of the study is the little girl's purposeful physical and bodily mediation of her activity, with the different modes having distinct functions in the meaning-making process; another is the naturalistic and interactive setting in which it takes place. The activity from which this evidence is derived has been recorded on video, and is therefore open to a level of description and analysis that is not possible in the case of recalled experience, discussed in Part One. The events discussed are represented as multimodal transcripts, shown in Tables 7.1 and 7.2.

The participants in this activity are Anna, 23 months old at the time, and her father Rob. Rob is the film maker, with Anna the main actor, and her actions the prime focus of the camera. The filming took place early on a weekend morning, before the rest of the family were up, with all the activity-taking centred on and around the table in the kitchen. This was not an unusual happening since Rob habitually spent this time with his daughter. The video text arose out of both Rob's personal and professional roles: as a father interested in recording his daughter's development, but also as an educational professional with a particular interest in the very early stages of literacy. His keen awareness of semiotic practices associated with literacy means that dispositions to certain kinds of literate activity are likely to be strongly evident in the interactions between himself and his daughter.

The activity in which they engage is the making of a Mother's Day card using marking, drawing and writing. Much of this revolves around the representation of a cat, which becomes the centre of a complex narrative as the card evolves. Two common semiotic practices are evident here: that of giving a 'card' in order to acknowledge a particular cultural event; and that of young children constructing the card themselves using readily available materials and tools (at this age, it is the effort of production that is acknowledged as the gift as much as the material object). Rob has prepared the artefacts needed for the activity. On the table in front of them is an A2 sheet of blank orange cartridge paper. On Anna's right is a red-and-white cylindrical tin containing an assortment of different coloured felt tip pens.

Framing

Two levels of framing are used in the description and analysis of the events. The broader level of framing is that of 'scene', which is characterised by the particular topic or activity developed in the course of transforming the sheet of paper into a card. Broadly speaking, the scene is synonymous with the semiotic event as discussed above. Scene 1 revolves around the physical activity of folding the paper and organising the felt tip pens, and Scene 2 around the representation of cats. Within the scene, a more micro level of segmentation, that of 'episode', is used, with each episode covering one central semiotic event. Episode 1, for example, is concerned with Anna's anticipation and planning of the activity.

Levels

Three levels of evidence are drawn upon in the course of this semiotic analysis (see Thompson, 1990). Firstly, salient ethnographic evidence, such as the information about Rob's profession, has been gathered to be incorporated into the analysis. Secondly, a micro, multimodal description of the bodily modes used by Anna to mediate and generate meanings is derived through two stages. The video text was first interrogated to derive a set of descriptive categories. The descriptive categories reflect those mediating strategies consistently deployed by Anna in her interaction with Rob during her interpretative activity. The set of descriptive categories used are: *language, vocalisation, gesture, gaze* and *action*. These operate as a set, which applies across the whole event; subsets apply to particular episodes within the event. So, for example, 'gesture' is a category that operates across the event as a whole, but not in the particular episodes to be discussed. Sub-divisions of these modes, based on their differential functions, are evolved in the course of the analysis that is derived from this description. Anna is the agent of all activity described in the tables, except where Rob is specifically identified. The marks made on the paper by Anna, which constitute the evolving Mother's Day card, are described under the category heading *semiotic object*. The third level of analysis is a hermeneutic explanation based on 'thick description' (Geertz, 1983), drawing on both the other levels. However, the boundaries between these three levels of evidence and explanation are flexible, providing opportunities for comparison, confirmation and reflection.

Hermeneutic Analysis

This stage involves a micro-level interpretative analysis derived from the multimodal description, and incorporating and drawing on the personal, social and cultural insights provided by the ethnographic information. The interpretation involves an adult's reconstruction of the process involved when a very young child works on the difficult job of structuring an event involving the symbolic representation of meaning. Central to an explication of how Anna does this is a focus on the way she orchestrates the different modalities used as she anticipates and plans what she is going to do. A traditional reliance on linguistic descriptors alone would have produced a very limited interpretation, given that her use of language in the first episode is minimal. Indeed, it would suggest that she plays a rather passive role, rather than, as is the case, an active and creative one; language at this point is not highly relevant to the activity in which she is engaged.

Gaze is a particularly significant tool throughout this process. Very little research has been carried out on the role of gaze during social interaction, and even less on its role during activity involving the interpretation of symbolic representation. Work with children under the age of two has tended to concentrate on looking at gaze to establish things like visual attention: for example, the way in which babies and very young children follow the line of an adult's gaze so that they are mutually attuned to the same object; and the ways in which they use adult expressions to help them understand new or difficult situations (Nelson, 1996; Rogoff, 1990). This approach concentrates on the description of the way in which a single mode can provide insights into how infants and young children follow the model provided by an adult. In this chapter, however, the focus is on the ways in which gaze is used in systematic configurations with other bodily modes, informed by the active and independent analytic concerns of young children in the course of structuring semiotic events. The description and analysis used here also shows that gaze, as is the case with other modes, is multiply constituted. For example, it has a number of distinct functions in the process of constructing beginnings and endings to these events: not just interpersonal and expressive, but also predictive and analytic. However, this is far from an exhaustive description, of the full range of its semiotic potential.

Anticipating and Planning—Scene 1, Episode 1 (see Table 7.1)

By focusing on the coordination of the full repertoire of mediational resources, it becomes apparent that there is a whole planning stage well before the business of drawing on the page, 'making the card', takes place. No precise starting point is announced for this activity; just a suggestion by Rob that something might be done. Preparations for the event have started off-camera, with the material paraphernalia typically brought out when children want to draw or write, readily at hand. Set out on the table is the unmarked sheet of paper and as Rob sits down, he puts the ink pot on the table. Already Anna is anticipating action, standing rather than sitting on the kitchen chair in order to be better able to survey the scene. She turns her gaze to the pot of pens, first in Rob's hand and holding it there as he places it on the table. At this point, her gaze has a predictive function; she is already starting to structure an activity, based on the artefacts that Rob is assembling. Berthoz (2000) points to the way in which, when we perceive an object, we already have within our minds the action we associate with it. Perception, he suggests, is 'simulated action' (p. 10). Anna, standing still on the chair, is able to envisage other times when she has used these pens, recalling images of previous experiences when such pens have been involved. This envisaging is multisensory and multimodal, involving perhaps colours, shape, tactile qualities, the smells and sounds in the room at the time; the position of the body in relation to what was going on; what else was happening, and so on. Developing his concept of recalled images, Damasio (1999) points to the way in which 'images allow us to choose among repertoires of previously available patterns of action' and we can 'more or less deliberately, more or less automatically, review mentally the images which represent different options of action' (p. 24). For Anna, the event starts with anticipation: with the construction and prediction of possibilities centred around the pot of felt-tipped pens and the things she likes to do and make with them.

All this takes place in the infinitesimal period of time before Rob speaks. He then proposes his own frame of activity around the pens and paper. His emphasis is on 'doing', repeating 'shall we do' three times and ending by asking 'do you want to do'. The activity revolves around the proposition that it is Mother's Day: he derives three proposals from this: that a card could be made to mark the occasion, that they could make a card together, and that Anna could make a card on her own. The setting, with paper and pens to the ready, indicates that these questions are rhetorical, and designed to elicit Anna's interest rather than her agreement; not unlike the 'Are you sitting comfortably?' of the radio programme I discussed earlier. It is likely that Rob has already decided that making the card is something that Anna needs to do to mark this particular cultural event. Two social dispositions would seem to be operating at this point: firstly, an engagement in symbolic activity as part of an act of giving and celebration; and secondly, there is the connection between a material and symbolic process and an identifiable social outcome; the beginning of a generic connection. In other words, there is a purpose that needs to be established for all this making and marking beyond the sheer pleasure of doing it.

Table 7.1. Scene 1 – Beginning

Local Setting: Rob and Anna are seated at the kitchen table. There is a large sheet of orange cartridge paper on the table and a pot of different coloured felt-tip pens.

Language	Vocalisation	Gaze	Action	Semiotic object
Episode 1 [11 secs]				
Rob: shall we do, shall we do a [k] its mummy's day today Mother's Day, shall we do do you want to do one for mummy		gaze on pens	Rob puts pens on table stands on chair	sheet of plain orange cartridge paper A2 size
Anna: yes		gaze on Rob		
Rob: shall I make it into a card shall I fold it for a card		gaze on pens	leans towards pen pot takes out a black felt tip	
Anna: yes		gaze on paper	Rob folds the paper	paper folded in half to become Mother's Day card
Rob: and then can you do a picture on the front	high fall		stands up holding the black felt tip Rob turns card so opening is on right	
Episode 2 [4 of 19 secs]				
Anna: I a drawing		gaze on page	kneels on the seat	
Rob: there you are				
Anna: there			places point of felt tip on bottom right-hand section of paper	a small black indented felt-tip mark about two-thirds of the way down the page on the right-hand side

Whilst Rob is talking to her, Anna continues to stand on the kitchen chair, and as he says 'mummy', she moves her gaze sharply towards him, the affective significance of the word drawing her attention. Here, her gaze has an interpersonal function (Kendon 1967; 1990). The suggestion that Rob makes provides a social and affective resource which elicits new images to draw on, amending her simulation of how this event is to proceed. Her predicted activity with the pens now has a further purpose: not just making marks with the pens, but making them and then giving them to someone who will demonstrate her appreciation of them. As Rob starts to articulate his third suggestion, she moves her gaze back to the pen pot, then reaches across the table and takes one out. This apparently preparatory routine marks the completion of a micro segment of activity: Anna has already envisaged what she will do, the tool she will use and a purpose for what she is doing; the design phase complete, she is now ready to start production.

Rob's question, 'shall I fold it into a card?', combined with the gestures of folding, has a performative quality to it: not only changing the paper physically from a single flat sheet to a folded sheet with two pages, but also transforming the social purpose of the paper from something relatively open, a resource that could be used for drawing, painting, cutting or myriad other uses, to something much more closed, the card to be given to a specific person as acknowledgement of a specific event. Both this and Anna's previous 'yes' act as discourse markers (Carter, 2001), enabling her to maintain an interactive role while keeping all her attention on the activity on the table. She stands on the chair, watching Rob transform the paper, her pen lifted above the page, action suspended while the paper is organised. All of Anna's attention is directed towards the page, the gesture of her hand and her gaze mediating her anticipated action around the card. Whilst the folding of the cartridge paper is going on, Rob suggests, 'and then can you do a picture on the front'. As with the question in his previous turn, Rob's choice of words here reflects a particular style of discourse in which the modal modifies, in the sense of softening, the impact of the embedded imperative. Anna, however, is still concentrating on the folding activity: holding her pen aloft, she responds with a vocalisation. This vocalisation is non-committal or vague, as if at this point she is way ahead of him in thinking about what she is going to do next. As soon as Rob has completed folding the paper, he places it in front of Anna on the table in the conventionally accepted position with the opening on the right-hand side.

Beginning—Scene 1, Episode 2 (see Table 7.1)

Her purpose, which was so meticulously constructed in that first episode of the event, is now fully incorporated in the movement of her body. First she leans across the table so that she is in closer physical contact with the page; then her hand reaches towards the paper and she kneels down on the seat, putting the point of the black felt tip on the bottom right-hand side of the page in a definite and purposeful action. As she does this, she ascribes a function to her intended action 'I a drawing / '. Her use of this term is a clear indication of her independent construction of the event, since this is not a term Rob has used at all on this occasion: synonymous terms and phrases, but never the word 'drawing'. The frame she has been constructing in the opening Episode of the event, taking into account all the available social and material resources, is that of *'I am planning how to use all these things to do a drawing for mummy'*.

As she moves into the second episode, it is the space, the blank sheet of orange paper, that becomes the principal focus of her interest. On the face of it this seems to be a spatial problem, but it is also a problem of beginning: where to put the first mark, and what its relationship to the surrounding space might be, and how the placing of this first mark might affect the placing of future marks. She places the point of the felt tip precisely and emphatically on the page, about two-thirds of the way down on the right-hand side, and then confirms this as signifying 'drawing' by her use of the deictic: 'I have done the drawing *there*'. 'Drawing' here referring not to the visual representation of a particular object, but to the action of making the mark; 'there' refers to the location of the resulting mark on the empty page.

In these opening episodes, the materials, pens and paper, are the material focus of Anna's predictive activity. Her structuring of each episode of the event is mediated through coordinated configurations of gaze and action, with each movement of her gaze being indicative of the stages of her construction (see also Figure 7.1).

Ending—Scene 2, Episode 4 (see Table 7.2)

I now want to look at how Anna interprets and constructs the finishing of the card. As the scene unfolds, Anna and Rob make the card, with Anna representing 'drawings' and 'cats', by their intentional location on different sections of the page. Ten episodes have taken place in reaching this point, seven in Scene 1, and three in Scene 2. Rob is persuaded by Anna to draw a cat too, and Episode 3 in Scene 2 shows the process by which she completes his cat by adding the facial features, eyes, nose and mouth, which Rob has 'forgotten'. This 'forgetting' has raised questions about completion: about how and when something you have been drawing or writing might be considered as being finished. This is a complex matter. Although the boundaries of the opening of an event are often fuzzy, nevertheless there are often material happenings that start the ball rolling, or act as the focus of anticipation, such as the placing of paper and pens on the table, or the switching on of a radio, as in the previous example. This is not always the case when it comes to deciding what is enough. Sometimes things external to the event provide an arbitrary cut-off point: time for some other important event or activity is reached, or sheer lack of further interest or stamina. However, where this is not the case, critical decisions are required which pertain to practical and qualitative judgements to be applied to particular cultural objects—in this case, judgements about whether the card was complete in the sense of having all the necessary attributes of such a card, or in the sense of satisfying certain aesthetic criteria.

Table 7.2. Scene 2—Ending
Local Setting: Anna is seated at the table looking at the card. She has just finished adding the features to Rob's picture of a cat.

Language	Vocalisation	Gaze	Action	Semiotic object
Episode 4 [7.5 secs]		Anna looks at Rob's cat and then down the page to her cat, across to the red zigzag on her right in the bottom centre, then to the left away from the page to the blue pen top lying on the table on the left of the page		On the bottom right of the page, zigzags representing drawings, and on the left, representing cats. In the centre of the page a drawing of a cat, on which Anna has added features
Anna: let's finish		gaze on pen and top	Anna picks up the pen top starts to put top back on pen continues pushing pen into top completes putting pen back in top	
finish.				
Rob: you finished				
Anna: yes				

So in what is to be the final episode of the scene, following her completion of the cat's features, Anna looks intently at the page. The function of her gaze in this process is analytic and interpretative (Lancaster, 2001), in that she is reviewing the visual outcome of the semiotic activity in which she and Rob have been engaging. This is quite distinct from the predictive and interpersonal functions of gaze identified previously. What she looks at, in the sense of what is salient on the page, and what she sees are informed by her prior interests and experiences: recalled images again. Le Corbusier (in Gardner, 1993) suggests that the view of an object acts as 'a shutter release' for the knowledge of it acquired through sensory, tactile, material, spatial and social experience of its properties. She scans the cat's face first, and then moves her gaze carefully down its body and down the page to her first 'cat' mark at the bottom left of the page. Her eyes then move across the page to the right, to the second of her cat marks, particularly to a section on the right-hand side where the physical production of the marks was more vigorous. At this point, however, her gaze turns sharply to the left, away from the page and towards the pen top lying on the table beside the paper.

The pen top signifies the potential completion of an activity, involving recollections and images of procedures and patterns of action around placing the top back on the pen and putting it away. As was the case in the first scene, recalled experience is mediated by gaze, but here with a reflective rather than a predictive function. Incorporated into the framework of production of a semiotic object of this kind is the making a critical judgement about its sufficiency, in this case its sufficiency to be considered finished or unfinished. Anna's turning away from the page at this point reflects the completion of her critical review of the text. It has to fulfil her criteria of representing cats both completely and pleasingly if it is to be judged as finished. Such a judgement is a reflective one, which involves Anna relating the visual constituents materially present on the page to salient textual experiences, as well as her wider social and aesthetic experience of what constitutes completeness.

Different 'completeness' criteria are involved here. Anna first studies the cat that Rob drew and whose face she worked on afterwards. The face now signifies a face complete with eyes, mouth and nose in the manner of other pictures of faces in other texts in her experience, though with the features represented according to Anna's own system of representation. The cat's body and tail, which Anna reviews next, signifies completion on an affective level in the sense that it represents the rest of the cat which Anna had been trying to encourage Rob to draw for her throughout Scenes 1 and 2. She then moves her gaze down to the cat which she drew in Scene 1 and then across to the cat drawn in Episode 2 of this scene. At the time of making these marks Anna had signalled completeness by her statement, her linguistic ascription, 'at's tat'. Now, reviewing these marks after a little time has elapsed, she is still satisfied, at both textual and affective levels, with the way they have been represented. Both these marks now signify completed cats. And finally, the very fact that she reviews the images that she has created with a view to deciding whether or not the card, or part of it, is finished, reflects a meta-semiotic awareness: an awareness that certain criteria need to be established and applied in these circumstances. These might include criteria that are numerical (an accepted number of features on a face, for example), ontological (the cats are cats because I have said they are cats), or affective (the promise of drawing a cat on this space has been fulfilled); the principles, once established, can now be applied in different situations and circumstances.

Following the critical review of the page, she returns her gaze to the pen top, and concentrates on the physical action of putting it back on the pen. She suggests to Rob that the activity is complete by her use of the imperative. This has a performative sense to it. As Rob's 'shall I make it into a card' is part of the opening episode, so Anna's 'let's finish' closes things down. She continues the process of pushing the pen top back onto the pen, lifting them up from the table and moving the focus of her gaze from the table itself to the technical matter at hand. This material process has now become an absorbing activity in its own right for Anna, distinct from its role in signifying the completion of the drawing. The manner in which Anna finishes the activity demonstrates the way in which 'completeness' is signified by a sequence of temporal acts closed down by various material routines: putting a pen top back on and putting things away, or stating that the activity is complete; all in all, restoring certain aspects of the environment to the state they were in before the activity started.

Consciousness of Time

The very 'micro-ness' of this kind of description raises questions about the extent to which the activity discussed can be said to involve conscious, knowing behaviour or non-conscious physical actions. Much of the physiological and sensorimotor activity that is involved as Anna speaks, listens, gazes and moves would probably be considered by most people to be non-conscious. However, by slowing the video film right down, it becomes possible to identify the order of operation of these mediating modes and see Anna's construction of the semiotic event as an intentional, progressive activity. This process is represented in Figure 7.1.

Each time Rob makes a suggestion, Anna would seem to amend her plans. At point 3 in Figure 7.1, following Rob's suggestion that something be made for her mother, she looks back at the pot of pens, her gaze predictive, as if reviewing her plans in the light of new information. At point 7, there is another review as she watches Rob fold the piece of paper to make it into a card. Long before any pen touches any part of the paper, she is systematically and progressively making use of all the semiotic resources provided, to plan what she is going to do. In this 'blown-up' version of events, it all seems to involve very conscious behaviour. At a normal speed, though, that can seem fanciful, since it all happens so fast it would seem hard to imagine that there would be enough time for conscious thought. A solution that would go some way to accommodating both views is that there is a persistent awareness of self in the act of doing, which takes into account the need for nonconscious behaviour, particularly where physical activity is concerned. Things

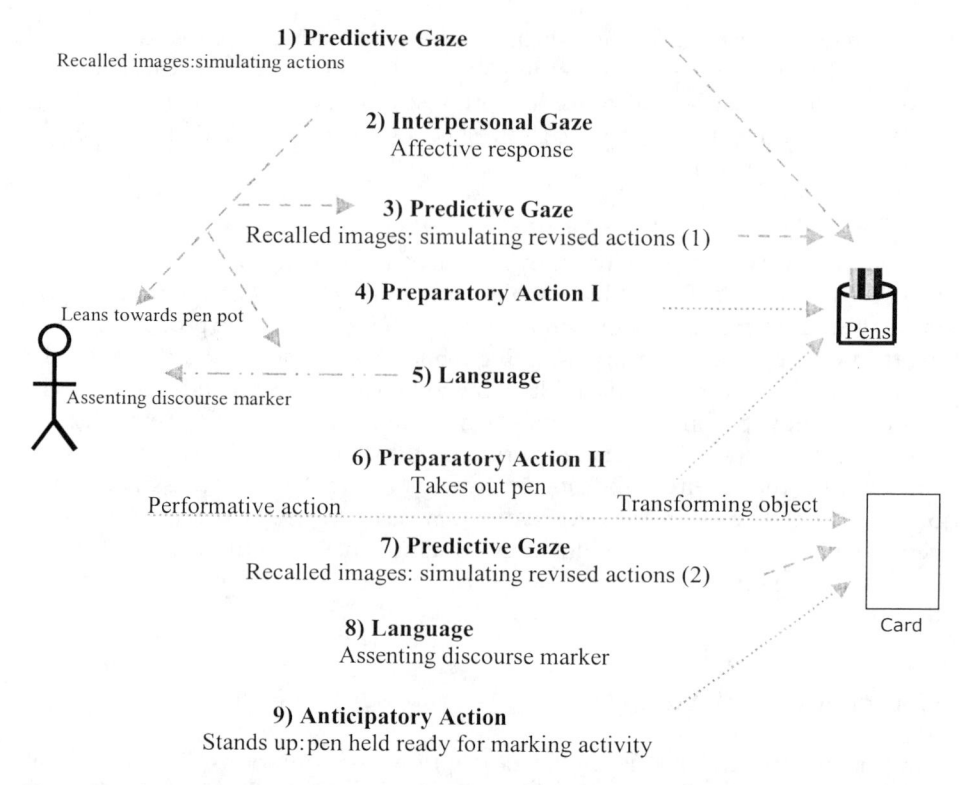

1) Predictive Gaze
Recalled images: simulating actions

2) Interpersonal Gaze
Affective response

3) Predictive Gaze
Recalled images: simulating revised actions (1)

4) Preparatory Action I
Leans towards pen pot

Pens

5) Language
Assenting discourse marker

6) Preparatory Action II
Takes out pen

Performative action   Transforming object

7) Predictive Gaze
Recalled images: simulating revised actions (2)

8) Language
Assenting discourse marker

Card

9) Anticipatory Action
Stands up: pen held ready for marking activity

Figure 7.1. A representation of Anna's construction of Episode 1, as a progressive sequence of multimodal activity

can be got on with, unless, of course, other factors arise which call for their being put on hold for some period of time; at this point, conscious control is reasserted. Point 9 in Figure 7.1 is a case in point: movement and activity is suddenly suspended while Rob prepares the 'card'; Anna holds her pen still in the air, her action changed from preparatory to anticipatory whilst waiting for Rob to fold the page. In her very conscious response to his suggestion, she interrupts a seemingly unconscious movement of hand and pen towards the paper, in the light of the change of circumstances produced by the transformation of page into card.

Conclusion

Both the examples discussed in this chapter demonstrate the range of modalities involved in the everyday activities of young children's lives. This applies not only to the material objects, paraphernalia and forms of representation, but also to the modes of bodily mediation involved. Anna, at 23 months, is already confident around abstract and symbolic forms of representation like drawing and writing, using an ensemble of bodily modes both to interpret and generate meanings. The presence, suggestions and support of a very interested adult provide additional resources for her to use, but does not intrude on her independence. All of the modes she uses are multiply constituted, having the capacity to fulfil a range of functions appropriate to the requirements of the task. Crucially, this enables her to work independently and to try things out and operate on her hunches in her own way. Gaze is particularly significant in mediating the reflective recall of images, enabling past experiences to inform present thinking and decisions about future actions.

Participating in the kinds of socially and educationally significant semiotic events that are discussed in this chapter involves perceiving them as not just being about what happens, in some clearly defined and material sense such as turning something on and off or starting and finishing the making of a mark. The question of when such events can be said to actually start and finish is a matter of social and cultural agreement, often involving considerable variation. The surrounding mass of things and actions and interactions also need to be organised and structured so that the whole thing fits together and makes sense. What this chapter has attempted to show is that children are interested in these rather ontological problems from a very early age, and are actively and ingeniously constructing their own solutions, using all available resources. It also demonstrates the value of this kind of multimodal micro-analysis in helping to reconstruct the thinking processes involved. The description and analysis of the means by which the child constructs the abstract parameters of the beginning and ending of an event, reveal this to be a physical, bodily process, with the different modes coordinated in different configurations in order to communicate and generate a wide range of meanings. The interpretative analysis derived from this goes some way to providing a window into some of both the child's conscious and non-conscious thinking. In other words, cognitive behaviour, consciousness and mind are closely allied to modalities of external bodily behaviours which can be observed and described by other people. As educators we need to take heed of this.

References

Berthoz, A. (2000) *The Brain's Sense of Movement,* trans. Weiss, G. London: Harvard University Press.

Bourdieu, P. (1986) *Distinction: A Social Critique of the Judgement of Taste.* Cambridge, Mass.: Harvard University Press.

———. (1991) *Language and Symbolic Power.* trans. Raymond, G. and Adamson, M. Cambridge, United Kingdom: Polity Press.

Carter, R. (2001) The Grammar of Talk; Spoken English, Grammar and the Classroom. Draft introduction to QCA publication. University of Nottingham, United Kingdom.

Damasio, A. (1994) *Descartes' Error: Emotion, Reason and the Human Brain.* London: Papermac.

———. (1999) *The Feeling of What Happens: Body, Emotion and the Making of Consciousness.* London: Vintage.

Gardner, H. (1993) *Frames of Mind: The Theory of Multiple Intelligences*. London: HarperCollins.

Geertz, C. (1983) *Local Knowledge*. London: HarperCollins.

Goffman, E. (1986) *Frame Analysis: An Essay on the Organisation of Experience*. Boston: Northeastern University Press.

Heath, S. (1983) *Ways with Words*. Cambridge, United Kingdom: Cambridge University Press.

Johnson, M. (1987) *The Body in the Mind: The Bodily Basis of Meaning, Imagination, and Reason*. Chicago and London: University of Chicago Press.

Kendon, A. (1967) Some Functions of Gaze-direction in Social Interaction. *Acta Psychologica*, 26, 22–63.

——.(1990) *Conducting Interaction: Patterns of Behavior in Focused Encounters.*Cambridge, United Kingdom: Cambridge University Press.

Kress, G.R. and van Leeuwen, T. (2001) *Multimodal Discourse: The Modes and Media of Contemporary Communication*. London: Arnold.

Lakoff, G. and Johnson, M. (1999) *Philosophy in the Flesh: The Embodied Mind and its Challenge to Western Thought*. New York: Basic Books.

Lancaster, L. (2001) Staring at the Page: The Function of Gaze in a Young Child's Interpretation of Symbolic Forms. *Journal of Childhood Literacy*, Vol. 1, No 2.

Nelson, K. (1985) *Making Sense: The Acquisition of Shared Meaning*. Orlando, Florida: Academic Press, Inc.

——(1996) *Language in Cognitive Development: The Emergence of the Mediated Mind*. Cambridge, United Kingdom: Cambridge University Press.

Rogoff, B. (1990) *Apprenticeship in Thinking: Cognitive Development in Social Context*. New York: Oxford University Press.

Scribner, S. and Cole, M. (1981) *The Psychology of Literacy*. Cambridge, Mass.: Harvard University Press.

Street, B.V. (1995) *Social Literacies: Critical Approaches to Literacy in Development, Ethnography and Education*. London: Longman.

Thompson, J. (1990) *Ideology and Modern Culture*. Cambridge, University Press: Polity Press.

Weinberg, M.K. and Tronick E.Z. (1994) Beyond the Face: An Empirical Study of Infant Affective Configurations of Facial, Vocal, Gestural, and Regulatory Behaviors. *Child Development*, 65, pp. 1503–1515.

Pippa Stein 8

THE OLIFANTSVLEI FRESH STORIES PROJECT: MULTIMODALITY, CREATIVITY AND FIXING IN THE SEMIOTIC CHAIN

The focus of this chapter is on an early literacy project in narrative, The Olifantsvlei Fresh Stories Project, which was carried out during 2001 with Grade 1 and 2 teachers and children at Olifantsvlei Primary School, which serves children from unemployed and migrant families living in informal settlements on the borders of the city of Johannesburg. The aim of the six-month project was to develop a body of imaginative fresh stories based on and arising from the children's lives and local experiences. Within a broader political frame, this interest in the local is central to the post-apartheid historical moment in South Africa in which issues of identity, language, culture, redress and equity are central to the national debate and nation-building project that began in 1994 with the first democratic election and the transformation of the South African state.

Multimodal pedagogies work consciously and systematically across semiotic modes in order to unleash creativity, reshape knowledge and develop different forms of learning beyond the linguistic (Kress and van Leeuwen, 2001; Kress, Jewitt, Ogborn and Tsatsarelis, 2000; Stein and Newfield 2001; 2002). The use of multimodal pedagogies in working through this project led to the production of multiple semiotic objects in different sequenced stages and in different modes: 2D drawings, writing, 3D figures, spoken dialogues and multimodal play performances. The production of these textual objects was in response to a central concept that ran through the project—namely, the creation of a body of characters who would form the basis of storytelling, play making and writing. These multimodal textual objects have been described by Kress as points of 'fixing' in the chain of semiosis. In this chapter, I focus on the 3D doll/child figures produced by the children because, *in relation to the semiotic chain,* they illuminate a number of important issues concerning multimodality, materiality and creativity within different social contexts of meaning-making. Through the particular ways in which the making of the doll/child figures happened, in other words, *the process of making,* I raise issues around agency, cultural memory and home and school learning within the South African context.

The Olifantsvlei 'Fresh Stories' Project

The Olifantsvlei Fresh Stories Project was a collaborative project between two Grade 1 and 2 teachers and two researchers. It facilitated a process of narrative storytelling and writing in which the Grade 1 and 2 children would create 'fresh stories', as distinct from traditional African folkloric tales that they had heard, or stories that they had read or heard from their class readers. Although the medium of instruction in this school from Grade 1 is English, the project emphasised that the children, who are all multilingual speakers of African languages, could work in and through any languages they wished, including Zulu, Sotho, Tswana and English. As the teachers were accustomed to providing scaffolding and direction for all learning activities, the intention was to create a more relaxed and playful environment for making, which would allow the children to respond to the creative tasks with little or no intervention from teachers. The purpose of this was to construct what we call within the constraints of school *'an unpoliced zone'* in order to investigate the choices the children would made in terms of the 'stuff' which was at hand—their resources for representation—and their interests within the specific social context of making.

In order to provide an entry point or stimulus for inventing stories, the children were asked to think of someone in their homes, neighbourhoods or on their streets who interested them and who could become a 'character' in a story that they would create later on as a whole class. The idea was that the class would invent, through various multimodal transformatory processes, a cast of well-developed characters who would form the basis of play-making, storytelling and story writing.

After the children had 'fixed' on a particular person, they were asked to act out how this person moved, walked, talked, laughed, sat down and ate supper. Through dramatic action, the 'person' was evolving into a 'character'. The children were then asked to draw 2D figures of the character and write something about this character in any language they wished. In the next stage of the process, the children were to make 3D figures of their characters in class. Their teachers made a papier-mâché mixture; but according to the children, 'the mixture flopped and our characters turned into puddles'. At this point, the children turned to their teachers and said, 'Don't worry, we'll make our own figures', and over the next few days, many of them brought into class a collection of 3D doll/child like figures and cardboard cut-out figures that they had made at home. These doll/child figures were then used as puppet characters in a number of dialogues and plays which they subsequently improvised in class and performed. At the end of the process, the children were asked to write any story about their doll figures in any language they wished.

The Dolls/Child Figures as Socio-cultural Manifestation

In this section I compare the features of the contemporary doll/child figures that the children produced to traditional fertility doll/child figures of the Southern African region in order to gain a deeper understanding of the children's uses of materiality, creativity and mutation of aesthetic form within culturally and historically situated practices of representation. I claim that the children's doll figures form part of the ongoing semiotic chain of social, cultural and aesthetic practices around fertility doll/child figures which have existed in Southern Africa for hundreds of years and which continue to exist in some communities today. In terms of their material, aesthetic and symbolic characteristics they show remarkable similarities as well as significant differences to the grammar of such fertility child figures in terms of their internal and external characteristics, their use of materials, external adornments and their overall design. The symbolic resonance of materials in traditional fertility doll/child figures (Nel and Leibhammer, 1998) is echoed in the children's choices and use of the representational resources available to them in their home and community contexts, as well as in their processes of making. This social semiotic analysis thus provides a way of reading the children's dolls/child figures against shifting backdrops of cultural memory and communicative practices that have been reflected in material solutions arising out of specific contexts of use, interests and historical moments. These layers of association are revealed through the form the figures take, the materials from which they are made and the words with which they are associated in the semiotic chain.

Definition of Fertility Doll/Child Figures

The term 'fertility dolls' or 'child figures' refers to small objects with anthropomorphic forms, traditionally made by women for girls' and women's use in a range of contexts and domains relating to women's fertility, child rearing and marriage rituals. Their symbolism in form and materials is talisman-like, suggestive and affective (Nel and Leibhammer, 1998). As this genre of culture-making emerges from female domains and relates to intimate areas of female identities and fertility, the dolls' use in puberty and adolescent initiation practices have been kept secret from public scrutiny. As pointed out by Dell (1998), these objects are polyvalent, fulfilling multiple symbolic functions: as objects of play by girl children in the same way as children play with dolls the world over, as fertility charms, and as figures that have magical powers to act as 'evocations of the child' in fertility, puberty and marriage rituals in which the dolls function as intermediate between living and dead—between women and their powers to reproduce. Such dolls have been granted magical and metaphoric powers, acting as ciphers through which a wished-for child or ancestral soul can pass through and enter into her owner's womb.

Shapes

Traditionally Southern African doll/child figures across regions and communities share a cylindrical or conical shape and are abstract, rather than figurative, in form (see Figure 8.1). These primary forms, which allude to women as receptacles or containers, result from the female body and dress forms that characterise the way that women clothe themselves traditionally, for example, the shape made by Ndebele women who wrap their beaded blankets or wear conical rings around their necks in Ndebele style dress. Their internal and external characteristics are achieved through multiple forms of layering: the conical and cylindrical shapes of the dolls are produced through the use of an inner core around which is folded and draped in stylised systems of multiple layerings, various types of cloth material and adornments. The inner cores are usually constructed from grass, reeds, bottles, gourds,

Figure 8.1

Figure 8.2

calabashes, wild oranges, tins and wood. The containers such as the wild oranges and gourds are filled with talisman-like powders and seeds, then wrapped with different cloths, and finally adorned with glass beads, seeds, grasses, plant fibres, safety pins, metal and leather.

It is important to point out that the doll/child figures are represented as female adults, capable of procreation. They do not take the form of babies or children, although they evoke the idea of the potential child in how they are used as playthings and fertility charms.

Shapes of the Olifantsvlei Dolls

The majority of doll/child figures made by the Olifantsvlei children were conical in shape and abstract in form. This effect was achieved through the use of plastic and glass bottles associated with the food and drink in domestic settings, namely cold drinks (Sprite, Virgin and Coke) and cooking oil bottles. In one doll (Figure 8.1) which was made entirely out of paper and plastic, the conical shape was achieved through cutting out a cardboard shape which when turned, formed a conical shape in an abstract and highly suggestive way. Another doll (Figure 8.2) had a more figurative body shape than the rest: it was constructed out of a pair of sticks for the legs around which was moulded an old stocking in an elaborate set of ties, folds and knots. This doll had a more defined body shape, which emphasised large buttocks and large breasts moulded in counterpoint to one another.

Weight and Height

The bottle interiors of the Olifantsvlei dolls had different degrees of weightiness. Some bottles were empty; some were filled with materials like foam chips, sand and stones in varying proportions. The weight of the dolls enabled them to remain standing solidly upright facing the viewer, a singular characteristic of all the dolls made. In the same way that the containers of the traditional dolls (wild oranges, tins, gourds) were often filled with talisman-like powders and seeds, the detailed attention by the children to the range of materials gathered to fill the interiors points to evidence of their 'interests', both functional and symbolic, in relation to this aspect of doll-making. In terms of the height of the dolls, they were all more or less the same height, with a few variations. The height of 25cms was determined by the choice of the size of 'cooldrink bottle': one doll made from a cooking bottle was slightly taller than the rest. However, like their ancestors', all the children's dolls could be described as small objects with few variations in size.

Exterior Attachments: Heads, Arms and Breasts

In traditional doll figures, heads were made in a variety of ways, including the use of stoppers adorned with beads or clay. In the Olifantsvlei figures, heads were constructed out of scrunched-up newspaper covered in stretch knit cloth or fabric rolled into a ball and attached by wire, string, glue or fabric to the neck of the bottles. One doll had a piece of cloth cut into shreds resembling hair. In traditional figures, arms were usually made out of clay, strings of beads or reeds, if they were made at all. In the children's dolls, they used nails, dowel sticks and twigs inserted into the bottles to suggest arms. In traditional doll figures, breasts are rarely defined except in the clay figures and more abstractly represented through beads, for example. However, in the children's doll figures, marked attention is paid to more figurative representations of breasts. One doll, wrapped in several cloths suggesting layers of blankets, looks like a baby, however, on lifting up the blankets, a pair of fully developed breasts are revealed, centrally defined and prominent, which have been 'hidden' beneath the clothing. The boundaries between 'baby' 'girl' and 'woman' remain fluid. Another doll made from an artfully wrapped women's stocking has clearly defined breasts made from two stones covered with stocking. The absence and presence of breasts, and the different ways in which they are defined, shaped and revealed, are evidence of social and cultural attitudes towards breasts as well as marking the dolls as adolescent and adult female figures.

Use of Fabric

In traditional doll figures, the inner conical or cylindrical cores are usually covered in various types of cloth in earth colours. In styles of multilayering, different

Figure 8.3

adornments are then attached to the cloth. According to Nel and Leibhammer (1998), the use of cloth firmly locates the tradition and practices around doll-making in the domain of women. The wrapping of the inner core with folds of cloth is highly symbolic of the union of male and female principles: the female cloth envelops the male phallic core in a symbolic representation of the procreative act.

The use of a rich variety of cloth in different textures, weaves, weights and colours, and folded in different ways, is a salient feature of the Olifantsvlei dolls. The range of cloth, and the choices made regarding texture, design, colour and style of folds reveals a high level of care and interest in fashion styles and the aesthetics of cloth which take traditional forms of doll-making into new arenas and redefine the female form. The use of women's stockings to symbolise a 'second skin' (Figure 8.2), the use of fake fur in zebra stripes to cover a stylised body shape of prominent buttocks and breasts, the use of plastic bubble wrap brilliantly folded to suggest a billowing dress (Figure 8.3), the use of different cloths for 'doeks' and head coverings, lace, socks, old duvet covers and dishcloths in hues of blue, red, black, green, brown and off-white all suggest that the children had many fabric resources on hand in their environment from which to select the particular cloth they wanted. The use of fresh, clean cloth on the dolls is rare: they are mostly wrapped in 'waste' pieces of cloth that have been refashioned into the desired shape and style.

Whilst hand- or machine-sewn seams on the dolls are rare, the varieties of ways in that the cloth has been wrapped can be linked to the multiple twists and folds that African women invent around the use of cloth as forms of body clothing and headdress. In other words, the use of cloth on the dolls in its various forms can be located within a historical and cultural milieu of cloth wraps and folds which are used as identity and status markers within local communities.

Use of Adornments and Face Markings

Whilst a key feature of traditional Southern African dolls is the use of varied forms of adornment such as glass beads, ostrich shells, safety pins, coins, badges, buttons, chains and elaborate beadwork designs, reflecting specific regional influences, the children's doll figures in this study had relatively few adornments. One doll (Figure 8.2) was decorated with two necklaces: a plastic colourful necklace for a little girl with punched-out starfish and conical shell shapes, and a second black bead necklace distinctly African in style. This doll had 'ears' symbolised by small brass safety pins on each side of the head. The children used a variety of marks in pen or koki to signal facial features, including eyes, noses and mouths. Some faces had no markings at all.

The Process of Making the Doll/Child Figures

Interviews were conducted with eight children who made dolls in order to investigate in more depth the processes of making, including who made the dolls, how they were made, where the children obtained the materials for making them, who the dolls represented, and how the children had used them. It emerged from their responses that in every case, the child had been helped by an adult woman—a mother, grandmother, aunt or neighbour—in the making of the doll. This help took different forms: in some cases, the child and the grandmother or mother physically constructed the doll together. So, for example, in one case the mother sewed the cloth and gave suggestions for the structure of the doll, whilst the child chose the cloth and adornments. In the case of the bubblewrap doll (Figure 8.3), which was made by a boy, an aunt suggested to him that he make the doll out of plastic bags and showed him how to tie a plastic bag to give the impression of a doek around the head. In the case of Figure 8.2 made by a boy and his mother, the mother constructed the inner body shape emphasising breast and buttocks in a complex use of stocking ties and twigs, and then allowed her son to 'dress' the doll in a fake zebra fur skirt and top. In some cases, the children were emphatic about the fact that they made them 'themselves'. When I asked the girl who made the stocking doll, she said 'myself' and when asked how she learnt how to make such a doll, she replied, 'My granny from Lesotho taught me', adding that she had made three other dolls like this before. Another girl said that, 'my mother from the Transkei' helped her to make her doll. This information is invaluable in coming to understand the social context of making such dolls within local households, and clearly points to the continuing role of adult women in the processes of making. Significantly, no child mentioned that an adult man helped to make the doll. However, what is interesting are the clear shifts in gendered patterns of making at the level of the children: several dolls were made by boy children with mothers or aunts acting as mentors in passing on knowledge, skills and practices regarding a formerly strictly female cultural domain.

Another important point arising from the children's reports on the process of making is the collaborative nature of the making: how children knew how and where to recruit cultural and community knowledge in the family or neighbourhood in order to realise their needs. This process of recruitment and the multimodal products themselves point to a sense of 'deep knowledge' rooted in families and communities, in urban and rural mixes, which finds its expression in the continuities and transformations of ideas around what constitutes doll-making within the Gauteng region.

Taking the Ordinary and Making the Extraordinary

In interviewing the children on their use of materials, it became evident that they had consciously looked for materials to suit their needs and had made careful decisions, sometimes with an adult, about how to use these materials. The child who had shaped a doll figure from folds fashioned from one large piece of discarded dishcloth (Figure 8.2) told me she had gone into the 'veld' to look for materials and had found this cloth. Another child told me he had found the bottle for his conical-shaped inner core 'in a rubbish bin outside the disco'. No child had the means to purchase any materials for making the dolls: they had found all the resources in their environments and had reshaped them according to their affective, symbolic and aesthetic interests. What these figures reveal is the dynamic relationship between creativity, innovation and resources: the term 'resources' takes on different values and meanings in different contexts of use. A discarded plastic bag on a rubbish dump becomes a doek: that which cannot be eaten is fashioned into a doll. A safety pin becomes an ear, a button an eye, a nail an arm and a breast a stone. The point is that these children had no other choice but to forage in the veld and through the rubbish dumps around them to find what they needed. Such limits can be very generative: these children were able to see potential in the ordinary and transform it into the extraordinary.

These 3D figures illustrate the hybridity and fluidity of contemporary urban cultural life and the degree to which cultural and generic transformation have taken place at multiple levels. At the level of 'making', it is traditionally women who make such dolls; but in this project, boys participated in the making of their own dolls. The traditional boundaries around what constitutes 'child fertility dolls' within ethnic and gender classifications have collapsed, and in this process, the traditional in all its multiplicity of forms and materiality is redesigned into the contemporary using available contextual materials. These doll/child figures illustrate how individuals have many layers of representational resources available to them, not only from one culture, but from many cultures. As Hamilton (1998) has noted in her work on African women's material culture as markers of identity, the analysis of the production of material culture has the potential to change the way in which discussions about identity are framed: material culture 'speaks to identity as at once conservatively continuous with the past and as creatively innovative, as bounded and as porous, as transportable and as rooted.' This children's process of remaking is not reproductive but innovative and transformative, both of the objects that are extending the 'grammar' of doll-making culture, and in relation to the children's identities.

Shifting Contexts of Use in the Semiotic Chain

In this section I return to the Olifantsvlei 'Fresh Stories' Project to focus on how the dolls were used by some children as points of 'fixing' in the semiotic chain—a chain that began with drawing and writing about a 'character' (Stage 1), the making of a character in 3D (the doll figures) (Stage 2), the invention of dialogues and plays using the 3D character (Stage 3), and a final writing task—a story on the character (Stage 4). I have chosen examples to give readers a sense of the range of texts produced.

Cawekazi's Semiotic Chain

Cawekazi, a Grade 2 girl, drew a picture of her 'mother' in Stage 1, the first drawing project, and anchored the image with the written text, 'The name of my mother is Nthabiseng is my mother Nthabiseng His cook after school His cook a porridge'. In Stage 2, she went home and made her own 3D doll figure out of wrapped stockings. She did not use her doll figure in a play. In Stage 4, she did a new drawing and wrote a story about her 'baby' whom she named 'Dineo'. The period of time between the first piece of writing and the second was two months (13 March–28 May).

In Cawekazi's 2D drawings, 3D doll figure and written texts, her points of fixing reveal interesting 'slippage' in her semiotic chain. Her semiotic chain starts, in the sense that she produces the 'first sign' with a 2D drawing of 'her mother', accompanied by a written text in which she writes about 'her mother' who 'cooks porridge' and who is named Nthabsieng. She then makes a 3D doll figure at home on her own, who is at once a representation of fertility: herself, her mother as a fertile mother, herself as a fertile mother, and her wished-for baby. This fertile mother (herself) symbolically and magically gives birth to a child who becomes Cawekazi's child in her written story, which follows (Stage 4), in which Cawekazi tells the tale of 'her baby Dineo'. In the realm of the symbolic and fantasy, Cawekazi takes on the role of the mother, gives birth to her own child and through this act of making (both the doll as material and the doll as child), Cawekazi perpetuates the generation. The child/doll figure is made and used by Cawekazi to serve her own desires and interests in the semiotic chain: in the transformation from her focus on her mother to the focus on the baby Dineo, Cawekazi uses her doll to fulfill its symbolic function, which is to create another body in which the spirit of the child would evolve.

Sonti's Semiotic Chain

Sonti's doll/child figure, whom she names Ntswaki, is a syncretic mix of the traditional African doll figure and the contemporary. With safety pins for ears, a traditional African black bead necklace and a Taiwanese pink, green and purple plastic seashell necklace wound around her neck, Ntswaki straddles the African and the Western, the local and the global, the past and the present. She is at once child, plaything, woman and mother. Sonti uses this doll/child figure in an improvised dialogue in Sotho:

> Sonti: Lebitso la hae ke Ntswaki. Ntswaki o ne a rata ho bapala le bana. Jwale a itebala a fihla bosiu. Ntate a ba a mo fihlele pele. Mme ke hona a kenang ka tlung. *[Her name is Ntswaki. Ntswaki likes to play with the children. She used to be relaxed while she played and used to come back home late. Her husband would get home first. It's then that the mother, Ntswaki, came into the house.]*
> Father/Husband: (in a deep voice) Mme o tswa kae ka nako e? *[Mother/wife, where do you come from at this time?]*
> Ntswaki: (trembling) A . . . a . . . .a. ./nna ke ne ke ilo bapala le bana. *[A . . . ah . . . ah. . I went to play with the children.]*
> Father/Husband: Why o rata ho bapala le bana? *[Why do you like to play with children?]*
> Ntswaki: Nna ke rata bana. *[I like children.]*

(A ba a setse a mo mathisa.) *[He chases her out of the house.]*
Father/Husband: Mme, why o itebala hore o tlo pheha? *[Mother/wife, why do you forget that you have to cook?]*
Ntswaki: Ha ke a itebala. Ke ne ke tlile. Ke ne ke nahana hore wena ha wa mphihlela pele. A ba a re. *[I am not relaxed. I came here. I thought that you would not be home before me (she said).]*
Father/Husband: O-*[Oh.]*
Ntswaki: A ba a re nna ha ke sa tla hlola ke bapala le bana. *[I'm not going to play with the children again.]*

Sonti's dialogue plays with the theme of the marriage, children and patriarchy. The doll/child figure Ntswaki is out playing with 'the children' and neglects to come home in time to cook supper for her husband. He instructs her to 'stop playing' and to 'start cooking', in other words, to stop being a 'child' and become a 'woman/wife'. Ntswaki challenges him initially but this turns into submission. Ntswaki is simultaneously a child-bride, a plaything, a mother and a wife. In this extract Sonti takes further the iconic power of the male and female principles symbolised in the doll figures in a self-reflexive and playful enactment of the notions of play: the consequences of being a child and a bride are that the time for 'play' is brief as you enter into patriarchy, marriage and motherhood.

It seems clear, from Cawekazi's and Sonti's use of the doll/child figures for writing and for dialogue, that these 3D figures provide an important identity function in the semiotic chain. Through their physicality—their shape, weight, density and use of materials—they become embodiments of 'ideas' and 'images' of characters in the children's imaginations which they become attached to and identify with. They can be felt, touched, held, gazed at, moved from place to place and destroyed in ways that 2D drawings cannot be. It is for these reasons that I think the 3D figures in the Olifantsvlei story project were absolutely central in shaping the children's narratives and providing them with something literally to hold on to in the making of meaning.

Creativity as Variations on a Theme

I have argued elsewhere (Stein and Newfield 2001; 2002) that multimodal pedagogies unleash creativity in unexpected, unpredictable ways. They *produce* creativity. What is the nature of this creativity and how does it get produced? Hofstadter's theory of creativity provides some insights into the process: 'Making variations on a theme is really the crux of creativity'. (1985, p. 233). He explains how a theme starts with a conceptual skeleton or 'wordless concept' which he compares to a black box with rows of plastic knobs on it which can be set at different levels, allowing for setting variations. By varying the setting and the different knobs, by introducing new knobs and new relationships to old knobs, an extraordinary array of different possibilities and variations are produced. For example, new knobs might be revealed as a consequence of the setting of old knobs. In addition, new knobs can be 'awakened' out of nowhere: they don't all have to be present at the outset in the concept. When the concept enters a new domain, it starts migrating and developing in ways that are unexpected and unanticipated. Another crucial idea in this theory is the notion of 'slippage', in which concepts have a way of 'slipping' into one another, with unpredictable results. Concepts, in their very structure, contain 'slippability'. The most productive form of slippage is 'nondeliberate yet nonaccidental' which permeates our mental processes, and is 'the very crux of fluid thought.' (1985, p. 237). Creativity is also produced when the context changes: one comes to view the phenomenon in new ways, which in itself generates new images. This sets up a 'closed loop':

- fresh situations get unconsciously framed in terms of familiar concepts
- those familiar concepts come equipped with standard knobs to twiddle
- twiddling those knobs carries you into fresh new conceptual territory (1985, p. 254)

Hofstadter's theory throws some light on the nature of the creativity that is produced in multimodal pedagogies. It seems that working with different modes of representation in semiotic chains is a form of 'knob twiddling': each mode has the potential to produce multiple variations on a concept. By varying different modes, introducing and adding new modes to existing modes in infinite chains, a huge number of variations on a concept are made possible. Recontextualising the concept in new domains allows it to migrate from familiar domains and attach itself to new conceptual territory, which in turn produces new variations on the concept.

The Olifantsvlei 'Fresh Stories' Project demonstrates this process at work: once the children had decided that the papier-mâché was not working for them, they consciously chose a new context (their homes) in which to make their doll figures. In the making of doll figures in the home contexts, 'doll-making' was framed by the participants (the children and their mothers, grandmothers and women informants) in terms of familiar concepts (traditional doll-making cultural practices). These practices form part of residual cultural memory and have conventions and styles that have been socially produced in African communities over many years. However, in the new context of production (making 3D figures in your home setting for a school project on stories), what gets made is dependent on which materials for representation are available and how these materials will serve each dollmaker's interests. Working with environmentally available materials such as old plastic bags, bubble wrap, safety pins and old stockings takes the concept of 'doll-making' into new conceptual territory, providing the makers with endless possibilities for variation on a 'traditional' doll theme. This is an instance of how 'fixing' works in the semiotic chain of continuities and innovations in doll-making culture.

The 'fixing' in terms of the semiotic chain of narrative is produced in a similar way. The theme or concept of 'Make a character from your world' starts off as a 2D drawing, is transformed into written language, then transformed into a 3D doll figure that has weight and substance. In the act of making, the 3D figure slips in and out of an intertextual response to the familiar 2D drawing and writing (looking backwards in the chain) into new conceptual territory (pointing forwards in the chain). Such a process reflects 'slippability' in the ways in which certain ideas about the character get dropped, migrate, new ideas are picked up on and developed in endless cycles of variations on the theme. Some of these variations involve conscious choices on the part of the sign maker (in terms of his or her interests) but choices can be made *unconsciously* in the act of making. Cawekazi's variations migrated from writing and drawing her mother, to making a doll figure that took on a symbolic life as simultaneously herself, her mother, herself as mother, and her baby. This polyvalent object gives 'birth' to baby Dineo, who becomes the main subject of her final story, in which Cawekazi evolves into the mother of baby Dineo. The point to be made is that although the object appears to be 'fixed' in the sense that it materialises into what appears to be a static text, the meanings attached to the text are unstable and fluid within the semiotic chain.

Conclusion

The main focus of this chapter has been on the context, process and production of the 3D doll figures by Grade 1 and 2 children and their relationship to other points of fixing in the semiotic chain set up by the 'Fresh Stories' project. Through an exploration of the children's transformation and recontextualisation of culturally and historically situated practices surrounding the representation of such doll/child figures and their symbolic meanings, we are able to gain a deeper understanding into the relations between creativity, multimodal pedagogies, resources for representation and learning. It seems that pedagogies that consciously work to structure and stimulate variations on concepts or themes, produce creativity. Conceptual skeletons are usually nameless and wordless. Multimodal pedagogies represent a paradigm shift from language to mode. They move in and out and across modes, in and out and beyond language. Through this capacity for slippage, they enable learners to play with nameless and wordless concepts and 'fix' them in multiple variations of shapes, colours, patterns, weights, densities, cloths, words, images. This 'slippage' is induced through play, through creating a healthy tension between 'unpoliced' and 'policed' zones in classrooms spaces.

Learners' choices surrounding resources for representation are determined to some extent by availability within the wider semiotic environment in which they move. However, the above examples from Olifantsvlei demonstrate that what a child finally produces is influenced by when and how the child takes agency in relation to his or her interests and needs around representation, and the degree of familiarity the child enjoys with the representational resources available. Some children exhibit more resource flexibility than others: Cawekazi seems to have more flexibility and familiarity with the language, English, than Lisebo. Lisebo, however, shows flexibility with minimal resources: bubblewrap, plastic bags and a Coke bottle. In terms of questions of 'value' it is possible to make an effective, beautiful object out of minimal resources, if the maker has confidence, resource flexibility and a 'deep knowledge' in that practice. However, Lisebo's access to linguistic resources in English is limited, and this is evident in his linguistic text.

In relation to the taking of agency and its consequences, the Olifantsvlei 'Fresh Stories' project shows the potential for more 'slippage' between home, communities and schools in our context. The children's statement, 'Don't worry, we'll make our own', in response to the failure of the papier-mâché mixture, can be read as a profound challenge to the authority of school ways of doing things which are alien and disconnected from children's worlds and experiences of making. When given the chance to create their own objects at home, they drew on people close to them who had knowledge of such practices and who assisted them in the making. It seems clear that through this assertion of identity, cultural practices and community, these children are showing their teachers that their home environments need to be more valued for their potential to speak back to the school, and that through such synergies, important forms of learning and teaching can take place.

Acknowledgments

I would like to thank the teachers, students and principal at Olifantsvlei Primary School; Denise Newfield and the Wits Multiliteracies Project; Joni Brenner; David Andrews; Gunther Kress; Jim Cummins; Karel Nel and Malcolm Purkey for their helpful ideas on the 'Fresh Stories' project.

References

Dell, E. (1998) 'Introduction' in Nel, K. Leibhammer, N., Dell, E. et al., *Evocations of the Child: Fertility Figures of the Southern African Region*. Cape Town: Human and Rousseau (Pty) Ltd and Johannesburg: The Johannesburg Art Gallery.

Hamilton, C. (1998) 'Women and Material Markers of Identity.' In Nel, K., Leibhammer, N. and Dell, E. et al., *Evocations of the Child: Fertility Figures of the Southern African Region*. Cape Town: Human and Rousseau (Pty) Ltd and Johannesburg: The Johannesburg Art Gallery.

Hofstadter, D. (1985) Metamagical Themas: Questing for the Essence of Mind and Pattern. London: New York: Penguin Books.

Kress, G.R. (1997) *Before Writing: Rethinking the Paths to Literacy*. London: Routledge.

Kress, G.R., Jewitt, C., Ogborn, J. and Tsatsarelis, C. (2000) *Multimodal Teaching and Learning*. London: Continuum.

Kress, G.R. and van Leeuwen, T. (2001) *Multimodal Discourse*. London: Arnold.

Nel, K., Leibhammer, N. and Dell, E. et al. (1998) *Evocations of the Child: Fertility Figures of the Southern African Region*. Cape Town: Human and Rousseau (Pty) Ltd and Johannesburg: The Johannesburg Art Gallery.

Nel, K. and Leibhammer, N. (1998) 'Evocations of the Child' in Nel, K. Leibhammer, N., Dell, E. et al., *Evocations of the Child: Fertility Figures of the Southern African Region.* Cape Town: Human and Rousseau (Pty) Ltd and Johannesburg: The Johannesburg Art Gallery.

Stein, P. and Newfield, D. (2001) 'Agency, Creativity, Access and Activism in Post-Apartheid South Africa'. Plenary presented at the Eighth International Literacy and Education Research Network Conference on Learning (LERN), Spetses, Greece, July, 2001, www.theLearner.com

Stein, P. and Newfield, D. (2002) 'Opening up the Third Ground: Multimodal Pedagogies, Representation and Identity in Post-Apartheid South Africa.', In Cummins, J. and Davison, C. (Eds). *Kluwer Handbook of English Language Teaching*. Amsterdam: Kluwer Academic Publishers.

Kate Pahl 9

CHILDREN'S TEXT-MAKING AT HOME: TRANSFORMING MEANING ACROSS MODES

A child is playing on the carpet of his bedroom floor. He places small figures in relation to each other, including a 'Woody' character from the film *Toy Story*, some models of Pokémon and assorted trucks and miniature animals. He lies low on the ground and takes a photograph. Then another, accompanied by a running commentary. When the film is developed, he cuts out the photographs and remounts them with a new commentary to create a newsletter about his favourite Pokémon creatures. The child collects the Pokémon cards. He cuts out images from a Pokémon magazine and sticks them onto a new card, to create a collage with different small creatures on it in his role as Pokémon trainer. In order to develop his identity as maker of Pokémon creatures he traces the outlines of figures on cards and places them together to make a representation of his own Pokémon factory. The child also makes miniature Pokémon creatures out of modeling material with which he plays on his bedroom floor and leaves about the house. The child's home is full of the detritus of his making. His mother tries to clear this up, and finally decides to create a display of the small creatures he makes. The house is re-arranged as a result of the display cabinet, which includes the small Pokémon creatures. They have been placed inside a glass cabinet, as a display.

These descriptions can be mapped onto an account of multimodality. The child decided to move across modes, from one mode, the two-dimensional images of the Pokémon creatures in a magazine, to another, the cut-out images as part of a collage, and then to a new mode, three-dimensional models of the creatures made of modeling material. In all these examples, the child has crossed from one mode to another, and in each mode different affordances are present and can be manipulated and used. By attending to the interplay between modes the importance of the transitions across modes can be appreciated and recognized. Moving across modes is revealed to be a crucial way in which children express and uphold meaning. When the affordances of one mode begin to lose their communicative possibility, another mode can be taken up.

This descriptive account gives rise to three key questions in relation to multimodal meaning-making:

- How did this child transform meaning as he took one particular theme or idea and followed it across modalities?
- How did the choice of mode affect meaning?
- How did mode affect identity construction?

I used the case study of Sam, the boy playing on the carpet, as a 'telling case' from which to make interpretative comments (Mitchell, 1984). The data presented comes from a three-year study of children's meaning-making in the home. Drawing on ethnographic research methods, three homes of five- to seven-year-old boys were visited regularly, over two years, to carry out a study of how meaning was constructed focusing on multimodal texts. In this case, Sam was six when the study began, and eight when it was concluded. The data was analyzed by coding for meaning and looking at meaning as it crossed modes, and also looking for themes over time, repeating patterns within homes which were followed and then interpreted with the families.

Sam's Home

Sam's mother, Parmjit, was a teacher in an inner-London borough and her family originally came from India. Her home was a house on a quiet street in North London in a mixed multiracial inner-London area. Sam attended the local school, and was in Year 2 (second grade) when this fieldwork was being carried out.

Visiting Sam's home on a regular basis yielded rich patterns of meaning-making. Sam's home and the artifacts within could be seen as a 'sign', which was the subject of research alongside Sam's text-making (Kress and van Leeuwen, 2001). The ethnographic focus on the way the home was constructed and the research involved tracking meaning-making by taking regular pictures of the decoration in the home, and how it shifted over time. Over the two years of the study Parmjit and Sam transformed and re-interpreted the space within which they lived, so that the home was subject to new readings and revisions. For example, Sam's bedroom shifted across the corridor during the time of the research. In order to get a sense of Sam's home, and to re-create it the concept of 'inventory' was used to analyze Sam's home meaning-making communicative practices. An inventory of Sam's bedroom gave an insight into the structuring of his home, and the representational and cultural resources that were available to him. Parmjit was preoccupied with ordering and classifying Sam's many toys and activities. Sam had acquired a considerable number of toys, a Game Boy, PlayStation, hundreds of Pokémon cards, a large rack of videos, some Meccano, little cars, toys and access to modeling materials like 'Femo'. Tracking Sam's meaning-making involved taking snapshots of the activities and objects he engaged with. On one particular evening as part of an ethnographic field visit the objects on the floor were recorded, and included:

Traced Pokémon cards

A box of Pokémon cards

A three-dimensional cardboard tray with as number of objects within it, referred to as a 'mini world'

Pokémon cards in clear plastic envelopes

Card, glue and scissors

A plastic 'bug'

The ethnographic analysis constructed floor space as a temporary 'text' where different family 'interests' were placed side by side, only to be tidied up subsequently. While floor space may not be a focus for deliberate 'meaning-making', often the household's key 'interests' could be discovered on the floor or on the coffee table in the living room. Sam and Parmjit both used the coffee table in the living room and often both Sam's work and Parmjit's teaching or leisure activities were juxtaposed on its surface. Sam's bedroom was also a focus for research. Since children's bedrooms often have floor space available to play, this was an important interpretative site when making a home visit, and many of the photographs taken by Sam were taken of his bedroom floor. Sam created meanings using his bedroom space, and his bedroom was changed through adding new furnishings, curtains and artifacts. I regarded Sam's bedroom as a text to be 'read', and I explored the meanings created within the room as well as recognizing it as a space for new meanings to be made.

During the research period it was observed that Sam and Parmjit were closely connected, their descriptions of Sam's activities echoed each other, and sometimes Parmjit helped interpret Sam's drawings. Tidying up was a habitual activity in the home. Parmjit often tidied up and assigned places to the objects in the house. Sometimes these were hard to classify (shells, models, bits of paper, bills, photographs, cards, plastic items and magazines) and she complained about the 'miscellaneous piles' she encountered in her home.

In order to analyze Sam's texts, I engaged him in conversation. I often failed to keep track of his copious making. A lot of the time Sam explained to me, in patient tones, how you make something. Sam came to see me as a friend who shared his interests and was willing to sit and listen to him. I made a particular relationship with Sam away from Parmjit, and discussed things separately with her. Classification of things was often left up to Sam, with Parmjit working with him to structure the classification, as in the decisions on which 'Femo' models to put in a display cabinet.

142   MULTIMODAL LITERACY

Part of the ethnography involved tracing where the origins of Sam's texts could be found. Sam and Parmjit's household drew on many cultural resources such as places visited, museums, Parmjit's work in schools, design materials, television, videos and games. Sam also engaged fully with popular culture such as the 'Pokémon' craze (see below) and made full use of a wide range of representational resources. The house drew on a number of different texts, moving from Parmjit's interest in design magazines, and how things looked, to Sam's reading of his Pokémon magazines, and interest in tiny figures. These 'voices' interwove within the texts of the household; their echoes could be heard both in the surroundings, in the home and in their texts (Bakhtin, 1981).

The Pokémon Phenomenon—A Brief History

The Pokémon phenomenon, popular around the world, started out as a game, with accompanying cards each carrying the slogan 'Gotta catch them all'. Pokémon creatures were hybrids derived from the insect and dinosaur and animal world. They are figments of a Japanese game inventor's imagination. They are manifested or realized in:

- Cards, which could be collected and bought in newsagents by parents for their children in packs of 11;
- TV programmes, which told a tale of Ash, who is a Pokémon trainer, and his friends, particularly his pet Pokémon, Pikachu;
- a game, which can be bought for 'Game Boy';
- T-shirts, caps, pyjamas, duvet covers and paraphernalia such as small plastic versions of Pokémons;
- Two films that are now videos.

Children collected the cards, traded them, watched the TV programme, went to see the movie and bought the merchandise. At the time of the fieldwork, at the end of 1999 through to 2000, the craze was very intense.

Sam's Interest in Mode

In order to explore how Sam made meaning, I focussed on how Sam related to mode. Sam explored the possibilities of mode while becoming interested in particular subjects. He drew figures and cut out images in order to make his own custom-made Pokémon cards. This interest quickly spread to modeling Pokémon creatures, and then he began to model different figures using 'Femo', a modeling substance, drawing on a wide variety of themes. These included friends of his mothers', himself, furniture and other home items, which he called 'homey touches'; Christmas objects; Halloween objects; and Egyptian artifacts. Sam was

Children's Text-Making at Home   143

very clear about how he lived with different interests in order to produce his sense of identity:

> 'I've always liked gore. I've always been changing my subject. When I was a baby I liked wheels, then I liked Thomas the Tank Engine, then I liked Robots, I liked Space then I liked Pokémon through seven and a little bit of eight, then I'm into Warhammer now I've moved on from the rest of my—I was getting bigger all those eight life years.'
>
> (Sam, November 20, 2001, on tape)

Sam's words reveal how strongly he connects his sense of identity with the cultural resources around him. By tracing the context of Sam's meaning-making back to the cultural resources upon which he drew, I was able to provide a more nuanced account of each text he produced as it emerged in the home.

In the following examples, fieldnotes, alongside photographs and transcribed oral narratives, build up an ethnographic account of each text. Sam worked mainly in a visual sphere, drawing, modeling and using photography to represent his meanings, but he also used writing, and speaking to present meaning.

In order to make new signs, Sam drew on children's popular culture and made artifacts using cultural resources which acted as 'tools of identity', supporting and upholding who he was (Holland, Lachicotte, Skinner and Cain, 2001, p. 42). Sam took artifacts out of context, from one 'figured world' such as the imaginary landscape of Pokémon, to another, for example, his bedroom floor, and re-contextualized them, placing them in another context (Holland, Lachicotte, Skinner and Cain, 2001, p. 41; Bernstein, 1996). In doing so, he deployed cultural resources that in some cases, he chose to support this identity formation. Sam used these resources to create meanings and in doing so, often entered different 'figured worlds' (Holland, Lachicotte, Skinner and Cain, 2001, p. 41). These new texts could then be worked upon and transformed across modes, so that the text was 're-figured' (Holland, Lachicotte, Skinner and Cain 2001, p. 236).

The following examples reveal Sam's making and re-making of his identity through text-making. By looking at moment-by-moment points of transformation in the following texts, Sam's identity shifts can be tracked over a three-month time period. Some texts were produced as a response to work generated during field visits, some texts had been drawn already, and were described to me in the context of a focus on Pokémon. The texts can be sequenced as follows:

1. Professor Sam's Pokémon Factory (drawing) (Figure 9.1)
2. The colour collage Pokémon card—'Trainer' (Figure 9.2)
3. The photograph taken by Sam which shows his bedroom carpet and Pokémon characters in play (Figure 9.3)

Sam discussed and produced many other examples of text production during the research period. These included copying Pokémon cards from the web and making

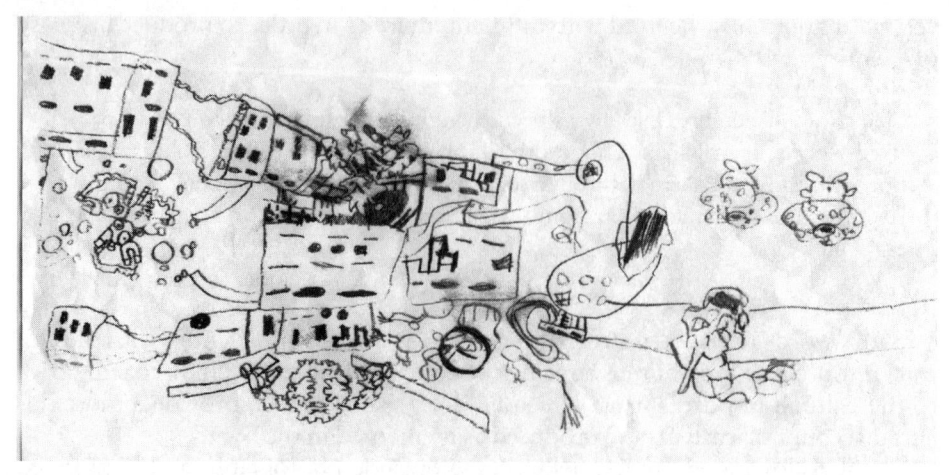

Figure 9.1

them into hand-made cards, making Christmas cards with Pokémon creatures on them, making models of Pokémon characters and placing Pokémon characters in dramatic poses when on holiday to be photographed and made into mini books.

Sam often began by using tracing paper to construct his images, lifting images from other sources, and then customizing them into a new, inter-textual multi-modal artifact. Sam found tracing a useful way of lifting characters from one mode to another, as he explains here:

>Fieldnotes 3 April 01
>
>Sam: I actually traced them,
>   turned the piece of tracing paper round
>   you know that one which you do,
>   you know when you trace something
>   you turn the piece of tracing paper
>   you draw it again and then it comes out on a piece of paper.
>   That's what I did for the Pokémons.
>   Look.

An example of this is Professor Sam's Pokémon factory (Figure 9.1). In this example, Sam has traced over using his cards as a basis. Sam said of this:

>Fieldnotes 11 April 00
>
>Sam: It's a Palectric lab.
>   They're where Professor Oak presses the buttons
>   and a new body comes out and makes a Pokémon.

> I don't think that is his real lab I just made his lab up.
> My name is Professor Sam.
> I made a trainer card for Professor Sam.

Here Sam used tracing paper to develop a laboratory for his own Pokémon creatures. By inserting his own self, Professor Sam, into the existing narrative, Sam then transformed the Pokémon narrative and made it his own. The text then became imbued with Sam's subjectivity. Instead of Professor Oak, from the original Pokémon script, Sam became the maker of Pokémon creatures, changing their qualities, and making up new cards with new qualities. Sam identified the names of the Pokémon creatures in the traced drawing: Magneton is on the right-hand side of the drawing, being 'created', Electrobuzz is in the middle, at the bottom of the drawing, and clockwise, are Vileplume, Onyx, Geodude and Gravalye. The same creatures recur in Figure 9.2, the trainer card: and in Figure 9.3, one of the animated figures on his bedroom carpet includes Electrobuzz as well as Blastoise and Poliwhirl. The shapes of the creatures recur across modes, as Sam carried his 'interest' into different areas of play. The process of 'tracing' using tracing paper and re-framing is the way in which Sam used to literally 'lift' an image from one context to another. Tracing paper involves an attention to the correct duplication of an object, but then facilitates the transformation of the object as here, in which the Pokémon creatures are placed within the new context of the Pokémon factory.

Sam continued to manipulate images of Pokémon creatures. In the collage colour example (Figure 9.2) the card has been made up of a number of different cut-out bits and has acquired a life of its own. The card is a 'trainer card' for 'Professor Sam', as described above. Sam described the process:

> I got Japanese Pokémons from a magazine cut it out the picture and then I just got
> my Porygon card cos I got 2 of them.
> It has the same moves I cut out trainer and sticked on its name.
> I cutted the picture out and stuck it on there.

Sam later in the visit referred back to this process as he played in his bedroom,

Fieldnotes 9 May 00

That was a Porygon card but he's made of collage but he's stuck together and I made him because of that.

Here, the 'cutting out' involves a transformation, from one kind of Pokémon card to another, a trainer (Kress, 1997). Sam effects his transformation with the representational resources available to him. The materiality of this card, and this emphasis on the new name, using new bits of Pokémon card, is how Sam signaled the difference between the 'real' Pokémon card and his new one. Sam had made many 'Pokémon cards at home, some of which were 'shinies'. Shiny cards were very high

TRAINER 30 HP

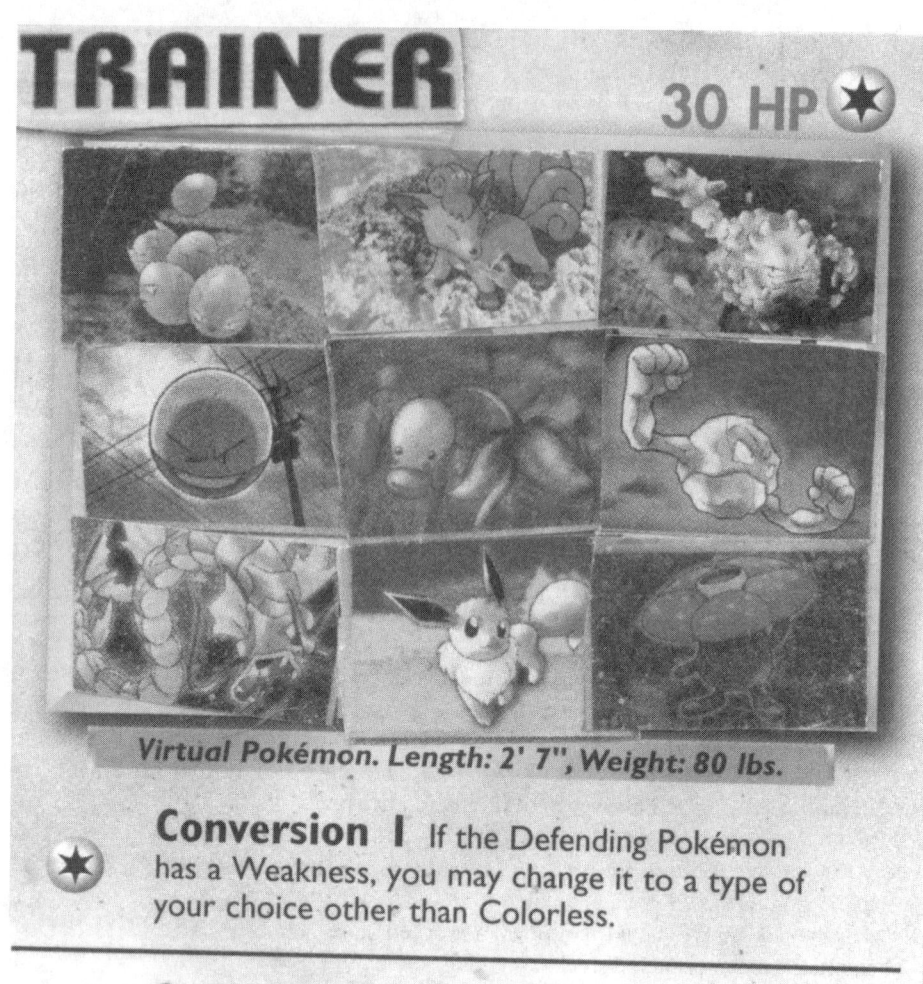

Virtual Pokémon. Length: 2' 7", Weight: 80 lbs.

Conversion 1 If the Defending Pokémon has a Weakness, you may change it to a type of your choice other than Colorless.

Conversion 2 Change Porygon's Resistance to a type of your choice other than Colorless.

weakness	resistance	retreat cost
	-30	

Figure 9.2

Children's Text-Making at Home 147

up in the pecking order of Pokémon cards. Sam, however, found his own way of making a shiny card:

> Fieldnotes 11 April 00 (from notes taken down as Sam spoke):
>
> Sam: First you get some cardboard I think you'd better save a card.
> To draw round on the cardboard.
> Then you'll have a piece of a shape of a Pokémon card.
> Then you get some shiny wrapping paper
> and you turn it round on the white
> bit and draw a triangle like the space to put the Pokémon picture in
> and then you simply put in all the detail
> like all the hit points and all the weakness and you choose what it does.
> But first you've got to draw a picture of your own Pokémon
> and then you put it to one side.
> Then you cut it out at the end
> and you've got to cut it out right on the edges and then you turn it around
> and get the Pokémon card the real one the real Pokémon card
> and try and copy out all the detail at the back and then it's finished.

The detailed discussion of the making process is articulated in relation to the child's interest and pleasure. Sam made the Pokémon cards because this is what he wanted to do. His focus on the making included instructions about holding on to material, 'you'd better save a card' and getting hold of wrapping paper of a particular kind, 'shiny'. The description alternates in register between an invitation to a friend, 'then you' and the more formal 'How you do it' way of describing whereby the object has a serious quality: 'First you've got to draw a picture'. Sam has listened to different discourses taken from popular programmes on cooking, art and 'making things', and embedded them into his description. The description includes a notion of making as play, but also serious, on the cusp of entertainment and work. Sam emphasized this with verbal rhetorical devices such as 'you simply put', which draws from the genre of the expert telling the uninitiated novice about what to do.

The materiality of the process is very important to Sam. The multi-modal nature of the object is a key part of its identity as a fully fashioned card, not two-dimensional but three, with shiny paper and specific material characteristics. He describes very precisely the 'affordances' of the medium, what is available to him in terms of representational resources. Sam uses the materials that are at hand within the home, and draws on a wide range of representational resources in order to make his card (Kress, 1997). His interest is the driving force behind his description of making a Pokémon card.

Moving from the making of [cards to the assembling of Pokémon creatures on the bedroom carpet involves another transition across modes. As part of the ethno-

Figure 9.3

graphic research, the children were all given cameras, in order to record their home environments from their own perspective and, if possible, to record some moments of play. This is what Sam did. He was playing in his bedroom one evening, using a variety of small toys, including some Pokémon figurines, some cars, trains and dolphins. He then used the camera to 'set up' dramatic action, and to produce a commentary. Figure 9.3 reveals how Sam then placed the figures in poses, and took photographs of the figures on the carpet. He moved the figures about and activated the play so that it became semi-cinematic. The 'carpet road' and his bedroom became in his imagination the backdrop for a film. Here Sam is seeing his room as film set — space to be used for imaginative play. The commentary ran continuously as he shot poses of his characters:

Fieldnotes 9 May 00

Sam: Charizard and Charmeleon are getting an ice cream.
Blastoise is in the pond he went over the track and into the aeroplane.
Electrobuzz and Blastoise are talking.
The one in the aeroplane is Blastoise.
Blastoise and Electrobuzz they look good. [Sam takes a photograph].
In the water are the water Pokémons — Poliwhirl.
Seadra's got out.
He's tired of being in the water.

> He's lying down.
> I am going to draw a sunset over that photo
> [of Charmeleon and Charmender].
> Blastoise is getting angry with Poliwhirl.
> The train has topped suddenly and this one's sunk.
> They've just bashed together the motorbike now bashed over there.
> Electrobuzz is watching there.
> He's over there.
> He fell into the pond.

Spoken commentary was characteristic of Sam's play, which interspersed action and small world play with his most beloved Pokémon creatures, Blastoise, Charmander, Charmeleon and Electrobuzz, taking centre stage as protagonists. The commentary operates like instructions on a film set, with each creature activated in response to the commentary. Sam suggested film as a genre in which the play could be set.

The play crossed boundaries in that traditional toys, such as cars and dolphins, are displayed, as well as 'Woody' from the film *Toy Story*. Play frequently had this hybrid quality, as Sam re-made and re-configured playing across boundaries created by toy manufacturers (Hilton, 1996). Play became a movement into different identities embodied in different forms. Holland writes about play:

> It is the opening out of thought within the activity of play, what we might call the cultural production of virtualities, that allows for the emergence of new figured world, of refigured worlds that come eventually to reshape selves and lives in all seriousness. (Holland, Lachicotte, Skinner and Cain, 2001, p. 236)

In analyzing Sam's play, I drew on the notion of 'refigured worlds' and on the 'cultural production of virtualities' which could be combined across genres to create new worlds (Holland, Lachicotte, Skinner and Cain, 2001, p. 236). Sam combined worlds to create spaces where he could experience new combinations of actions. These included the 'figured world' of Pokémon, Cops and Robbers and chases, *Toy Story* and so on (Holland, Lachicotte, Skinner and Cain, 2001, p. 41). Sam's spoken commentary went in different directions as he moved his characters about. Action was indicated with the word 'bashed', while the visual 'look' of the characters was also incorporated into the spoken commentary, 'they look good'. Sam re-positioned his toys and took 'action shots' with the camera in order to make spatial meanings that could then be turned into a fantasy script. Figure 9.3 shows how Sam has moved in very close to the play, and shot his characters from the position of the carpet, so that they appear larger and more 'life-like'. While the foreground is fuzzy, Sam has chosen to present his characters as dramatic actors in a complex play world, looming over the spectator like characters in a film.

The text here became a complex process of transformation. Beginning as dramatic play, the presence of the camera fixed the shifting semiotic landscape and recorded a moment in the 'small worlds' play of the child. Some of this small world play was then re-written with an adult friend, who helped him construct a narrative that was placed within a mini newspaper, called 'Sam's Worlds' from the initial small world play.

Narrative from 'Sam's Worlds':

> Our helicopter was travelling over the Pokémon land when it saw the island. We wanted to see what was happening in the Pokémon land. We could see Charmander coming to the zoo and Blastoise was in the pool with Seadra and Polywhirl. Charmeleon and Charizard were looking around the zoo. Polywag was waiting for the truck to pass.

This narrative has been re-written within the context of 'The Pokémon Land'. By supplying Sam with his camera, as part of my work as an ethnographer, I enabled him to incorporate his small world play into a new text, and with the help of an adult friend, he has been able to transform his narratives once more. Finally, the whole process became one in which Sam now saw the potential for new 'framing' of his characters; on holiday in Crete, he used the camera to capture moments when his favourite Pokémon figurine, Blastoise, was engaged in exciting dramatic action, such as speeding in a speed boat. One of these images was then placed inside the frame of a yellow 'Post-it' note to become a new Pokémon card.

I traced back the origin of the texts produced in the home. The photographic texts could be traced back to the notion of film. Sam said to me that the next stage could be using a video camera. The genre seems to be that of action movies, and the framing of objects in dramatic positions suggests cartoons. The re-framing of the text into a newspaper was achieved by the help of an adult friend which then gave another modal layer to the process. The complexity of Sam's response to the Pokémon narratives he encountered revealed an interest in the processes of transformation, and in materiality.

Tracking Sam's meaning-making across modes, and following the number of moments of re-contextualisation begins to open out a complex, shifting world of semiosis in which the child's interest is expressed in a number of fragmented and dispersed textual forms, including tracing paper, cut-out cards, photographs, collages and modeling material (Bernstein 1996). Texts here can be seen to be fluid, moving into one another, and sometimes the boundaries between texts are less clear. A momentary text operated as a 'punctuation mark' in a shifting semiotic world. While some texts could be taken away and kept, much of Sam's text-making was ephemeral in that it could not be caught directly. He re-arranged his characters to form a 'text', and then moved them a second later. Text-making becomes a moment by moment process which then 'sediments' into home artifacts such as a display cabinet. I use the word 'sedimentation' to describe the settling of texts placed as artifacts in specific spaces in the home, and incorporated into the family's 'habitus'—that is, the habitual ways of being observed within the home (Bourdieu, 1990).

Sam's meaning-making flowed through play, the making of cards, the taking of photographs and the re-framing of them, the use of props and toy artifacts as well as the making of new ones. This took place in a communicational environment that provided a rich set of cultural resources on which to draw. The resources available to Sam were not so much material resources, but *the resource to move across modes,* from play to the creation of a temporary text, to drawing and then to play again. This resource to move from play to drawing, to play to cutting out, and then back to construction or model making, was one observed in all the homes where the research was carried out (Pahl, 2001).

Sam's activities were shaped by the affordances of the bedroom floor, the Pokémon creatures, the use of paper, pen and card to create new cards. In inserting his own narratives into the making of things, the new Pokémon factory, the action play on the carpet, Sam was transforming cultural resources, and shifting both his identity in practice and the mode in which the sign has been realized. Materiality, mode and subjectivity were engaged together, within 'interest', which describes the motivation of process by which the child is engaged in a practice. The same forms recurred in all the modes, but the meaning was different, according to the affordances available to Sam. He moved from being 'Professor Sam' to being a trainer, to being an animator of creatures. Sam was interacting with the affordances available to him to create new 'tools of identity', which in turn created new affordances and re-interpretations (Kress, 1997, Holland, Lachicotte, Skinner and Cain, 2001, p. 42). In order to pay attention to the affordances available to the child, an ethnographic perspective was used to study Sam's home, and his mother's view of what he did. The habitus both constructed and supported what Sam did, and then was transformed by his activities (Bourdieu, 1990).

Sam's Modeling and Parmjit's Home: 'Homey Touches'

In order to examine Sam's view of mode, I will turn to his meaning-making using modeling material. Sam liked to make models out of 'Femo', a material similar to Play-Doh, which can be baked in the oven and which allows the maker to use colour and shape. Sam discovered Femo soon after his seventh birthday:

He was asked why he was dissatisfied with two-dimensional models, and replied,

Sam, 3 October 01 on Tape, and Subsequently Revised by Sam 27 February 02

Sam: I don't like stuff like flat stuff,
     I mostly like big sort of 3D models.
     Do you know how I thought of this Femo making?

K: Why tell me.

Sam: Well it was near my 7th birthday, very near,
     And I was sitting on my bed and I said to my mum um how can I like

152   MULTIMODAL LITERACY

>   have something like Play-Doh but dries?
>   [she said]
>   'Well . . . I know your brother built this model of you when you was a baby'

This piece of transcript reveals Sam's thoughts about the relationship between mode and his identity. Sam started by rejecting 'flat stuff' and then articulated how he came to decide upon Femo modeling, which became his passion. Sam's brother had originally started Femo modeling by making a model of Sam when he was born. Sam described how the use of 3D, using modeling material such as Femo, facilitated 'life-like' replicas of, in this case, a baby. Like Kress's example of 'cutting out', the move from two-dimensional to three-dimensional facilitates a more 'life-like' identity formation, which in turn allowed Sam to re-fashion his 'identity-in-practice' (Kress, 1997, p. 27; Holland, Lachicotte, Skinner and Cain, 2001, p. 40). Sam's identity as a baby who has been modeled and his interest in modeling cohered at the point at which he wanted to move across modes, from 2D to 3D. Sam articulated his interest in 'Femo' models in relation to their affordances, to the possibilities they offered him:

Fieldnotes 7 May 01

Sam: I used to get my Femo models and like, have a battle.
I used to make really big ones and I pretend that they crashed through and they start fighting.'

The use of the models allowed Sam to enter a mini world, and to experience as if 'for real' the world he had created. Sam liked to explore his own worlds through constructing new worlds using the modeling material. One such example is the 'homey touches'. At the end of the fieldwork he was asked about his collection of small models. After some deliberation, Parmjit decided to create a display cabinet for Sam's small models, and Sam was interviewed about these in order to gain an understanding of what they meant to him. He had made with Femo a small model of a sofa, some chairs, and a bed. Sam said of them,

From Transcript 3 oct 01

Kate: What other things are there in there?
Sam: There's homey touches.
Kate: Homey touches, what are they?
Sam: Homey touches, touches.
Kate: What are they?
Sam: They're like just little things that you can put in a home.
       There's a bed there's another bed over there there's a table there's a cup there's a TV there's a sofa there's a little bouncy castle at the back (laughs).

Sam's 'homey touches' corresponded to his notion of 'home'. The Femo models activated 'home as sign' and his collection provided the backdrop, like a doll's house, to 'playing house'. Sam has constructed mini worlds, by using multimodal resources. By moving into 3 D Sam has been able to activate what he thinks of as 'home' and give his pieces a name, 'Homey touches'. Sam's own sense of identity is bound up with these 'homey touches' as Parmjit herself admits in an interview,

Interview Transcript 11 April 01

Parmjit: And because Sam is just a bit person,
his life is these little miniature figures,
and they're just, and he is interesting,
because he had to leave things

Parmjit both acknowledged that the miniature figures are part of him, and talked about how the home was littered with tiny objects. Multimodal meaning-making becomes both valued and contested, as children attempt to people their spaces with objects that can then be used for small play, but then are left at the point at which they become 'mess'. The 'habitus' is transformed moment by moment by text-making (Bourdieu, 1990). By constructing this kind of activity as multimodal and attending to how miniaturized multimodal play produces shifts in subjectivity, as Parmjit herself admits, a more nuanced notion of children's meaning-making is possible.

Conclusion

By opening up the densely patterned world of Sam's meaning-making to an interpretative ethnographic gaze, and by exploring the worlds beyond the linguistic a complex pattern of communicative practices has been revealed. Scored within these patterns are the specific moves across modes. For example, in Professor Sam's Pokémon factory the use of tracing paper realized a different kind of sign, in which several Pokémon cards could be traced and then recontextualized within a new space, a sheet of A4 paper. The 'trainer card' for the new Professor Sam, whose creation was facilitated through the tracing paper and drawing, was created using cut-out card and 'bits' from other Pokémon cards. The finished product was hybrid and adapted to the identity of the maker. The process took place over a few months, but could be tracked back and forth, across modes, and could be seen as a flowing semiotic process.

By attending to the interplay between modes, Sam's leaps in imaginative conception can also be fully appreciated as rich and complex learning experiences. Sam's movement across modes could then be traced back, and conceptualized in relation to the shifts in identity he achieved through each leap. Semiotic ethnography has enabled the researcher to watch the process step by step so that the child's unique learning paths through modes can be recognized and understood. The challenge would be to extend this in work at school, where the child could be supported in a multimodal learning environment to invent meaning as creatively as Professor Sam, who produced creatures in his own Pokémon factory to be turned into new and different cards.

Acknowledgments

Many thanks to Sam and Parmjit for their support for the research.
Names have been changed to preserve anonymity where appropriate.

References

Bakhtin, M. (1981) Ed. Holquist, M.; Trans. Holquist, M. and Emerson, C. *The Dialogic Imagination*. Austin: University of Texas Press.
Bernstein, B. (1996) *Pedagogy, Symbolic Control and Identity*. London: Taylor and Francis.
Bourdieu, P. (1990) trans. Richard Nice. *The Logic of Practice*. Cambridge, United Kingdom: Polity Press.
Hilton, M. (ed.) (1996) *Potent Fictions: Children's Literacy and the Challenge of Popular Culture*. London and New York: Routledge.
Holland, D., Lachicotte Jr., W. Skinner, D. and Cain, C. (2001) *Identity and Agency in Cultural Worlds*. Cambridge, Mass. and London: Harvard University Press.
Kress, G.R. (1997) *Before Writing: Rethinking the Paths to Literacy*. London and New York: Routledge.
Kress, G.R. and van Leeuwen, T. (2001) *Multimodal Discourse: the Modes and Media of Contemporary Communication*. London and New York: Arnold.
Mitchell, J.C. (1984) 'Typicality and the Case Study' in Ellen, R.F. *Ethnographic Research: A Guide to General Conduct*. (pp. 238–241) London: Academic Press, Harcourt Brace Jovanovich.
Pahl, K. (2001, November) 'Texts as Artefacts Crossing Sites: Map Making at Home and School' *Reading: Literacy and Language*. Vol. 35, No. 3. 2001.

Anton Franks 10

PALMERS' KISS: SHAKESPEARE, SCHOOL DRAMA AND SEMIOTICS

The 'study' of Shakespearean text in schools is prevalent in the English-speaking world, where high value is attached to the study of Shakespeare as 'canonical' literature. But, the text presents students with archaic forms of language and historically remote cultural conventions and so it is difficult stuff to 'penetrate'. Learners have differential access to the wider resources of cultural and specifically textual knowledge that can enable them to make sense of the text. At the same time, teachers often want to mobilise their students' experience and knowledge of the world, of home and school, of other texts—books, films and television—and bring them to bear on their reading of the printed page. Sometimes, teachers decide that students will better understand the meaning of the text if they move beyond sedentary readings toward acting out some part of Shakespeare. Through the processes of dramatisation, the bodily enactment of the text in voice, action and interaction, value might be added to the reading of Shakespeare.

To lead students through such complex activity with a Shakespearean text requires great skill on the part of the teacher. The teacher orchestrates action that leads from readings of the printed text and moves towards its dramatisation. Experienced teachers are likely to have these ways of working 'at their fingertips'—they *know* how to set these complex patterns of learning into motion. In this chapter I will look closely at parts of such a lesson. Teachers may know how to do these things well, but neither they nor interested observers of such lessons may know of adequate ways to observe, describe and analyse them. Traditional modes of describing and analysing classroom action and interaction tend to present verbal transcripts and descriptive narrative as data. When we look at the subtle shifts of meaning-making involved in moving between a group reading of a 'literary' dramatic text, social action and dramatised activity, however, something else might be needed.

One way is to focus on the role and function of the body, the socially organised body, situated in particular places and social settings, as a locus of multimodal meaning making activity. Here I shall be looking for transitions between social action and dramatic action, focussing particularly on bodily action and interaction in its particular social and cultural setting and using methods of multimodal semiotic analysis.

There are several reasons that serve as an impetus for this approach. In the first place, the pre-eminent way of making dramatic meaning, whether scripted or improvised, is through the representative action of socially organised persons, and the main material for making meaning in drama is the human body. But then if we look at drama, we find that the ways that meaning is made is very close to the ways that we make meaning in everyday social life. In both the social and dramatic communication we use combinations of speech, movement, gesture, posture, face work, movement in and through space, relative positioning in space in relation to particular settings, other people, objects and so forth. Multimodal social semiotics allows us to bring into focus the physical meaning-making action of socially organised people in specific cultural settings. What separates drama from everyday life is perhaps the way that physicalised social action is selected, framed and shaped in particular settings. Drama seen in this way is the crystallisation of human relations represented in and through physically realised social interaction. The framing of dramatic action, that which marks boundaries between social and dramatic action, is one of the key elements of the analysis to be explored here. The final reason is that, although there is much work on the analysis of English and drama in education, the focus on description, transcription and analysis of verbal exchanges tends to represent these situations as stripped of physical presence and co-presence. In this field of study, there is comparatively little systematic work on description and analysis of physicalised social action and interaction.

Method

Selection of Data

The example I shall be examining is selected from a data set of 32 videotaped English lessons with 14- to 15-year-old students; it is early on in a sequence of lessons in which a class is working on *Romeo and Juliet*. The data have been gathered from three inner-London schools as part of a project to investigate the production of school English. As a proportion of the sample, it is one of two lessons around playtexts in which drama is used as a mode of learning. There are four phases of the lesson and these are comparable to other such lesson formats. In the opening stage, the teacher gives instructions, emphasising key concepts to be explored, and lays out a sequence of action and how time and space are to be divided and used. In the next phase, sitting in groups of five around tables, students work on the same small section of the text that the teacher has excerpted and had printed out onto sheets of paper. They practise speaking lines aloud and then annotate their texts in the manner of a 'director's script', indicating line delivery and accompanying action. In the third part of the lesson, groups of students move into various spaces to practise acting-out a section of the text. Finally, at the end of the lesson, the students show each other their scenes as 'work in progress' rather than as polished performance.

What is striking about this particular example, and what makes it usefully representative of this kind of active approach with dramatic text, however, is the sheer amount of effort—mental, physical and emotional—that the teacher and students put into reading and dramatising the text. What we see emerging from this effort cannot be described as fully realised drama. For various reasons, the students struggle to act out the text and make the drama fluent. It is both the progressive nature of the sequence of activity and the struggle to make meaning of the text that is of particular interest. The students make dramatic meaning, but it is 'emergent drama' rather than fully formed. Because it is 'on the way to becoming drama' we might see the multimodal *processes* of meaning making emerging more clearly in the shifts between the action of reading the text, and the social and dramatic interactions that spring from the reading.

To analyse such complex communicational processes is never easy. In order to select points of entry into the video data the tape of the lesson was viewed repeatedly and in different ways—at normal speed with and without sound, at double speed forwards and backwards without sound. This technique was used to identify patterns of progression and to select excerpts that were representative of a particular phase, capturing a sense of the complexity of communicative activity, but bounded and brief enough to make them amenable to description and analysis. Two excerpts have been chosen. The first illustrates the business of sitting around a table preparing lines, speaking them aloud in a group and preparing an annotated 'director's script'. At this stage, 'the drama' is mostly in the voice. The second excerpt shows another group of students rehearsing a dramatised 'staging' of the same section of the text in the corridor. These two instances were selected because they illustrate how the process of dramatisation moves from sedentary dramatised reading towards an enactment of the text that is realised in terms of voice, gesture, posture, space and spatial positioning in relation both to other actors and to the audience. Once selected, the video clips were again repeatedly viewed with and without sound, at normal and double speed and then sections of dialogue, action and reaction were transcribed. The broad categories of speech and action can be seen as the main modes of communication in the productive activity of the teacher and the students and serve as the broad modes of analysis.

In both excerpts the teacher can be seen to be the leading social and dramatic actor and is at the same time the main audience for the drama that students produce: she becomes a key figure in the analysis of the lesson. In analysing the progression of activity from sedentary reading to active dramatised reading there is a concentration on ways that this process uncovers and makes dramatic resources available for the students.

Parameters of Description

The broad framework of multimodal social semiotics allows us to bring into view the ways that the complex layering of signs, forms, modes and functions of socially organised people work together to make meaning through and in bodily communication. This is the predominant viewpoint from which I shall analyse the ways that teachers and learners realise meaning in the movement between written text (the Shakespeare play), speech (classroom discussion and dramatised reading) and socially directed action in particular settings of time and place (drama shared in the classroom with and shown to teacher and fellow students). These are seen as combinatory semiotic resources that social actors pattern, produce, and perform to others. Different subjects on the curriculum tend to operate within specific discursive formations and lead to patterns of physical and mental activity that require particular forms of engagements with the world (see especially Kress, 2001; Kress and van Leeuwen 2001; and Kress et al. 2001).

There are two connected and concentric spheres of bodily communicative action that are taken into account here. First in looking at gesture, posture and facial expression we are describing the ways that the body moves in and around its own axis. Second, there is an outer sphere described by the body's movement through space. The direction taken here is elaborated from multimodal perspectives specifically focussed on bodily communication in drama and learning situations (see Franks 1995; 1996; Franks and Jewitt, 2001). In viewing bodily communication there is a particular concentration on the upper body, especially on the use of arms and face in communicative work. This focus becomes even tighter when we come to look for signs of dramatised reading. Even small movements of the eyes and eyebrows are seen to be significant here, which might put us in mind of Birdwhistell's work on 'kinesics' (1975). The main focus, therefore, is on what might be described as the 'surface features' of bodily communication. At the same time, it has to be acknowledged, however, that combinations of speech, gesture and action relate in differential, diverse but important ways to thinking and feeling (see McNeill, 1979).

The ways in which boundaries of time and place are co-ordinated and combined give us the *setting*. At the same time, the 'micro-history' of the lesson, the place of the English lesson in the timetable of the school day and then, within the boundaries of the lesson its progressive sequence of action over time, is set within a wider history of the development of schooling and the curriculum. Within this setting, conceptual and material boundaries around meaningful action are described here under the concept of *frame*. However, that concept functions not only to map out or mark boundaries of time and space, it is 'meta-communicative' in that it helps us to understand the accents and inflections operating in particular sequences, or 'strips' of communicative action. How we interpret the raising of an eyebrow whilst reading from a script, for example, will depend on how this movement is given a context in a flow of dialogue and interaction over time (Bateson 1973; Goffman 1974).

In the approach taken here, bodily communication is seen as a global undertaking of particular persons, and atomised description, or complicated notation systems might impede our sense of how signs, forms and modes work together in sequences action over time (Greimas, 1987). This 'global' approach to analysis of sequences and combinations of action, identifying repetitions and patterns of sign-making emerging over time can be found in work on the semiotics of drama and theatre, which is helpful when we come to look at dramatic activity (Pavis, 1982). In examining repetitions and patterns of gesture, movement, spatial arrangement and so forth, we can look out for the arrangements that simultaneously dramatise and crystallise social arrangements. Here we might think about Brecht's technique and concept of *gestus*— the embodied dramatic sign that simultaneously represents and comments on, or evaluates social arrangements (see Brecht 1964, p. 198, Franks and Jones, 1999). This consideration will assist in the selection and identification of significant, representative or 'emblematic' moments in particular sequences of this particular lesson, and serve to guide the ways that aspects of speech, gesture, movement, posture and relative positioning can be grouped together for the purposes of analysis. Finally, from both theatrical and social semiotic perspectives, the notion of *audience* is significant—who is participating in, watching, listening and responding to these social and dramatic interactions in this English classroom? How does a consciousness of audience affect what is done and said?

This approach is less about 'reading off' the signs of the body and involves more interpretation and 'reading into' the social and dramatic action. The labour of interpretation takes into account the actors as persons involved in sequences of interaction, working with and between a range of resources for communication, text, speech, gesture, posture and so on (Kendon, 1990). Knowledge derived from the wider body of data that this lesson is drawn from, as well as my own observation, experience and knowledge of the field of English and drama teaching helps in the task of interpretation.

Setting of the Lesson—Frame, Conceptual Boundaries and Patterns of Action

At the start of the lesson, the teacher spends just two minutes talking about the nature and pattern of the lesson, speaking from her seat behind her desk. She talks using particular emphases and clear diction throughout the lesson, often repeating important points in different ways and accompanying her words with hand gestures 'accenting' speech. The whole lesson of over an hour and a half, she tells them first, is about the students *developing* their scene and a sense of the *characters* they are playing. For this they are to develop and practise the *tone of voice, facial expressions, ways of standing and moving* appropriate for the characters they are playing. They are to think about the emotions that underlie and give emphasis to the words they speak. Because it had seemed to work well in the previous lesson, she has selected just a few particular *lines* for them to concentrate on in this lesson. She suggests that they might start off by playing with just a few *lines* of one *character's* speech out of the excerpt.

The terms in italics here are those given particular weight and emphasis, through intonation, variation (for instance, the general concept of 'character' is, after the opening few words, made in specific reference to Romeo, and the notion of scene becomes reduced to 'lines') and repetition, in the teacher's opening instructions. She emphasises the idea that comprehending the emotional states of characters will give them clues about how to speak the lines with more meaning. If these are emphases in terms of the content, focus and outcome of the work, a stress on 'group work' and repeated 'practise' (she does not once use the term 'rehearsal') give direction on particular modes of working.

There are several overlapping layers to the rhetorical frame being established by the teacher in this brief introduction to the lesson. Towards the outermost layers, the teacher and students share an awareness of the relatively high value placed on Shakespearean text in wider cultural domains—Shakespeare as 'cultural capital' (Bourdieu 1991; 1993). As an adult, an English teacher, the teacher is a more experienced 'other' and her understanding of this is likely to be more developed. The students look to the teacher to be able to mediate and elucidate the nature of the value of the text. In wider culture, as in schools, Shakespeare as cultural artefact is mediated in two forms—as printed text and, whether in film, theatre, CD-ROM, or television, as dramatic performance. In framing this lesson there is an emphasis on an articulation between text and performance in a continuum that moves from a close concentration on lines of text, through the idea of character and ending with ways that character is realised through dramatised speech and action. There are implicit pointers here to the ways that, in the wider world, actors, especially those trained in the conventional modes of naturalism, work to realise character. On a similar view, in repeatedly talking about 'lines' of the text the teacher is connecting the discourse of theatre, in which actors learn their 'lines' for performance, with the discourse of the English literature classroom. Here, reference to particular lines of source texts is seen as important evidence to support analytical argument. The overlap between the actors' and the teacher's idea of engaging school students in an understanding of text is in the concept of 'empathy' with the characters. Two considerations are likely to lie behind the teacher's reference to 'practise' rather than 'rehearsal': first that she is speaking to a range of students who have English as an additional language, but second, 'practise' locates the purpose of the activity more in the domain of schooling and learning about the play, rather than preparing to perform the play in the theatre.

Students will have had schooled experience of 'doing' Shakespeare prior to this set of lessons. The previous year, for example, these students will have had to study a Shakespeare play in preparation for national standardised tests (it is possible that *Romeo and Juliet* was the text studied by these particular students). Seen within the context of their previous experience of Shakespeare on the curriculum, we might assume that there is likely to be some level of shared understanding between teacher and students of the ways in which the value of Shakespeare is enacted and valorised through educational policy and pedagogical practices. Here we deal with another layer of the frame for the lesson that makes reference to the requirements of the curriculum and, as these students are studying towards public examinations in English, the specifications of the English syllabus. Of such requirements that bear on this lesson, those that deal with how Shakespeare works as a text for performance, developing understandings of characters and their motivations, and how texts are adapted to different media are particularly germane. Students will have to write analytical pieces that will show something of these categories of understanding to submit for examination. Behind the teacher's direction to focus on a short section of text, there is also a pedagogical idea that a tight focus on short key sections of text will transfer and feed into a student's ability to engage with and understand the whole text.

In the centre of the frame is the action and interaction that takes place in the lesson. This is the focus of attention. Around this action, however, there is an approach to contextual frame here that works something like the 'layers of an onion' rather than representing frame as a single boundary line. (This is not quite the right metaphor, perhaps, as it is an image that might seem to be too solid and 'organic' to adequately represent and evoke complex social patterning.) Tightest to the action of the lesson is a layer defined by approaches developed in the interaction of particular teachers and students in a specific school with a particular constituency, what might be described as particular 'pedagogic arrangements'. Surrounding this layer of the frame are the requirements of the national curriculum and examination syllabi that also bear on the development of these pedagogic arrangements. At the outermost layers, the place of Shakespeare in wider culture—for example, in film, television and theatre, in 'popular imagination'—works in certain ways to frame the action that takes place in this particular lesson.

Reading the Lines

At the teacher's direction, the whole class is to work on a portion of Act 1 Scene 5, in which Juliet and Romeo first meet at the Capulets' masked ball. Prior to this scene in the play, it has been significantly established that Juliet's family, the Capulets, have a long-standing feud with Romeo's family, the Montagues and, moreover, that Romeo professes his love for Rosalind (who never appears in the play). This scene of 'love at first sight' is a pivotal scene in the play and the story of the lovers and the (tragic) course of their relationship runs from this point. The students are to work at tables in groups of five practising lines and marking their texts for when they are to leave their seats and rehearse a more active dramatic presentation of the scene. Although fairly cramped, the teacher has arranged the classroom with desks pushed together to make the tables, and these placed at angles rather than 'square' with the walls of the room. This arrangement of space facilitates 'sight lines' in the classroom, with the teacher and students better able to see each other and be seen, and this signals an openness and emphasis on interactive and collaborative group work in this place with this teacher. The arrangement of the room is a resource that maximises the potential to engage in group work.

162   MULTIMODAL LITERACY

The teacher approaches a group that is sitting by a window in the corner of the room, furthest from the teacher's desk and board (that indicates 'front' of room) and opposite the door. There are four girls and one boy. By name and appearance, the three girls and boy are from a South Asian background and one girl is from a northeast African background. She and another girl wear hijabs (Muslim headscarves). When this last girl in the group speaks, it is with heavily accented English. The others have mainly London accents, tinged to a greater or lesser extent with Caribbean and Ssouth Asian pronunciation. Of the five students, three appear to be looking at the text, two of them with heads bent as if in close study, and the two others are directing their gaze towards each other or towards the approaching teacher. 'There's a lot of silence over here, what's happening?' the teacher observes, as she moves into position. She leans over the table slightly and looks around at the students. By her side, C looks up and replies, 'Miss, we've read, we read it through'.

From an observer's viewpoint, the physical appearance of the students, their relative positions in space, their postures and their direction of gaze point us towards something about how they are orientated toward the text and the tasks. Clearly there are differences in the knowledge, skills and resources that these students will be able or willing to bring to reading and dramatising this text. They have followed instructions up to a point and then have ground to a halt. Perhaps from the teacher's point of view it appears that (so far as can be judged from the following sequence of action) this group needs some sort of structured intervention and an injection of 'energy' to get them moving, so that they can gather some momentum that will carry them through the rest of the lesson. In response to A, the teacher looks around the group, then leans across and picks up a slip of paper on which are printed a few lines. She asks whether they're 'absolutely happy with these lines?' and 'ready to go now?' From their response, she gathers that the work has scarcely begun. Overall, the teacher stays with this group for about seven minutes and the following sequence emerges from this point:

1. Teacher checks on the allocation of parts (11 sec.)
2. She draws attention to a four-line speech of Juliet's and makes sure everyone has a copy to read from (38 sec.)
3. Teacher questions the students on what action and feelings have led up to the point where Juliet makes this speech and checks on their understanding of what is actually going on at this point of the play (1 min. 36 sec.)
4. Students each read the speech. Teacher comments briefly after the first three readings (1 min. 44 sec.)
5. More commentary on reading and then extended talk to provide a focus and motivation for voicing the lines (48 sec.)
6. A student asks the teacher to read the speech and, with some reluctance, she accedes to the request and offers her own interpretation in speaking the lines (33 sec.)

7. Teacher reinforces her instructions—they are to use this experience of voicing the lines as a basis for annotating their sheets, giving indications of how they should be spoken and to think about action, posture and gesture accompanying the speech. She departs (1 min. 3 sec.)

(Total time 6:31)

Much of the time is spent talking around the text, mostly before the reading but also with some talk following that. I will look more closely at stage three of the sequence to gain some sense of how the discussion around the text plays out. At this stage there is only glancing reference to the printed text and so the sequence is tabulated in two columns describing the modes of speech and action.

The teacher reduces both the physical and social distance between herself and the students when she sits at the table. Exploring intimate thoughts and motivations perhaps requires this proximity. Three concurrent approaches appear here. First the teacher elicits what students know about the play, what has happened prior to the speech that is chosen for a run-through. At the same time, without prying, the teacher is finessing the students' experience, whether from their personal lives or mediated by other written texts, film or television, about 'young love'. This will help them to 'understand [Romeo and Juliet's] characters more'. Alongside questioning and exposition, the teacher is involved in dramatising, elaborating a dramatic context for the students through dramatised narrative, facial expression and gesture. Even without visual images, the pantomimic and exaggerated kissing sequence shows this approach most clearly in the transcript. In using these kinds of energetic and heightened ways of communicating, the teacher's performance serves as an affective prompt and resource for the students when it comes to their reading of the speech from the play.

In the following sequence, the teacher encourages the students to read this well-known speech of Juliet's:

> Good pilgrim, you do wrong your hand too much,
> Which mannerly devotion shows in this.
> For saints have hands that pilgrims' hands do touch,
> And palm to palm is a holy palmers' kiss.

The students read from the text and rehearse the speech. In tabulating this section I have decided that two columns of speech and action used in analysis of the previous section of dialogue do not adequately capture the significance of this sequence. Their reading is a move towards a dramatisation of the speech and it is marked mainly in the use of their voices, and this category of voice is set down in the first column. The manner in which the students hold the text appears to me to signify something of their relation to the text and their response to the task of doing this dramatised reading and so this has been included as a second category. The third category of 'face' is set out because there is a certain amount of face work involved in realising the characterisation. Although the audience for the reading includes other students in this small group, repeated viewing of this section of videotape shows

Table 10.1

Speech	Action
T: What was happening before this? *Why* is the character saying this? So Juliet's just about to say 'Good pilgrim you do wrong your hand too much'. What's just happened before? A: He's kissed her hand, he's just kissed, he's just kissed her. T: Who has Romeo just kissed?/ A: /Romeo's kissed Juliet's hand. T: So they're at a nobleman's party, they are of noble family, and they are at a party. And they've just started kissing each other! Is this acceptable?	Teacher stands and leans on table. Students look mostly at the text, sometimes at the teacher, and odd glances at each other. Teacher sits. The teacher's left arm is tucked in close to her body on the table, gestures with right arm towards text on table and uses her hands to accent her words Teacher makes wide-eyed, dramatic face
Two young people running up to each other, never seen each other before, and kiss, kiss, kiss, kiss! So it's a bit shocking isn't it? No? Their emotions have overtaken them. And of course they're probably not sure where it's come from either.	Teacher makes exaggerated kissing gesture with mouth three times Student C giggles and others look at each other and smile.
But of course, if you look at the bottom of this sheet, there are some ideas about why some people think that Romeo and Juliet fell in love so quickly. You might like to look at those and to think, 'Well why did they?'	Teacher picks up sheet and points, students shuffle papers and look. Teacher makes circular gesture to the left of her temple.
Because if you can understand, or have a reason why, you might be able to understand their characters more. So, what do you think, how do you think Juliet will say these lines? Is she going to be shouting them? A: Sh . . . shocked miss T: Shocked. Surprised. Unsure of herself. Her voice.	 Hands under chin, looking from text to teacher.

Note: Transcription of this section is complete. The conventions are in the style of playscript with '/' indicating overlapping speech.

that the main audience for the reading is the teacher. Her responses after the reading are marked down in the remaining column.

Watching and listening repeatedly to this sequence, it becomes apparent that the words themselves and their spatial layout on the page promote a marked tendency towards rhythmical utterance. Students' feeling towards and about the text is in some ways signalled by their physical relation to it. Students A and C, for example, have a very relaxed relation to the text and this may free them up to work on an attempt at characterisation as is signalled by C's adjustment before she reads. Eyebrow work is most noted in A's work with the speech. As the teacher comments, B's reading is 'sweet' and she too communicates some sense of modesty and shyness, but her final gesture with the book suggests a certain diffidence in her attitude to the text and task of reading aloud. All students look towards the teacher at the end of their reading—she is the main audience for this 'performance of the voice'.

More work on intention and feeling follows, starting with a generalised review of the readings.

T: Quiet. Calm. Yes, you were all *that*. Erm . . . *[pause]* Wasn't there a bit of excitement there as well?
A: Quite happy.
T: Sorry?
A: Quite happy.
T: Quite happy and *excited*. But it's controlled excitement. I don't know where it's coming from. It's confused. So, I don't know, if it was Leonardo di Caprio coming in when you were doing this. If I said, well look, to help you, I don't know, I've got some famous superstar to come in, how would you say it?
Ss: *[Giggle]*.
T: *[To male student]* Perhaps you wouldn't be interested in Leonardo di Caprio.
B: No, no Miss.
T: Well, you can pick *your* person.

First we find the teacher helps to construct a sense of character with her interpretative commentary on the reading. Next the teacher shifts into first person, and through this shows identification, empathy perhaps, with Juliet's character. She follows this through with another move designed to stimulate the students' empathetic sense with her reference to film stars. Who might be the object of their passion? She is only momentarily and humorously arrested in this train of thought when she realises that the boy might not feel too 'interested in Leonardo di Caprio'. This sequence is immediately followed by the request from C that they hear the teacher's interpretation of Juliet's speech. Given the progressive flow of interaction so far, asking the teacher to 'model' a reading of the speech is an entirely appropriate move at this stage. Already she has done much to provide the foundation and scaffolding for the students to build a dramatic realisation of character. She has led a small investigation into the subjective position of a young person experiencing a dizzying surge of attraction for another. Now, when she is

Table 10.2

Student	Voice	Physical relation to text	Face	Teacher response
A	Fluent reading, with intonation and rhythm soft voice	Text flat on table, straight posture, hands below table on lap, head inclined and still	Subtle shifts of eyebrows, eyes and mouth to accent aspects of speech and show emotion. Looks towards teacher at end of reading	After reading says, 'Can we feel the kind of, the kind of chill in her voice there? The unsurety [sic] about where it's come from? The uncertainty?'
B	Mostly fluent but with some elongated pauses, retains some rhythmic quality, soft voice	Grips book at ~60° just above table, at end of reading drops book down and knocks its spine against table	Mostly in concentrating mode, raises eyebrows when pausing over 'pilgrims', casts eyes down at end of reading and then looks towards teacher	Concentrated look whilst reading, eyes narrowed. After reading, says, 'That's very sweet.'
C	Mostly fluent, with lilting intonation and rhythm, stumbles slightly and swallows at 'hands do touch'	Adjusts her posture before reading. Text flat on table, elbows either side with hands clasped between text and chest—resembles gesture of modesty	Mostly concentrating on reading	Concentrated look whilst reading, eyes narrowed. After reading, presses lips together and nods three times slowly
D	Fluent, clear and rhythmic, but with little tonal variation	Text held just above table at ~60°	Head inclined down, placid expression and concentrated on reading	Concentrated look whilst reading, eyes narrowed. 'OK' after reading
E	Starts reasonably well, but reading gets choppier as she progresses. Is prompted with help of A. Appears to be in relatively early stage of learning English	Has both arms on table with hands cupped around text and follows words with right hand	Inclined down and very concentrated on reading. Little movement but for eyes following text and around mouth to form words	Teacher stands during reading and gives a concentrated look. After reading, she echoes last phrase 'Holy Palmers' kiss. OK'

asked to do her interpretation, she too displays some modesty, but nonetheless she agrees. She first thinks aloud about who could be the focus of her passion, her Romeo, and then she reads from a standing position, leaning over the text and into the middle of the table. There is intimacy in this proximity to the students that suits the rendering of this speech. After this, she changes tone, and issues reminders about annotating the text and urges them forward after this preparation to work on acting out the scene.

Corridor Drama

In the next phase of the lesson, groups move from their seats out into various spaces around and outside the classroom to work on dramatising the scenes. Another group of five students have moved just outside the door of the classroom and concentrate on the short section of the scene where Juliet and Romeo first meet. The masked ball is going on around them and the group practise a lengthier section of the scene that involves three other characters. The focus here is on two boys who are working on the section of dialogue in which 'love at first sight' is played out. Looking at how available space is used, the diagram below shows how the students arranged themselves.

This corridor, a rather awkward and public space, is their 'studio space' for the rehearsal. We can see how they have positioned themselves in relation to the space and to each other. This grouping maximises the potential of the space to signify 'stage' and 'banquet hall' as setting for the scene and, at the same time, arranges characters together in such a way as to map out and represent the sequence of social interaction between particular characters as the scene progresses. The excerpt begins with a conversation between Tybalt and Capulet, then moves its focus to Romeo and Juliet and their face-to-face meeting, and ends when Juliet's nurse joins the couple.

We can see how the boys playing Juliet and Romeo have positioned themselves near the wall of the corridor, their backs angled close to the wall, and that they are standing at an angle to each other, rather than facing the opposite wall. Their position allows them to see and be seen by a notional 'audience' who, if there was an audience, might be positioned looking onto the scene from the opposite wall of the corridor. This does show that an idea about staging is being realised here. However, if this were a real stage, and the audience were somewhere behind the line of the left-hand wall, then Romeo and Juliet would be playing their intimate scene upstage. In a theatre we might expect it to signal the electric intimacy of the meeting to be best represented if it were to be played downstage in close proximity to the audience. The upstage position is common in student drama and signifies the discomfort of public exposure that many of us feel when we are required to act in this way. The sense of discomfort is more acute in this age group, and is likely to be further exacerbated, alongside other factors, by the fact that they are two teenage boys playing out a love scene between a girl and a boy and that they are being filmed.

168   MULTIMODAL LITERACY

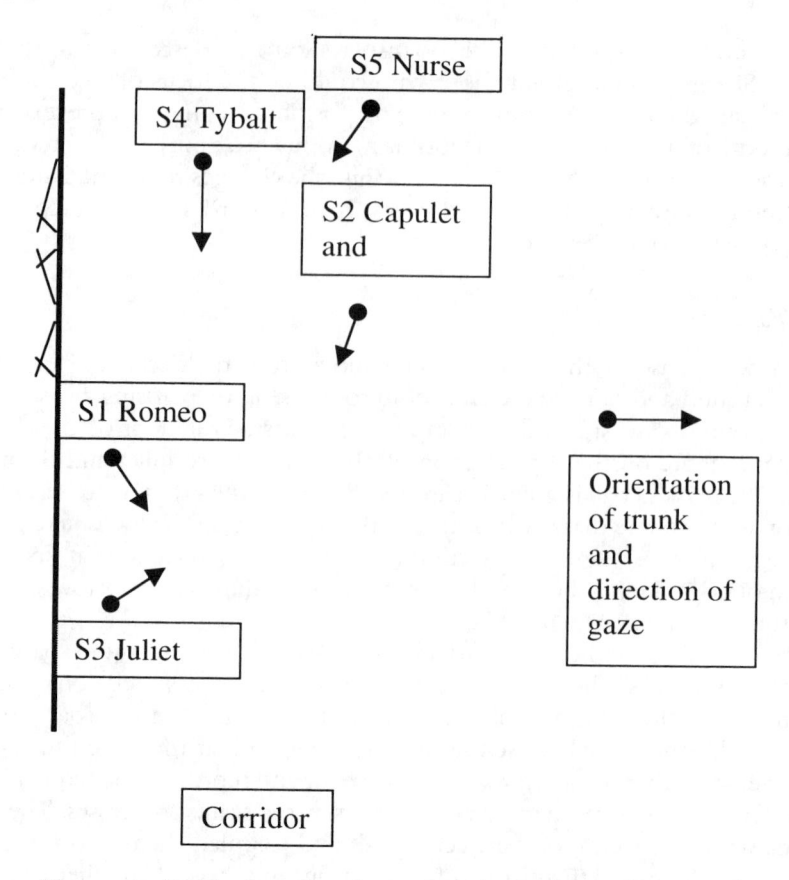

Figure 10.1. Positioning of students rehearsing in the corridor

Next, we can look more closely at the way that gesture, posture, face and voice work together in interaction between the dramatised reading and interplay with the teacher and other students. The boys' feet remain planted in the same position throughout the playing of the scene. The grip on the text and the relatively rigid posture does give some sense of the technical demands and difficulties of simultaneous reading and action, leaving aside the archaic forms of words used in Shakespeare. S1 playing Romeo is set in the posture, slightly bowed over his script for most of the playing, looking out towards S2 only when she intervenes with points of direction at the start of the one-minute sequence of dialogue.

> S1: If I perform [sic, should read 'profane'] with my unworthiest hand
>   This holy shrine/
> S2: /Hold your, your hand, his hand, his hand/
> S1: /the gentle sin in this.

Palmers' Kiss 169

>   My lips, two blushing pilgrims, ready stand
>   To smooth that rough touch/
> S2: /A kiss a kiss/
> S1: /with a tender kiss

Watching the videotape, it appears that S1's gaze flicks rapidly between reading the text and glancing at S2 at this stage and after these interventions his grip and gaze on the text intensifies until another intervention from S2 when she gestures that he should be kissing S1. He wavers even more towards the end as the teacher approaches closer. Juliet, S2, on the other hand, starts off reading fluently, as it is the scene that the class has been practising in the classroom, and looking toward 'his Romeo'.

The teacher has moved slowly and quietly up the corridor and arrives at the end of the sequence, around the time when Romeo is directed to kiss Juliet. She stands close to S2's shoulder watching the boys from that angle.

Again we find the teacher engaged in pantomimic gesture (in its heightened form), playing with her hands in the manner of a puppet show for the two boys who are struggling with reading the words, the meaning of the words and the concomitant sequence of action. There is a rhythmic and stylised quality to their

Figure 10.2. The boys playing Romeo and Juliet

Table 10.3

Speech	Action
S3: You kiss thy [sic] book.	
T: Right, I think, isn't the line. 'You kiss by the book'?	Teacher checks S2's script
S3: Yes.	
T: Yes, do you remember on the film?	Looks towards S1 and S3
I mean they're talking about pilgrims and palms, so, you don't need to worry about kiss . . . kissing.	Teacher stretches out arms, gazing at hands in thought
T: You know it's palm to palm isn't it, like this.	Teacher, hands palm facing palm, slightly apart, centre of chest with elbows out stylised gesture of prayer. Echoing, S2 holds one palm towards S1 and S3
T: So, it could be you don't even have to touch, it could be very close, it could just be very electric, that little space in between your hands	Teacher sweeps hands to and fro in front of chest, with palms facing out to give gesture of distance.
S2: See you're so childish.	Brings hands back palm to palm with 'electric' gap.
It's just a drama thing.	She gestures towards S1 and S3 with R hand, in mock exasperation.

reading noted in the previous stage of the lesson. And more, there is a move towards characterisation and an attempt at signifying intimacy through some tonal qualities of speech, relative posture and some putative moves towards intimate gesture. It is on the way towards drama. But their reading and dramatic action deteriorates, becomes less fluent and more jagged, as the playing of the scene progresses. The teacher's show of hands is a way to let them out of the discomfort of touching each other. She has the image of the gap between electrodes that the 'spark' of Romeo and Juliet's first flush of love might leap across. She suggests that this might be more powerful than passionate embrace, that in any case would not be appropriate for the characters under the gaze of Juliet's parents at their masked ball. Her reference to the film, which allows one to gaze at the faces and expressions of intimate action from close up, draws in another resource for the design of their scene, and is another way of helping them to be dramatic and justifies a stylised manoeuvre. Their love has to be represented in these circumstances as potential energy, massed and waiting to be released. This is clearly awkward stuff for the boys, and the comment from S2, a girl, 'See, it's only drama' underlines their embarrassment as the thing about live drama is that it is lived in the present modes of everyday communication. It is, at the same time, simultaneously really represented, and fictional.

Focussing on how a sense of audience affects action, the miscue in S3's reading of Juliet's last line in this sequence is indicative of how his reading of the speech fragments as he senses the teacher's approach. He and S1 have had their concentration on reading wobbled prior to this by S2's directorial interventions—mostly she is insisting that they should make some attempt at kissing each other. These interventions are perhaps entirely reasonable if they are to make a credible dramatic representation of this scene in which the two main protagonists of the play fall in love at first meeting. When they are able to concentrate on a sphere of attention between themselves—that is, that they can concentrate to the exclusion of spectators—then their acting has more flow. At each intervention the performers become more self-monitoring and self-conscious and this affects their ability to enter the role and more fully realise the drama of the text. Watching the video, it is arguable that one can discern another shift towards self-consciousness as the teacher creeps into the field of their peripheral vision. The teacher is clearly conscious of the effect she has on the performance by becoming part of the audience. Within seconds she asks them to 'remember the film' and then she does the 'puppetry' with her hands. The conjunction of these two moves shifts the attention off the boys as performers and positions them as audience. In so doing, she attempts to liberate two connected sets of resources—their familiarity, comfort and possibly expertise as viewers of film and their ability as people to understand the play with the hands as a way of distancing themselves from culturally and emotionally difficult (but not impossible) dramatic action.

Conclusion

I have followed here a progressive sequence of action, from the teacher establishing the purposes of the lesson, familiarisation with a section of text through utterance of lines and then towards more animated dramatic action. This is broadly typical of the pattern of a lesson that involves the dramatisation of a Shakespearean play text. The complexities of moving between (an authoritative and canonical) printed text, students' understandings of the text, drawing on their wider experience of other texts and life in cultural locations and mediated by the interventions of the teacher and fellow students, are not easy to describe or penetrate for the purposes of analysis. As the materials and forms of meaning-making action in everyday social life and drama show extensive overlap, the shifts between social and dramatic action are also difficult to identify. A multimodal semiotic perspective has been used here to look at and analyse the process of developing drama from a reading of printed Shakespearean text in order to mark out the (subtle) shifts between dramatic and social action. To help understand the nature and boundaries of these shifts, the concept of frame has been used; that is, how the action in the lesson has been framed. Although it has to be acknowledged that there is more work to do in this area, I have attempted to bring into view how modes of bodily communication are orchestrated and work together to realise dramatic meaning in a particular inner-city classroom. The attempt is governed by a desire not simply to read through classroom activity for meaning, treating physical activity as if it is transparent, but to focus on the physicalised aspects of the meaning-making process in social and cultural settings.

It is finally important for me to comment that I am aware of the potential afforded by a multimodal approach to explore important issues of subjectivity, dimensions of cultural background, ethnicity, gender and social class. These central issues have merely been touched on, but have by no means been fully explored or exhausted in my account and there remains the need for future work in this area.

References

Bateson, G. (1973) 'A Theory of Play and Fantasy', in: *Steps to an Ecology of Mind*. St. Albans, United Kingdom: Paladin.

Birdwhistell, R. (1975) *Introduction to Kinesics: An Annotation System for Analysis of Body Motion and Gesture*. Louisville, Ky.: University of Louisville.

Bourdieu, P. (1993) *The Field of Cultural Production*. Cambridge, UK: Polity Press.

Bourdieu, P. (1991) *Language and Symbolic Power*. Thompson, J. B. (Ed.) Raymond, G. and Adamson, M. (trans). Cambridge, United Kingdom: Polity Press.

Brecht, B. (1964) *Brecht on Theatre*. Willett, J. (Ed.). London, Eyre Methuen.

Franks, A. (1996) 'Drama Education, the Body and Representation (or, the Mystery of the Missing Bodies)' in *Research in Drama Education*, 1/1, pp. 105–120.

Franks, A. (1995) 'The Body as a Form of Representation' in *Social Semiotics*, 5/1, pp. 1–21.

Franks, A. and Jewitt, C. (2001) 'The Meaning of Action in Learning and Teaching', *British Educational Research Journal*, 27(2): 201-18.

Franks, A. and Jones, K. (1999) '"Lessons from Brecht: a Brechtian Approach to Drama, Texts and Education' with Ken Jones in *Research in Drama Education Vol. 4 No. 2 Autumn 1999*, pp. 181–200.

Goffman, E. (1974) *Frame Analysis*. Cambridge, Mass.: Harvard University Press.

Greimas, A. J. (1987) 'Towards a Semiotics of the Natural World' in: *On Meaning: Selected Writings in Semiotic Theory*. P. J. Perron & F. H. Collins (trans.). London: Pinter.

Kendon, A. (1990) *Conducting Interaction: Patterns of Behaviour in Focused Encounters*. Cambridge, United Kingdom: Cambridge University Press.

Kress, G.R. (2001) '"You've Just Got to Learn How to See": Curriculum Subjects, Young People and Schooled Engagement with the World' in *Linguistics and Education*, 11(4), Elsevier Science Inc.

Kress, G.R., Jewitt, C. Ogborn, J. and Tsatsarelis, C. (2001) *Multimodal Teaching and Learning: Rhetorics of the Science Classroom*. London: Cassell.

Kress, G.R. and van Leeuwen, T. (2001) *Multimodal Discourse: The Modes and Media of Contemporary Communication*. London: Arnold.

McNeill, D. (1979) *The Conceptual Basis of Language*. Hillsdale N.J.: Lawrence Erlbaum Associates.

Pavis, P. (1982) *Languages of the Stage*. New York, Performing Arts Journal Publications.

Gunther Kress   11

GENRES AND THE MULTIMODAL PRODUCTION OF 'SCIENTIFICNESS'

In this chapter I want to do two things: on the one hand I want to explore two questions in a semiotic theory of multimodality. The first is, How is knowledge reconfigured when 'it' is moved from one mode to another, the matter of transduction. The second question is, What can we learn about learning in the process of sign-making, and the reading of signs? On the other hand I have a more theoretical issue in mind, which is this, We have taken many of our terms from linguistic descriptions and theories of language. Do these terms still work when we want to apply them to other modes? Take the category of genre, for instance. Much of the work done over the last 20 or 30 years assumes that genres are linguistic phenomena. Yes, film, or video and television, have been described by using this term, and of course these consist of much more than 'just' language. And literary texts have been described in genre-terms for a very long time. But in the broad area of literacy the work that underpins the interest in genre treats it as a purely linguistic phenomenon.

I'll defer the question about genre for the moment, and concentrate on the first two issues. The 'knowledge' that is at issue is at one level fairly straightforward: What is an onion cell like, as an instance of the more general knowledge: what is a plant cell like? But the knowledge that is at issue is also much broader still: What is it to be and act scientifically? How do I demonstrate scientificness? The examples that I will use to discuss these questions draws on research on the multimodal character of science teaching in a secondary school in England (Kress et al., 2001); the young people—all girls—are 11 years old; that is, in the English system they are in Year 7. 'Knowledge' arises in a social context; it is a social category. Here the social context is school, itself part of wider social institutions—'education' and 'science'. 'Scientificness' is a social construct, a meaning that arises in and signals belonging to a community and its practices. It is at this point that we can use the term 'meaning' to indicate the semiotic aspect of social practices: to be able to act in certain ways is to be able to mean certain things.

So the question is, What is it that we want to mean, and what modes (and genres) are best for realising that meaning? I wish to make this concrete by looking at two texts. The texts are entirely usual. They come from a science classroom in a secondary school in inner-city London. The series of lessons in which the texts were produced had as its topic 'plant-cells'. Four children—all girls—had worked together in a group around a microscope, first preparing a slide with a piece of the epidermis of an onion, then looking at this slide through a microscope, and afterwards carrying out the task, given by the teacher, of 'doing a report'. Each had to 'record' the experiment: 'to draw what they had seen through the microscope'; and 'to write what they had done' in conducting the experiment. The teacher had given them just two specific instructions: 'put your writing at the top of the page (the teacher was anxious that the drawing should not take up too much of the space on the page, so as to leave enough room for writing), and 'use only your lead pencil—do not use coloured pencils in your drawings' (to distinguish 'scientificness' [black and white drawing] from 'artisticness' [using colour pens] or from 'everyday realism').

Here I will look at two of the four texts produced.

The first example, Figure 11.1 has the drawing at the top of the page, and the written part of the text at the bottom. Image and writing are clearly separated on the page; each has its own, slightly differing, heading. At this point it becomes essential to introduce the notion of genre. The written text has the generic form of a 'recount'. That is, it is a temporally ordered/sequenced presentation of events, reported in sentences. The image part of the text has the form of a line drawing; it is not clear that there is a suitable generic label—such as diagram, or flowchart, for instance—available to name it.

I will first say something briefly about the written part of the text as a *recount*, then I will attempt to uncover the generic form of the visual part. After that I speculate on the generic form of the text as a whole. My question is, How is 'scientificness' produced multimodally? To answer it I need to use the category of 'genre'.

I treat Genre as that textual/social category which realises in text the social relations of the participants involved in the social interaction that gives rise to the text. The social relations realised in the recount are of three types: those of the relations of the actors, objects and events that are *reported in* the recount; those of the relations between the participants in the act of communication, which are *implied by* the recount. The third type concerns the social world that is *represented in* the recount. At that point the question is, 'How is (the institution of) science represented/constructed as a social activity? Here we are in large part in the realm of the discursive organisation of the activity, in the sense of Foucault's use of 'discourse'.

The relations 'in' the recount are of actors acting in events with and on objects, either singly "I collected all the equipment" or jointly "We then sorted the microscope out . . ." This is recounted 'realistically'; that is, it is presented in the text as being a recount of what actually happened, of the actual, significant events re-

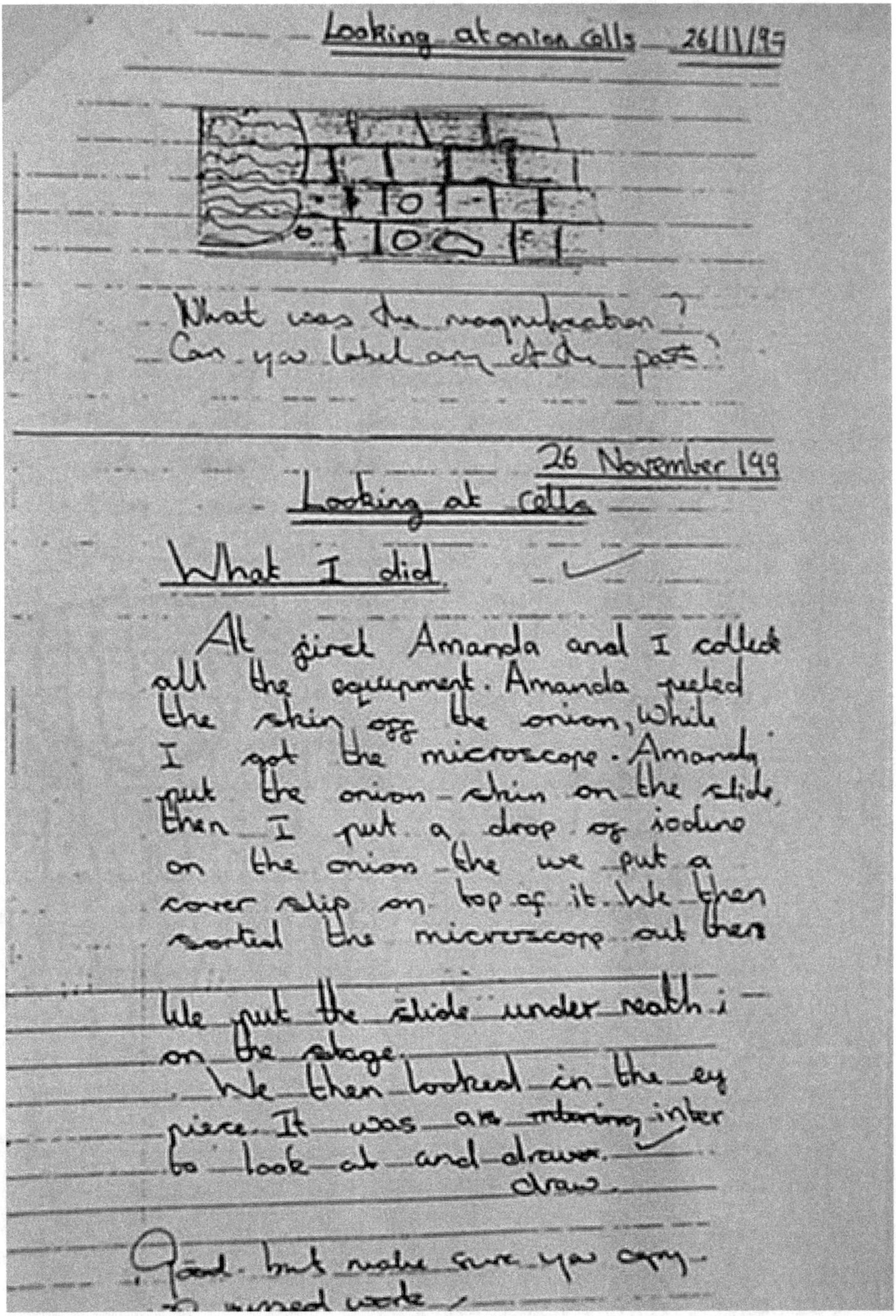

Looking at onion cells 26/11/99

[drawing of brick-like cells]

What was the magnification?
Can you label any of the parts?

26 November 199
Looking at cells

What I did ✓

At first Amanda and I collected all the equipment. Amanda peeled the skin off the onion, while I got the microscope. Amanda put the onion skin on the slide, then I put a drop of iodine on the onion, the we put a cover slip on top of it. We then sorted the microscope out then

We put the slide underneath on the stage.
We then looked in the eye piece. It was an interesting to look at and draw. draw.

Good, but make sure you copy missed work

Figure 11.1. Brickwall

counted in the temporal sequence in which they happened. There is a clear implication that no other (significant) events occurred. The recount is 'complete', there is closure: it is a completed, finished, rounded-off textual entity. The recount, as genre, makes an implicit claim about the relation of the events/practices recounted to other practices in the world, and of the relation of the domain of the practices to other domains. It is the claim of everyday realism, in the everyday world: implicitly, it claims 'this is, simply, how it was; these were the main participants, the main events and they occurred in this order'. It also claims, more specifically, that 'practices in science classroom are (like) practices in the everyday world'. (A *narrative*, by contrast, makes a different claim: 'that is how I have (re)constructed the world for you', and 'practices in the everyday world may be different to the way they are narrated here').

The social roles and relations established and implied by *the genre of recount as message* (that is, genre-oriented towards communication) are those of 'recounter'— I am someone who knows that which is being recounted—and 'recountee'—you are someone whom I regard as wishing to have the events recounted to you. If I am receiving the recount, the roles are those of being someone who is interested in having these events recounted to myself, in being the 'recountee', and in accepting you as the 'recounter'. The recount presents a world of action/event, temporally ordered and complete.

In asking about the generic form of the drawing, we bump up against the problem I mentioned: there are no genre-terms for describing what this drawing is or does, either in terms of the presentation of material—the content—or of its representation of the social relations between the 'participants' in the communicational event. What are these relations, as they are realised in the drawing, as they appear here? In answering this I will make use of the same terms for types of relations as I used just above. First, what is *shown* 'in' the drawing (analogous to what is *told* 'in' the recount) and by the drawing as a whole? The drawing shows a rectangular block with clearly distinct elements within it. The block is strongly framed along the top and the bottom, but is open at each end horizontally, suggesting that it is 'a part of', 'an extract from', 'a fragment of' a larger entity. This suggests that while the drawing is not *textually complete,* it is *conceptually complete:* were you to extend the drawing to the left or to the right, then any other part of the larger entity of which this is a fragment will also be like this fragment. The elements of which the drawing is composed are drawn as being broadly uniform in shape and size. One of the handouts used in the lead-up lessons had suggested to the students that in looking through the microscope, they would see something resembling 'bricks in a brick-wall', and, quite clearly, that metaphor—expressed in writing—has guided this student's 'seeing'. On the left-most edge there is a large 'irregularity'— the circular shape—and there are small bubble-like elements within the bricks (these are likely to be air-bubbles on the slide).

This is a structure of relatively uniform elements in regular arrangement: the blocks are arranged in even layers, arranged regularly. So while the recount *tells* of a world of *happenings,* of *actions*/*events,* what is *shown* here is a world of *objects as they are,* static, stable, regular elements in regular arrangement. While the world of the recount is complete in that *it represents all there is to recount,* the world of this *display* is complete in that *it represents all there is to know*—to show more would be to show more of the same. And while the world of the recount is set in time and is completed—it has happened—the world of this display is out of time—it just *is*—and it is complete in *being*.

The relation between the participants in the act of communication is an 'objective' one. The viewer is presented with this text-element 'front on'. It is objectively there, with maximal 'involvement' of the viewer; that is, the viewer is positioned as confronting this image straight on, at eye-level. The positioning is neither to the side—which would indicate lesser involvement—nor is the viewer below or above the element shown, something that would indicate difference in power. The entity is presented to the viewer in a maximally neutral manner: it is simply 'there', *objectively*. Instead of the relations of 'recounter' and 'recountee' of that which is 'recounted', we have the relation of 'displayer' and 'viewer' of that which is 'displayed'.

Speaking modally, we can say that in terms of a 'point of view' the *display* is maximally 'objective' and positions the viewer as fully 'involved'. This is realised through the spatial affordance of the image. The 'point of recounting' by contrast is realised through the temporal affordance of writing: from the present, a series of past events is recounted. The formal feature used is that of tense, past tense (from an implied present standpoint). This positions the recountee as somewhat distanced, not as fully involved. (Fuller involvement would be a report in the present tense: 'we go and collect the equipment; we place the slide...?') This contrasting assessment of kinds of involvement clearly realises a differing set of social relations in the act of communication. Generically speaking, the *recount* and the *display* are not only using different modes—writing and image—but they differ in the social relations of the participants in the process of communication.

We can, further, make comments on the third level, the relation between the world of practices represented here and that of the everyday world. The drawing is not a realist one: it is generalised away from everyday realism, both through the means of using the soft black pencil on the white page (rather than the use of colour, as in one of the other pieces of work) and the abstracting, generalising, diagrammatic form of representation. The former tells us that certain aspects of the everyday world, such as the colour of the viewed entity, are not relevant here. This is similarly true with other aspects, such as the actual, the 'real' boundaries of the object. The represented object does not have real boundaries; it is not (clearly) framed on either horizontal side: it is, after all, a theoretical object, not a 'natural', everyday one.

These are all pointers to the kind of social world into which we are invited. 'Diagram' is closer to serving as a genre-label, in that it suggests both a particular social purpose, and social relations, of those who use the diagram and those who make it. 'Diagram' also suggests a particular coding-orientation: not the realism of the everyday world, but the realism of the scientific-technological world.

Do we have, on this one page, a single textual entity? Clearly it is a single message entity, namely the in-class work demanded by the teacher. We might defer the question of whether we want to call this complex of image and writing a (single) text, or whether we invent another term for it; it is, however, a unified piece as a coherent, unified response to a specific communicational demand. The genre of the written part is clear; as indeed—even though we struggle with an appropriate label—is the genre of the image part. Equally clearly, each of the two genres realises different social relations, a different stance in the wider social world.

So what is the genre of this text-entity overall? And what consequences do these questions have not just for a view of writing, but for the actual uses of writing, and for likely changes to the uses, forms and values of technologies of multimodal text-making?

To answer the first question: we can say that there is a clear difference between the 'naturalism' (established within the realism of everyday life) of the written genre of recount, and the abstraction (within the world of scientific theorising) of the visual genre of the diagram-drawing. The first positions me as someone who hears an account of a completed, ordered, sequence of events. Although they are recounted as though they form part of my everyday, I am nevertheless somewhat distanced by the tense used—these are events that happened in a past relative to my present. The sense of everydayness is reinforced by the syntax of the writing, which is close to the clausal structures of everyday speech, as is its use of words—'we then *sorted* the microscope *out*', coming as it does from a quite casual register. Doing science, in this account, is like doing cooking, or doing the dishes. The genre of the recount would deal with them all equally. The second form, the visual genre, positions me as someone who is given a view of a fragment of an entity, but understands that the fragment 'stands for' the structure of the whole entity, in a form which is not part of the everyday world. I am shown a theoretical object, not one from my everyday. I am positioned, by the genre of the display in a different domain, out of time, in a world of regularity produced by the theory that I am applying.

The task of the science curriculum is, still, to induct young people into the practices that constitute 'doing science'. That practice is presented in two distinct ways here: 'doing science' in the *recount* presents me with a world of ordered actions/events that are like actions/events in the everyday world. 'Doing science' in the *display* is presented as being about another world: not of actions and events, but of objects existing in states of affairs with regularities, abstracted away from the everyday world. The drawing style does not belong to the everyday: neither in its abstraction away from colour, nor in its regularity of representation. The regularity is of course 'real', but it is the regularity of theory, and not that of the world. If the recount distances me somewhat from its world, this display involves me fully; though objectively and neutrally.

If this multimodal text-entity 'has' a genre, then it is, quite simply, a mixed genre, in which differently organised worlds appear differently: one a world of actions where the actors are like you and me, involved in events which are those of our everyday, the other a world without actors, a world of things as they are, things that do not belong to the world of the everyday. If one is the world of the everyday, then the other is the world of theory, abstraction. One draws me in by suggesting that I am like the actors in a world that is familiar to me. The other positions me as a neutral observer of an objectively present world, but an observer with a special status and a special lens. The contradiction inherent in this position is made relatively 'invisible' and therefore unproblematic, because the two distinct positions are realised in fundamentally different modes, with absolutely distinct logics. If that was not so, if both positions were realised in the one mode, then this young woman might have found it much more difficult to have both positions with their contradiction.

This is the meaning of this genre; these are the social relations and the social roles of the participants projected by the combined genre. If this mixed genre contains unreconciled contradictions, seen from the point of view of school science, then so be it. Of course, this is a genre produced by a non-expert. The fact that she mixes the social relations of the world of the everyday with social relations of the world of scientific work may be an effect of the teaching that she has had, or it may be her response to what she has taken from that teaching. She is able to form her own generic response; to see science in her way and to represent it in her way: on the one hand as actions that are like those of the everyday, but in relation to a world that is very differently constituted. The genre overall seems to position her somewhere between the everyday and the special world of technical/theoretical endeavour. We might say that epistemologically the mixed genre says: the world of science is one where you look at things that do not belong to the everyday world in ways that are entirely like those in the everyday.

If we allow ourselves a moment to reflect on the issue of learning, a large number of questions arise. Learning as sign-making asks about the interest of the sign-maker, and that leads immediately to the question of what the interest of this young woman was. Assume that there was no such contradiction in the presentation of all the materials from her teacher—something we cannot of course really assume—what guided the processes of her selection from all that material? Which modes had she been most attentive to, writing or image? We know that some scientific knowledge is presented in images as canonical form—magnetic fields, springs, wave-forms, etc. This young woman's drawing approaches 'canonicity', whereas her writing probably does not. Was she therefore much more focussed on image representation than on writing? In both writing and image she presents 'the truth': the truth of what happened; and the truth of what is. The problem—from the point of view of science—is that these are truths in different social domains.

Mixed genres are commonplace; though the kind of disjunction presented here would be a severe problem if both texts were written texts, or if this was the text of an expert. Because the two generic positions are realised in different modes, the disjunction is not readily apparent, or does not become a problem: it does not appear as a contradiction. In fact it may well be a very good representation of the social relations as they exist in the science teaching that she is experiencing. Is it a problem that we do not have labels for these 'mixes', or indeed do not have labels for many kinds of generic organisation? This is not, I think, the main issue at all; if we find that we need labels, we will make them up. What is important is to recognise that texts realise, among other things, the kinds of social relations pointed to here, and do so in complex ways, which themselves realise the affective and social positions of their makers.

In this text we see design at work. This young woman has made a number of design decisions in her multimodal representation: a decision about layout (in the decision where to place which element); a decision about generic (epistemological) form (everyday or scientific) for each of the two elements; a decision about which mode to use for the realisation of the knowledge represented here, and of each of the distinct epistemological positions; and no doubt others.

As far as labels for generic mixes is concerned, my analysis of the next example may show that this may not be a hugely useful aim.

Several differences are apparent immediately. The 'diagram' (the teacher's written comment: 'Diagram needs to be much larger') is below the written text, as indeed the teacher had asked. There is a clear separation/division between the written part and the visual; they are separated by a heading, 'what we saw'. Yet the image partly protrudes into that heading, and the heading is tightly linked to the written text, insisting, as it were, on a connectedness, even a unity, of writing and image. Where in the first example they had been clearly separate, here there is a real physical and visual integration of both.

The genre of the written text is that of *procedure:* a sequence of distinct (in this case numbered) steps, which, when followed, will lead to the achievement of the intended aim. The social relations expressed 'in' the procedure differ from those in the recount. The recount told someone what had happened, and an implicit assumption might have been that there might be those who would wish to follow those actions. In the procedure the social relations are entirely different: there are those with the power/authority to order actions to be taken, and those who are assumed to carry out those actions. This is very different to the recount. It is no longer the friendly, informal *telling of what happened* so that you might do the same; this is *being told what to do*. The claim made implicitly by the user of the genre of procedure is one of relations of power, of actions commanded to be done and of intended outcomes. This is not a realist genre in the manner of the recount: it is not about real events that happened, nor a *report* of real events/actions of actual people, of events that are happening or have happened. It is a set of commands (in the syntactic form of imperatives) for actions that are to happen.

As in the first example, the written text part is generically complete. Its relation to the world of the everyday is different; it is not the world of everyday happenings. This is a world in which power exists, and those with power can insist on actions being taken in a specific way, and in a certain sequence. Whereas in the recount sequence has the function of saying in what order things happened—though they might have happened in a different order, here sequence is fixed. It is a world in which everything is controlled ahead of its happening. These are social relations

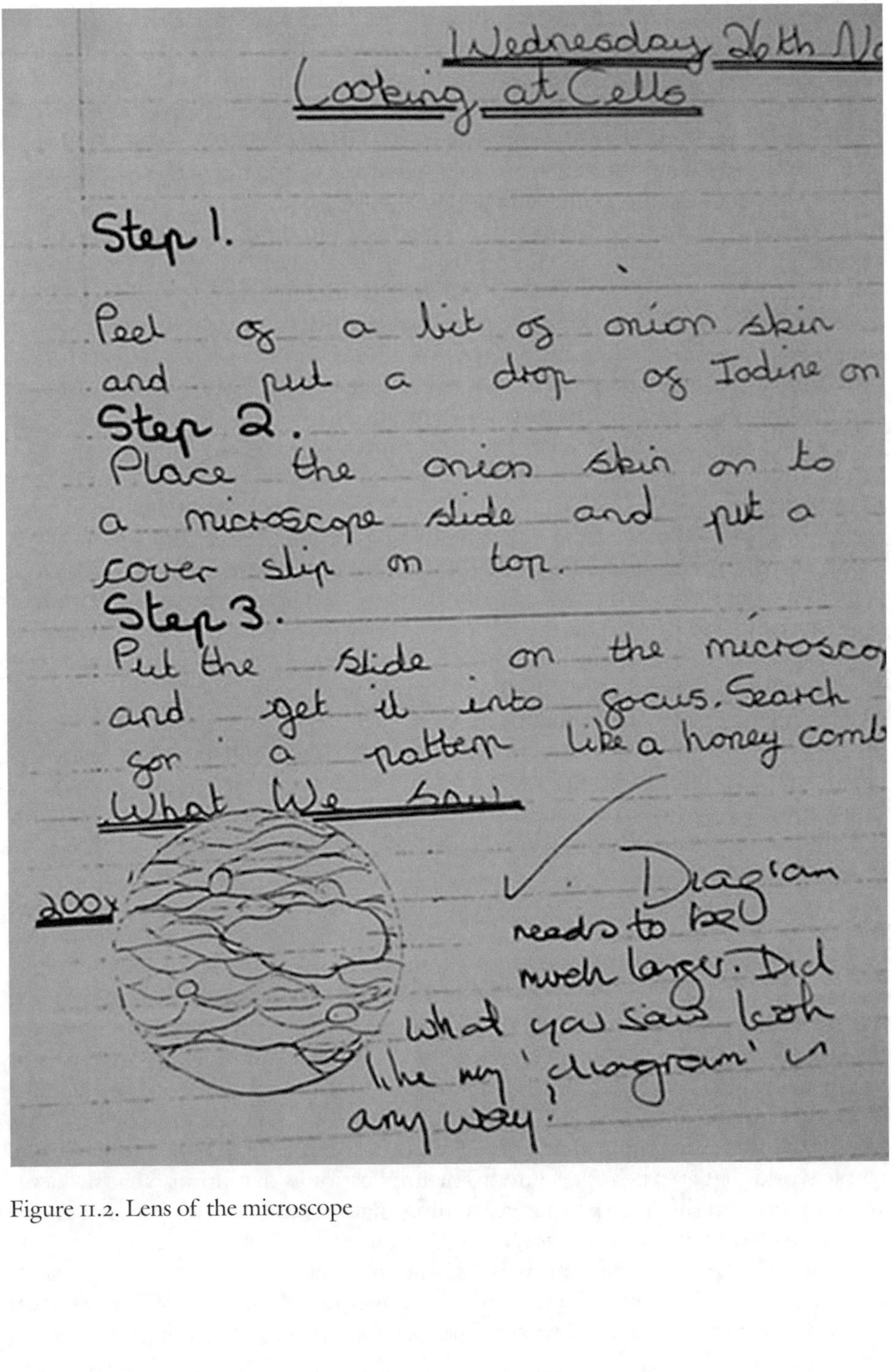

Wednesday 26th N[o]

Looking at Cells

Step 1.

Peel of a bit of onion skin and put a drop of Iodine on

Step 2.

Place the onion skin on to a microscope slide and put a cover slip on top.

Step 3.

Put the slide on the microsco[pe] and get it into focus. Search for a pattern like a honey comb

What We Saw

200x

✓ Diagram needs to be much larger. Did what you saw look like my 'diagram' in any way?

Figure 11.2. Lens of the microscope

of a very different kind. In the recount we could be sure that all the *significant* events were there, even though there might also have been others. For instance, in the recount we are told that 'it was interesting to look at and draw'. In the procedure we have only those (potential) actions (as commands) that are essential to the carrying out of a task which already exists as a pre-structured schema. If it mattered that the drawing should be interesting to look at and draw, then these would become imperatives, integrated appropriately in the sequence.

In terms of communicational roles, there is a big difference: the written text overall is a set of instructions, and the individual segments are commands to carry out the instructions in the sequence and as they are indicated. Consequently, the roles here are of a different kind: to act in a world in accord with the commands of some other who has power, with clear procedures and in accordance with those procedures. The reader is not in the world of their everyday. My role is to carry out commands issued by some (institutional) authority.

The relation between the world of this written text and the everyday world is one of difference. In this world I have less power than others, or that I might have in my everyday world. The manner in which I am drawn into the text is by command, by means of power, and not as before, by the pleasure or interest of the recount. Involvement differs from that of the recount: here I am positioned as someone who is expected to act. The world projected here is the world of precise procedures which those who are a part of this world must follow. It is not the everyday world of these students: there is no (implicit) claim here that the world of scientific practices is like the world of their everyday practices.

The drawing differs from that in the first example. One clue is provided in the instructions: 'Search for pattern like a honeycomb'. In his talk the teacher had provided the metaphor, among others, of a honeycomb: 'it might look like a honeycomb'. In the case of both texts a metaphor provided in language—in writing in the one instance ('what you will see will be like bricks in a brickwall')—and in talk in the other has been transducted by the pupils into visual form.

Here I will follow the same steps that I took in analysing both the written and the visual elements of the first example. The drawing shows a strongly delineated circle, with elements of different kinds contained in it. What is represented 'in' the image, and what is represented by the image overall, as a whole? Like her fellow students, this young woman saw air bubbles, larger and smaller ones. However, the cell entities that she saw are far less regular in shape, and their arrangement is not in any way as orderly as in the 'brickwall' example. Regularity of the elements or of their arrangements is not a feature of this image. The drawing differs from that in the first example in that what it *shows* is complete: here we are *shown* the whole world that is to be represented. The implication is that this is what she actually saw through the microscope: everything that was there to see is there, as she saw it. It is *textually* as well as *conceptually* complete.

In terms of point of view, this is like the first example: it is presented objectively, neutrally; front on, with the full involvement of the viewer. What is shown is an objective view of the real world. The form of realism, the coding-orientation is that of the everyday. Hence involvement suggested by the drawing differs from that of the writing.

In the drawing in the first example, scientificness lay in abstraction away from that which appeared in view in the microscope, abstraction guided by theory, through generalisation. There was no representation of the lens of the microscope, and in fact no real pretence that the drawing represented what the physical 'eye' had seen; what was represented what had been seen by the 'eye of theory'. Here, by contrast, scientificness lies in the precision of representing that which is there in view, the world that the human eye can see, in its messiness. In the first example, truth is the truth of abstraction, the truth of theory; here truth is the truth of actuality, of that which is there, the truth of the empirically real world. We are shown not only what she saw, but the means by which she saw what she saw. Hence we see the eyepiece through which the young woman looked: we see everything that she saw. For her, being scientific resides in the accuracy of observation and representation.

Compared to the first example, the relation of the written text and the image is inverted. There the written text was broadly realistic and the visual broadly non-realistic, theoretical. Here the written text is hypothetical; not an account of events as they happened, but of a schema for action in the world of science, which might lead to a set of actions in that world. The visual part, by contrast, is realistic. Jointly, the two parts of the text seem to suggest that the meaning of 'scientificness' might be that the world of science is defined by schemata for action which organise and underlie action; and that the essential task of science is to achieve an accurate account of the empirically real, aided by these schemata for actions.

If we contrast the two examples, they are an inversion of each other: in the first, the written part of the text is realist; in the second it is schematic/hypothetical; in the first text, the visual part is theoretical/abstract, while in the second it is empirical/realist. Scientificness is carried in distinctively different ways in the two cases. What unites them both is a concern for truth through accuracy: in the first case the concern for accuracy of what happened matched with accuracy of depiction of what exists in theory; in the second case, accuracy about hypothetical actions, matched with accuracy in the depiction of the empirical world. Underlying both are design decisions of great precision and subtlety—in choice of mode for contents, for (local) epistemology, and for the combination of the message complex.

What are the roles of the two modes of writing and image in these multimodal ensembles? Even though the written parts of the two ensembles are *generically* different from each other, they do share a significantly common feature: both are focussed on action and event, even if differently so; both of the visual elements by contrast are focussed on 'what is', the visual display of the world that is in focus. In each of the two texts as a whole, the component parts are incomplete without either the written and visual parts together. Each mode, writing and image, does distinctly different and specific things. The specificity is the same at one level: the affordance of the logic of time governs writing, and the affordance of the logic of space governs the image. Within that, there is the possibility of generic variation.

And the generic variation of the ensembles in each case produces an overall stance towards the notion of scientificness. That is the learning that has been achieved by each young woman for herself.

Genre as Design: Text and the New Media of Communication and Information

The two texts here are examples of *ensembles of modes,* brought together to realise particular meanings. The fact that the two school-texts are made by unpractised designers is in one way an advantage in that it shows how an untutored maker of such ensembles uses the affordances of the modes for their ends. The purpose of the science curriculum is, in one important way, to induct young people into the idea of scientificness. Here we see the response of two students to this demand, expressed through what we can see as design decisions in the realisation of that meaning. They are faced with the question, 'What is it to act or be scientific?' and each gives a distinct answer, which is expressed through choice of modes, and choice of genres, much more than through the issue of what aspects of curriculum content to represent. Both students understand the affordances of writing and of image: best of all, writing does the job of representing action and event — though of course, the teacher's demands, and previously encountered models will have given them resources in that respect; and image is best at showing the world objects and their relations, the world as it *is*. The teacher's inexplicit or 'open' framing of the task leaves much of the design decision to the students: how to interpret the relatively open request 'write what you did' in generically specific terms, and to do the same for the request 'draw what you saw'.

The first of the two examples shows a decision to go for realism in the written genre: to be truthful to science means that I am expected to report things as they were. I have to stay true to the empirically real. But this student also realised that science is about constructing general accounts of what this aspect of the world is (like), and she does that in her drawing: the truth of this world lies in this abstraction, which generalises away from the messiness of the empirical to a general truth. The truth of actions is reached via the mode of writing; and the truth of how the world looks, is reached via the mode of image.

For the second student there is a similar question, though she answers it differently: the truth of science lies in the generality of the procedures, in the generality of the practices, which must be the same each time they are performed, and not open to the chance of contingent event. This truth is reached via the mode of writing. The truth of what the world is like is reached via the mode of image, and the precise recording of what there actually is in that world, without concession to anything but strict observation.

These are epistemological decisions, but they are realised through design decisions focussed on the use of modes, the truth they harbour, the use of genres and the truths that they contain. On the face of it, these decisions have nothing to do with the existence of the new information and communication media. In reality they absolutely do: the manner in which these young people encounter school science owes much to the revolution in representation which has already in their world altered the status, the function, the uses, and the forms of writing. The 'books' that they use are transformed already by the joint effects of the emergence into central representational use of the mode of image, and the effect on the page of the organisations of the screens of the new media. The fact that there is now a design decision to be made, and that decisions about genre are now relatively open, is both a direct effect of the new media via their effect on the look of the page; and also an indirect effect of the new media in that teachers as much as designers of textbooks know that the young are attuned to a differently configured communicational world.

In that new communicational world there are now choices about how what is to be represented should be represented: in what mode, in what genre, in what ensembles of modes and genres on what occasions. These were not decisions open to students (or teachers or textbook makers) some 20 years earlier. Of course, with all this go questions not only of the potentials of the resources, but also of the new possibilities of arrangements, the new grammars of multimodal texts. These new grammars, barely coming into conventionality at the moment, and certainly very little understood, have effects in two ways at least. On the one hand, they order the arrangements of the elements in the ensembles; on the other hand, they design the functions that the different elements are to have in the ensembles. These are the kinds of decisions that I pointed to: writing used for the representation of event structures, and image used for the representations of displays of aspects of the world. This is 'functional specialisation' of the modes, and that in turn has the profoundest effects on the inner organisation and development of the modes.

Where before, up until 20, 30 years ago, writing carried all the communicational load of a message, and needed to have grammatical and syntactic structures that were equal to the complexities of that which had to be represented in that single mode, now there is a specialisation, which allows each of the modes to carry that part of the message for which it is best equipped. This brings with it the possibilities of great simplification of syntax for writing, for instance. It leads to some new questions, such as I have mentioned: What are the elements that come together in the multimodal ensembles? In the two text examples discussed above, there are image blocks and writing blocks, and it is these that form the first level of conjunction. At the first level of reading we note that the text is composed of 'blocks', and it is at that level not immediately relevant what modal realisation these elements have, whether they are image or writing. They are treated as elements of the same order. This is a bit like the analysis of a sentence where we might want to know what the main verb is, what its subject noun might be, and what complements—if any—there are. Reading at the next level down would then focus on the internal elements of these higher-level elements.

It is clear that the question of genre no longer rests with the written mode. If we wish to understand the social relations realised in these texts, we always need to look at the visual mode as well as the verbal.

Genre and Educational Strategies

The profound cultural diversity of all contemporary 'Western', post-industrial societies, as much as the new demands for education for participation in a fully globalised economy, has specific educational consequences. It means that the 'outcomes-based curriculum', or to use a better formulation, a curriculum that focusses on skills, disposition, essential processes and understanding of resources for representing and communicating, may be what all of 'us' in the anglophone and ever more globalising world will need to consider urgently. This will be a curriculum that focusses above all on giving students a full awareness of how to achieve their goals in the contexts of their social and personal lives, an ability for which I use the term 'design'. Much more goes with that change from content as stable knowledge to 'design'.

A new theory of text is essential to meet the demands of culturally plural societies in a globalising world. Theories of meaning will have to be rethought and remade. While there is a reality to genre, the conceptions that come from former social arrangements with their (relative) stabilities have left us with both the wrong theory and the wrong vocabulary. The wrong theory led us to believe that stability of language or of textform (as, indeed, of other social phenomena) is a feature of these phenomena in themselves, when it was—as it appears now—always a feature of these phenomena in a particular historical period, when relative social stability had obtained. So for instance, to speak of 'generic mixes' is in fact still to conceive of genre in the older fashion—of stable genres which can be and are mixed. A newer way of thinking might be that within a general awareness of the range of genres, of their shapes, their contexts, speakers and writers newly make the generic forms out of available resources. This is a much more 'generative' notion of genre: not one where you learn the shapes of existing kinds of texts alone in order to replicate them, but where you learn the generative rules of the constitution of generic form within the power structures of a society. And you learn what the shapes of these texts are out of those social conditions. That will permit (and account for) constant change, and makes the actions of the producer of the genre innovative and transformative. It encourages and normalises 'design' of text in response to the perceived needs of the maker of the text in a given environment. In such a theory all acts of representation are innovative; and creativity is the normal process of representation for all. The two texts that I have discussed are just such a response.

Reference

Kress, G.R., Jewitt, C., Ogborn, J., and Tsatsarelis, C. (2001) *Multimodal Teaching and Learning: The Rhetorics of the Science Classroom*. London: Continuum Press.

CONTRIBUTORS

Andrew Burn is Lecturer in Media Education in the Centre for the Study of Children, Youth and Media at the London University's Institute of Education. He has taught for over 20 years in comprehensive schools, and over the past four years has managed the Media Arts programme in the first government-designated specialist media school in the United Kingdom. His recent publications present research accounts of the use of digital video in schools.

Anton Franks was a teacher of drama and English in London schools and now teaches, researches and writes on drama and English in education at the Institute of Education and King's College, University of London. His recent publications include: 'Drama Education, the Body and Representation' in *Research in Drama Education* 1/1 and 'Drama, Desire and Schooling . . .' in *Changing English* 4/1.

Carey Jewitt is a researcher at the Institute of Education, University of London, and an editor of the journal Visual Communication. Her research interest is multimodal teaching and learning across the curriculum, and she is currently researching the multimodal production of school English and computer-mediated learning. Recent publications include *Multimodal Teaching and Learning: The Rhetorics of the Science Classroom* (2001) with Gunther Kress, Jon Ogborn and Charalampos Tsatsarelis, and *A Handbook of Visual Analysis* (2001), co-edited with Theo van Leeuwen.

Charmian Kenner is a researcher on bilingualism and family learning, with a particular interest in early literacy development. She has recently directed the ESRC-funded project 'Signs of Difference: How Children Learn to Write in Different Script Systems', based at the Institute of Education, University of London; and is a research fellow in the Department of Educational Studies, Goldsmiths College, University of London. Her publications include *Home Pages: Literacy Links for Bilingual Children* (2000).

Gunther Kress is professor of education and English at the Institute of Education, University of London. He has a specific interest in the interrelations in contemporary texts of different modes of communication, writing, image, speech, music—and their effects on forms of learning and knowing. His recent publications include: *Reading Images: The Grammar of Graphic Design* (1996); *Before Writing: Rethinking the Paths to Literacy* (1997); *Early Spelling: Between Convention and Creativity* (2001); *Multimodal Teaching and Learning: The Rhetorics of the Science Classroom* (2001); *Multimodal Discourse: The Modes and Media of Contemporary Communication* (2001); and *Literacy in the New Media Age* (2003).

Lesley Lancaster is an English co-ordinator at the Institute of Education, Manchester Metropolitan University. Her Ph.D. thesis, entitled, *Exploring the Need to Mean,* presents a multimodal analysis of a young child's use of semiotic resources in the mediation of symbolic meanings. She has published several articles using a multimodal perspective, most recently, 'Staring at the Page: The Functions of Gaze in a Young Child's Interpretation of Symbolic Forms' (2001) *Journal of Early Childhood Literacy* 1 (2) and 'Moving into Literacy: How it All Begins (2002), in N. Hall., J. Larson. and J. Marsh (eds.) *Handbook of Research in Early Childhood Literacy*.

Diane Mavers, a former primary school teacher and senior lecturer in primary education, is currently working as a researcher at the Institute of Education, Manchester Metropolitan University. She has worked on several evaluation projects relating to ICT and learning. Her research interests include multimodal communication, social semiotics, learning with new technologies, early years and primary education, and working with child researchers.

Gemma Moss is based in the Education Policy Research Unit, School of Educational Foundations and Policy Studies, Institute of Education, University of London. She is currently researching literacy policy in the United Kingdom. Her other interests include gender and literacy, the formation of the English curriculum, and the relationship between home and school literacy practices.

Kate Pahl works as a teaching fellow at the University of Sheffield. Her research interests include new literacy studies, multimodality, boys' literacies, and linguistic ethnography. Recent publications include *Transformations: Children's Meaning Making in a Nursery* (1999), and several articles, including, 'Texts as Artefacts Crossing Sites: Map Making at Home and at School' in *Reading: Literacy and Language,* pp. 120–125, Vol. 35. No. 3, November 2001. She is completing a Ph.D. thesis at King's College, London, entitled 'Ephemera, Mess and Miscellaneous Piles: Texts and Practices in Families'.

David Parker is research officer in the education projects department of the British Film Institute (bfi). His previous work includes a moving image and literacy research project with the BFI and King's College London. His recent publications address the use of the moving image and new technologies in education.

Pippa Stein is a senior lecturer in the School of Literature and Language Studies at the University of the Witwatersrand, Johannesburg, South Africa. Her research interests are in the field of literacy studies, multimodality and pedagogy, and social semiotics. Her recent publications include articles in *Multiliteracies: Literacy Learning and the Design of Social Futures* (Routledge), *Perspectives on Language and Literacy: Beyond the Here and Now* (Harvard Educational Review Reprint Series), and Kluwer Handbook on English *Language Teaching* (Kluwer Academic Publishers).

INDEX

action, 164, 170
  dramatic, 160–71
Adamson, R., 54
affect, affective, 12
affordance, 13–17, 20, 32, 39, 50–53, 71, 78, 79, 85, 139, 140, 147, 151, 183–84
  logic of space and image, 183
  logic of time and writing, 183
  modal, 32, 39, 52, 71, 78–79, 139–40, 183–84
  multimodal, 50, 53, 78, 79
  semiotic, 14
  of 'text-stuff', 85
agency, 9, 10, 41, 49
Al-Khatib, H., 106
alphabet, 93
  in Arabic, 93
  letter in, 93–94
Anansi and the Firefly, 56
Ancient Rome, 81
analogy, 11, 27
analysis, 159
  global, 159
  and notation, 159
Andrews, D., 137
animation, 6, 71
  multimodal production of, 6
anticipation of modes, 63
apt, aptness, 10, 20
  of signifier, 10
Arabic Community School, Hounslow, 105

arbitrariness/arbitrary, 10
  and convention, 10
  fusion of signifier and signified, 10
  of signs, 10
articulation, 63
  as anticipation, complementation, contradiction
  of modes, 63
  reiteration, 63
Attar, D., 82, 86
audience, 159

Bakhtin, M., 142
Barker, M., 76
Barthes, R., 31
Barton, D., 76
Bateson, G., 158
Baynham, M., 76
Berkeley Primary School, 105
Bernstein, B., 143, 150
Berthoz, A., 113
biliterate, 97, 105
Birdwhistell, R., 158
bodily/body, 114–21, 155–59
  communicative action, 158–59, 171
  enactment of text, 155
  and meaning-making, 156
  modes, 114–21
  signs of, 159
  socially organized, 156
Bordwell, D., 64

book, 16
  history of, 16
'bounce,' 6, 34, 41, 42, 44, 46, 52
boundary, 63, 67
Bourdieu, P., 110, 150, 151, 160
Brecht, B., 159
Brenner, J., 137
British Film Institute, 72
Burke, C.L., 89
Burn, A., 3, 5, 6, 62, 187
Buzan, T., 22

Cain, C., 143, 149, 151, 152
Cambridge Film Consortium, 72
Carter, R., 115
Chinese character(s), 92, 96–98, 100
Christensen, P., 20
cinematic, 59
closure, 66
cognitive, 12
Cole, M., 109
communication, 11–14, 17
  purposes and representation, 27
communication technologies, 4, 16
competence, 17
complementation of modes, 63
concept maps, 12
conjunction, 63, 67
contradiction of modes, 63
convention, 10
Cope, B., 89
creativity, 123–25, 132, 13–15, 186
criterial attributes, focus, 24, 26, 31
critique, 17
Cummings, J., 137
culture, 2, 11, 14, 35
  and materiality, 14
  and tools, 35
  and valuation, 15

Damasio, A., 109, 113
Dell, E., 125
design, 6, 9, 17, 34–41, 50, 52, 54, 56, 60–63, 70–73, 78–79, 80–81, 84, 105, 180, 183, 184–86
  of animated film, 70, 71
  choices, 54, 66, 71, 180
  decisions, 180, 183–85

and learning, 17, 183
logics, 80, 81
multimodal, 17, 36, 50, 52, 78
and moving image, 56
page, 80
principles of, 79
process, 34
spatial visual, 71
task, 79
temporal, 65
text-led, 79
visual, 39, 40, 60, 63
as work, 180
worlds, 80
diachronic axis, 64
directionality, 2, 32, 91–92, 96–98, 101, 103
  macro, 97
  micro, 98
  of line, 97
  of page, 95–96, 97
  of 'strokes,' 97
  textual, 98, 101
  vertical, 101
discourse(s), 6, 56, 58, 174
  marker, 115
  time, 66
display, 15, 177–78
  genre of, 177–78
distribution, 56
Dombey, H., 76
Dorling and Kindersley, 81–82, 84
drama, 157–85
  'corridor,' 167–68
  meaning-making, 157
dramatisation, 155, 160, 163
  as bodily enactment, 155
  of speech and action, 160, 163
drawing, 38
  affordances of, 38
Duncombe Primary School, 105
duration, 60, 65–66
  ellipsis, 65
  pause, 66
  scene, 66, 67
  stretch, 66
  summary, 65, 66
Dyson, A.H., 89

editing, 61
Eisenstein, S., 59, 63
ensembles of modes, 184
epistemology, 178, 180, 184
   and genre, 178, 180
   and mode, 178, 180, 184
ethnography, -ies, 7, 73, 75–78, 112, 141, 142, 147, 148
   analysis, 141
   and multimodality, 7, 73
   of reading, 76, 78
extra-linguistic, 2
   phenomena, 2
Eveline Lowe Primary School, 106
Eyewitness Guides, 81

face, 166
facilities (of media), 16
fertility doll, 123, 125
film/filmic, 6, 59, 60, 64
   animated, 6
   pre, 60
   pro, 60
Fisher, A., 32
'fixing,' 123, 132, 135–36
frame/framing, 16, 32, 116, 158, 171
Franks, A., 2, 5, 8, 9, 158, 159, 187
function(s), 64
   ideational, 64
   interpersonal, 64
   textual, 64
functional load, 15
functional specialization, 15, 20, 185

game(s), 37, 40
   narrative, 40
Gardner, H., 118
gaze, 112–18, 120, 169
   interpersonal function of, 115
   in performance, 169
Geertz, C., 112
genre, 9, 41, 173–80, 183, 185, 186
   change in, 41
   as design, 184
   of diagram, 177
   of *display*, 177
   epistemology of, 179
   labels, 180
   mixed, 179, 180
   and mode, 173, 176, 185
   as multimodal design, 9, 179
   of *procedure*, 180
   of *recount*, 174, 176–78
   variability of, 183–84
grammar(s), 2, 50, 185
   of editing, 59
   of film(ing), 59, 64
   kineikonic, 71
   multimodal texts, 185
   visual, 50
Greimas, A.J., 159
Goffman, E., 110, 158
Goodwyn, A., 32
Gowin, D.B., 21
graphisme, 89, 105
grouping, 67

habitus, 147, 151, 153
Halliday, M. A. K., 9
Hamilton, C., 132
Hamilton, M., 76
handwriting, 88–89
   kinaesthetic model of, 89
Harrison, C., 32
Harste, J.C., 89
Hawe, K., 32
Heap, J., 76
Heath, S., 76, 89, 109
hermeneutics, 112
Hilton, M., 149
Hodge, R.I.V., 9
Hofstadter, D., 134, 135
Holland, D., 143, 149, 151, 152
Hoyles, C., 54

ideational function, 64–68
identity, 8
   construction, 8
   and mode, 8
   and design, 80
illustration, 80
image, 2, 5, 16, 19, 38, 44, 52, 57, 59
   (spatial) affordances of, 38
   and discourse, 57
   moving, 57, 58, 59, 64
   moving, production, 58

image *(continued)*
  and provenance, 58
  relation of writing and, 2, 5
  site of, 16
  spatiality of, 2
information, 69
  distribution, 69
information technologies, 16
innovation, 132, 186
inscription, -al, 62
  technologies, 62
interest, 11, 12, 17, 131, 132, 150, 179
  aesthetic, 132
  affective, 131
  symbolic, 131
interpersonal function, 64, 68
interpretation, 159

James, A., 20
James, S., 81
Jewitt, C., 3, 5, 6, 15, 20, 30, 35, 53, 123, 158, 187
Johnson, M., 108, 109
Jones, K., 159

Kalantzis, M., 89
Kam, R., 106
Kendon, A., 115, 159
Kenner, C., 2, 5, 7, 20, 88, 89, 187
kineikonic mode, 59, 60–64, 70, 71
  mix, 70
  use of, 71
kinesics, 158
knowledge, 4, 173
  and (multi) mode, 4, 173
Krampen, M., 89
Kress, G.R., 2, 4, 5, 9, 12, 19, 20, 24, 25, 26, 27, 30, 32, 35, 56, 63, 64, 68, 78, 80, 81, 84, 89, 90, 106, 123, 137, 140, 145, 147, 152, 158, 173, 187

Lachicotte, Jr., 143, 149, 151, 152
Lambeth Chinese Community School, 105
Lancaster, L., 5, 7, 107, 118, 188
Lakoff, G., 108
language, 1
  as partial
lateralidad, 97

Latin American Saturday School, London, 105
layout, 81
Leibhammer, N., 125, 129
learning, 1, 2, 4, 5, 12, 35, 173, 179
  and computer applications, 35
  computer mediated, 35
  in formal sites, 3
  and multimode, 3, 4
  and semiotic form, 3
  and sign, 12
  as sign-making, 179
letters, 93, 94
Lewin, C., 33
Lewis, M., 77
linearity, 6, 32, 80–81, 85, 96, 105
  of writing, 6, 32, 80
links, 19, 28, 31, 32
  between images, 19
literacy, 4, 6, 7, 58, 85, 89, 111, 123
  curriculum
  events, 6, 7, 85, 109
  and multimodality, 6, 7
  practices, 4, 109, 111
  project, 123
  and text, 85
  visual, 32, 58
literacy event, 85, 89
logic(s), 15, 80, 81
  of image, 80, 183
  and mode of speech, 15
  (non-)linear, 80, 81
  and simultaneity
  of space/spatial, 15, 80, 81, 183
  of time, 15, 80, 81, 183
  of writing, 80, 183
Lovatt, A., 72
Lowe, S., 54

MacDonald, F., 83
Marsh, J., 20
material, materiality, 11, 14, 123, 125, 147
  affordance, 13, 15
  and culture, 14
  inherent qualities, 14
Mavers, D., 5, 20, 22, 25, 26, 188
Maybin, J., 76
McNeill, D., 158

meaning, 3, 173, 186
  differences in, 3
  facilities of, 4
  intention, 27
  of overall message
  and learning, 3
  mode and, 3, 173
  potential for, 13, 53
  theories of, 186
meaning making, 11, 13, 15, 19, 124, 140, 150, 155, 157
  in dramatization, 155, 157
  multimodal, 140, 150, 157
  outwardly, 19
  and text, 140
media, 3, 4
message, 4, 11, 12
  arrangements, 4
  and design, 4
metaphor, 11
Metz, C., 59, 71
Millard, E., 20
mind-maps, 2, 19, 20, 21, 22, 24, 32
Mitchell, J.C., 140
modality, 22, 66, 68
mode(s), 1, 2, 6, 13, 14, 34, 52, 54, 69, 78, 79, 110, 123, 135, 139, 140, 141, 150, 152, 179, 183, 184
  and affordance, 14–17, 20, 69, 78, 79, 183, 184
  arrangements of, 52, 54
  articulation of, 63
  bodily, 114–21
  and creativity, 135
  crossing, 139, 150
  ensembles of, 3, 69, 78–79, 114–21, 184
  and functional load, 15–16
  and functional specialization, 15
  grouping of, 63, 69
  and identity(-construction), 140, 152
  and information, 69
  and learning, 3
  logic of, 15, 179
  and meaning, 140
  partiality of, 3
  potentials of, 3
  reconfiguration, 53
  and representation, 3
  shifts across, 3, 150
  transitions across, 140, 150
montage, 59, 63
  vertical, 59
monomodal, 2
Morgan, W., 35
Moss. G., 3, 4, 5, 6, 7, 73, 76, 84, 85, 86, 188
motivated, motivation, 10
  of signs, 10
motricidad, 97, 105
movement, 45, 60, 61
  animated, 45
  design of, 61
  production of, 61
  variables in, 61
moving image, 56, 58, 59, 71
multimodal, 68, 70, 107, 112, 123, 134, 136, 139, 157, 158, 173, 185
  analysis, 107, 112
  description, 107
  grouping, 68
  meaning-making, 157
  pedagogies, 70, 123, 134, 136
  social semiotics, 155, 157, 158, 173
  texts, 140
  transcripts, 110
multimodality, 1, 4–9, 11, 54, 73, 78, 79, 88, 89, 105, 109, 123, 124, 136, 144, 156
  and communication, 2
  as emergent
  and ethnography, 73
  and learning, 1, 2, 4, 5, 11, 54
  and meaning making, 5, 156
  as methodology, 5
  and writing, 90

narrative, 123, 176
National Curriculum, 95, 161
  in English, 161
  and writing, 95
Nel, K., 125, 129, 137
Newfield, D., 123, 134, 137
Nelson, K., 112
Newnham Croft Primary School, 72
Noss, R., 36, 54
notation, 159
  of bodily communication, 159
Novak, J.D., 21

Oakhill, J., 76
Ogborn, J., 123
Olivantsvlei Primary School, 137
Omaya, R., 30
orchestration, 155, 171
  of action, 155
  of modes, 171

page, 4, 16, 32, 52, 80, 81, 85, 96, 101, 119, 185
  affordance of, 101
  and learning, 4
  and modal arrangement, 4
  move from, to screen, 52, 185
  space as linear, 96
  spatiality, 32, 80, 81
Pahl, K., 3, 5, 8, 139, 150, 188
Parkside Community College, 72
Parker, D., 3, 5, 6, 188
Pavis, P., 159
paragraph, 82, 83
Pearson, M., 25, 26
pedagogical arrangements, 161
pedagogy/-ies, 8, 58, 123, 136, 161
  monomodal, 71
  multimodal, 8, 58, 123, 136
'penhold,' 103, 104
performance, 160
  and text, 160
'Playground,' 34, 36, 41, 52, 53
  modal affordance of, 52, 53
Pokemon, 139, 140, 141
posture, 103, 104
  and writing, 103, 104
power, 10, 12
print, 90
  as multimodal, 90
  as complex semiotic system, 90
procedure, 180, 182
production, 56, 60, 61, 63
provenance, 15, 58
Purkey, M., 137

Raney, K., 58
reader(s), 7, 11, 13, 16, 17, 24, 76, 77, 85
  needs, 24
  non-fiction, 76
  and text, 77
reading, 7, 9, 12, 13, 73, 76, 77, 78, 85, 159

  as assessment, 12
  ethnographies of, 74, 78
  as hypothesis, 13
  models of, 77
  non-fiction, 73, 74
  'off,' 159
  as sign-making, 13
  as situated social practice, 13, 73
  successful, 76
reading path(s), 4, 6, 81, 83, 85
recount, 174, 176, 177, 178
Reed, M., 62
reiteration of modes, 63
remaking, 132
  as innovative, 132
  as transformative, 132
representation, 1, 11–17, 25, 46, 125, 186
  as creative, 186
  (-al) commitment, 38
  culturally mediated subjective, 25
  and multimodality, 15, 46
  partiality of, 11
  practices of, 125
representational practices, 32
representational resources, 1, 2, 14, 15, 90, 125, 142, 147
  regularities of, 1, 2
resources, 10, 14, 15, 35, 45, 107, 113, 132, 151
  and agency, 10
  bodily, 107
  change of, 10, 13
  and convention, 14
  and creativity, 132
  and materiality, 14
  mediational, 113
  physical, 107
  of screen, 35
  use of, 10
Restorick, J., 20, 22
Richard Atkins Primary School, 106
rhetorical frame, 160
Rogoff, B., 112
Russell, D., 35
rhythm, 69, 70
  spatial, 70

salience, 11
Saljo, R., 35

Sam, 154
Sassoon, R., 89, 95, 105
screen, 4, 16, 34, 35, 38, 52, 53, 185
  design of, 38
  and learning, 4
  and modal arrangements, 4
  move from page to, 52, 185
  organization of, 16
Scribner, S., 109
Scrimshaw, P., 33
script, 7
  learning of, 7, 88
semiosis, 13, 150
  of drawing, 19
  process of, 13
semiotic(s), 1, 9, 12, 36, 56, 68, 71, 109, 110, 111, 112, 114, 117, 118, 123, 125, 132, 133, 134, 135, 136
  activity, 118
  chain, 8, 125, 132, 133, 134, 135, 136
  combinatory, resources, 158
  event, 109, 110, 111, 112
  framework, 71
  and multimodality, 1, 9, 36
  objects, 112, 114, 117, 123
  potential, 36
  process, 12
  production, 56
  strata, 56
  resources, 59, 68, 71, 110
semiotic theory, 9, 10, 71, 173
  of multimodality, 9, 173
  traditional, 10
sequence, 15
  temporal, 15
setting, 158
sign(s), 10–13, 140
  inwardly made, 13
  and learning, 12
  outwardly made, 13
  and reading, 11
Shakespeare, 155–83
Sheil, T., 72
signified, 10–13, 19
signifier, 10–13, 19, 64
  material, 64
signifier stuff, 11, 12
sign-maker, 11, 12, 15

sign-making, 10, 12, 13, 15, 27
  as always new, 10
  internal, 67–68
  reading as, 13
Simon, O., 80
social power, 10
social semiotics, 9, 10, 17, 125, 156, 158–72, 173
  analysis, 125, 156
  multimodal, 156–72, 173
Skinner, D., 143, 149, 151, 152
Somekh, B., 20, 22, 25, 26, 32
spatial, 31, 64, 81
  arrangement, 31
  meaning, 64
  relationships, 81
spatiality, 2, 6, 19, 91, 92
  of image, 2, 6, 19
spectator, 68
  position, 68
speech, 2, 163, 164, 167, 170
Spraggon, L., 72
Stein, P., 3, 5, 8, 123, 188
Street, B., 32, 76, 109
stroke(s), 92, 96, 99, 100
  sequence, 96

technologies, 71
  digital, 71
temporal, 64
  meaning, 64
  shifts, 67, 70
temporality, 65, 66
text(s), 5, 7, 8, 9, 17, 46, 64, 68, 71, 74, 75, 77, 78, 79, 80, 83, 85, 136, 141, 149, 153, 155, 160, 178, 186
  constructing, 69
  and (multimodal) design, 78, 79, 85
  games as, 17
  knowledge, 155
  logic of (written), 80
  making, 140, 153
  moving image, 71
  in the National Curriculum, 83
  as play, 83
  and performance, 160
  and reader, 77, 79
  in reading research, 76

text(s) *(continued)*
  single, entity, 178
  temporary, 141
  theory of, 186
  as source of information, 78
  and spectator relations, 68
  as stable, 136
  as work, 83
  written, 80
textual function, 64, 69
textual objects, 123
Thomas, F., 89
Thompson, J., 111
Thompson, K., 64
time, 69, 70, 107
  multimodal construction, 107
trace, 39
  visual, 39
transduction, 173
transform, transformation, 11, 39, 40, 53, 58, 132, 133, 139, 140, 145, 149, 186
  meaning, 139
  modal, 39
Tronick, E.Z., 109
Tsai, A., 106
Tsatsarelis, C., 123

Van Leeuwen, T., 4, 20, 24, 26, 27, 30, 56, 63, 69, 80, 81, 109, 123, 140, 158

visual, 49, 60
  mode, 49, 60
  shot, 64, 68
  track, 64
voice, 163, 166
  student, 166

Weinberg, M.K., 109
Wellington Primary School, 106
Wits Multiliteracies Project, 137
Woodward, V.A., 89
writing, 2, 5, 16, 20, 38, 44, 52, 60, 86, 89, 90, 92, 100, 101, 102, 104
  actional aspects of, 90
  affordances of, 52
  and body, 104
  learning of, 89
  linearity of, 19
  and posture, 104
  predominance in curriculum, 20
  (analytic and synthetic) process, 91, 98, 100, 101, 102
  relation of image and, 5
  visual aspects of, 90
Wray, D., 77

new literacies
AND DIGITAL EPISTEMOLOGIES

Colin Lankshear, Michele Knobel,
Chris Bigum, & Michael Peters
General Editors

New literacies and new knowledges are being invented "in the streets" as people from all walks of life wrestle with new technologies, shifting values, changing institutions, and new structures of personality and temperament emerging in a global informational age. These new literacies and ways of knowing remain absent from classrooms. Many education administrators, teachers, teacher educators, and academics seem largely unaware of them. Others actively oppose them. Yet, they increasingly shape the engagements and worlds of young people in societies like our own. The *New Literacies and Digital Epistemologies* series will explore this terrain with a view to informing educational theory and practice in constructively critical ways.

For further information about the series and submitting manuscripts, please contact:

>Dr. Colin Lankshear
>"Papeleria Garabatos"
>Av Universidad #1894, Local 1
>Col. Oxtopulco Universidad
>Mexico City, CP 04310 MEXICO
>Fax 1-508-267 1287
>c.lankshear@yahoo.com

To order other books in this series, please contact our Customer Service Department at:

>(800) 770-LANG (within the U.S.)
>(212) 647-7706 (outside the U.S.)
>(212) 647-7707 FAX

Or browse online by series at:

>www.peterlangusa.com